PRAISE FOR JEN OLENICZAK BROWN AND
THINK ON YOUR FEET

"[*Think on Your Feet*] is a helpful maven's guide ideal for anyone who views a podium with fear and trembling."

—Publishers Weekly

"Think improv is just for comedians? Think again! Improv is about knowing where you are in the moment and being able to pivot to find what works. Jen Brown's book *Think On Your Feet* will help you and your team develop these skills to be successful in every business situation."

—Wendy Dailey,
Talent Advisor at Sanford Health

"Before reading this book, I was never one to study or practice for anything, especially when it came to communicating. I just figured that because I have the gift of gab, no practice was necessary. Sheesh, was I wrong! After being in numerous situations where the spotlight came to me unexpectedly, I can appreciate this 'bible' on perfecting your impromptu speaking and communications skills. I've always been one who commanded attention with only my voice, but with Jen's humorous yet intentional insight on how to maneuver in any situation, I can now command attention with intention!"

—Maleeka T. Hollaway,
founder of The Official Maleeka Group

"Too often fear of saying the wrong thing holds us back from our achievements. This book provides the tools and mental hacks to help you communicate confidently. Jen Brown's unique incorporation of improv frameworks and exercises are not only wholly effective, they're wildly engaging. This is a must-read for anyone looking to improve their communication skills."

—Katie Kapler,
CEO of CourseHorse

"*Think on Your Feet* is both super readable and relatable. It blends the best of a fun improv class with the career guidance books we devour because they set us straight. Jen's account of how best to apply improv basics to work and life moments bring a fun perspective and approach to age-old concerns. I fully recommend this book to anyone hoping or plotting how to get ahead with the next phase of their lives. Improv or scripted, Jen's explanations and samples of common professional moments make any scenario relatable, so that you'll feel prepared and ready."

—Eileen Cannon,
Senior Director, Content + Curriculum at PBS

"Jen Brown offers a refreshing new way of looking at human interactions and to ourselves. Everyone who aspires to become a more engaging and thoughtful communicator should follow Jen's ideas to bring a bit of improv to their lives. A must-read for college students!"

—Aída Martínez-Gómez, PhD,
Coordinator, Department of Modern Languages and Literature
at John Jay College of Criminal Justice

"Jen offers a way to break through one's preconceived notions and learn how to *really* collaborate with other people. She teaches how the reality that is created by using improv techniques in our conversations is powerful and can help to manifest the change that each of us desires, in work and in life!"

—Ashley Knight,
Program Coordinator, HR at Wake Baptist Health

"Through multiple real-life examples and suggested activities to guide the reader, Jen's enthusiasm for applying lessons from improv to communication is very evident."

—Jill Schiefelbein,
founder of The Dynamic Communicator

"Jen Brown not only makes improv accessible, she also weaves in lessons of empathy and strength. This is a read, learn, apply book. I've learned a new language that I already see sneaking into several conversations, and, more importantly, into my actions."

—Travis Sheridan,
Global Director at Venture Café

"*Think On Your Feet* is a self-improvement book that teaches you how to apply the brilliant lessons of improv to your daily life. As an HR professional, I know a thing or two about sensitive conversations and this book is filled with advice on how to master even the most difficult of conversations. Jen offers a wealth of great tips, fun tricks, and exercises and shows you how to work them into your day-to-day. 'Yes, and' I'll be recommending this book to my whole team."

—Jessica DeGrado,
HR People Partner at Atlassian

"Plenty of books tell you how to do planned comms work. This is the only one that explains the benefits of sometimes thinking on your feet and doing less planning, not more."

—Sree Sreenivasa,
Fast Company 100 Most Creative People in Business and
Loeb visiting professor at Stony Brook University

"I have seen Jen think on her feet and deftly respond to a wide variety of situations. Her background in improv, teaching and facilitating, make her eminently qualified to offer tips to make us all more adept at responding to the unexpected."

—Sharon Vatsky,
Director of Education, School and Family Programs,
Solomon R. Guggenheim Museum

THINK
ON YOUR
FEET

TIPS AND TRICKS
TO IMPROVE YOUR
**IMPROMPTU
COMMUNICATION
SKILLS**
ON THE JOB

JEN OLENICZAK
BROWN

NEW YORK   CHICAGO   SAN FRANCISCO   ATHENS
LONDON   MADRID   MEXICO CITY   MILAN
NEW DELHI   SINGAPORE   SYDNEY   TORONTO

1 2 3 4 5 6 7 8 9   LCR   24 23 22 21 20 19

ISBN   978-1-260-45703-2
MHID   1-260-45703-6

e-ISBN   978-1-260-45704-9
e-MHID   1-260-45704-4

Library of Congress Cataloging-in-Publication Data

Names: Brown, Jen Oleniczak, author.
Title: Think on your feet : tips and tricks to improve your impromptu
   communication skills on the job / Jen Oleniczak Brown.
Description: New York : McGraw-Hill Education, [2020] | Includes
   bibliographical references and index.
Identifiers: LCCN 2019028844 (print) | LCCN 2019028845 (ebook) |
   ISBN 9781260457032 | ISBN 1260457036 (MHID) | ISBN 9781260457049
   (e-ISBN) | ISBN 1260457044 (e-MHID)
Subjects: LCSH: Business communication. | Interpersonal communication.
Classification: LCC HF5718 .B73 2020 (print) | LCC HF5718 (ebook) |
   DDC 650.101/4—dc23
LC record available at https://lccn.loc.gov/2019028844
LC ebook record available at https://lccn.loc.gov/2019028845

McGraw-Hill Education books are available at special quantity discounts to use as premiums and sales promotions or for use in corporate training programs. To contact a representative, please visit the Contact Us pages at www.mhprofessional.com.

Contents

Introduction

When you think about presenting without planning ahead of time, how do you feel? Nervous, excited, anxious, stressed, happy? Take a moment to think about the following situations:

- You're asked to give a five-minute update on a project you know nothing about at the weekly staff meeting.

- You're asked one challenging question during an interview for a job you're really excited about, and you're thrown completely for a loop because you were not expecting it at all. And this isn't a survival job, this is something that would turn into a career and make moves for you. And now you might not get it, all because of that one question and your deer-in-the-headlights look.

- You're headed to a networking event, one that matters, not a company cocktail hour. You're looking for people to collaborate with and who can help advance your career. You walk in, and in that moment you freeze. What do you say to them now that they are here and oh God, are you staring? Yes, you're staring. Quick, look down at your shoes!

Do these situations sound familiar? Impromptu speaking in professional situations is tough business. How many times have you thought, "I wish I would have . . ." after a moment you were caught off-guard? Have you ever "prepared" for a situation, overthought every single moment that could possibly happen, only to be shocked when something you didn't actually plan for happens? Cue stress, anxiety, and the would-haves.

Preparing for the unexpected is one of the best ways to handle the unexpected: "I don't know what's going to happen in my meeting later today. I have an idea, and I've prepped items I'm interested in talking about, but things could go in a completely different direction than I expected." And that's OK! The key to that is learning how to prepare for the things you can't prepare for.

Sounds weird, right? Prepare for what you can't prepare for? Get ready to think on your feet! Take a class in the flexible!

Improv is the way to prepare for the unexpected. I'm not talking about the one person on stage telling jokes to an apathetic and potentially drunk audience. I'm talking about the team sport of improvisation, specifically improv comedy. Before you chuck the book across the room, consider this: improv is a heightened reality. You take things that happen in real life, and you practice your reactions and responses—while keeping in mind the rules of improv you've learned along the way. Then you take those improv rules and apply them to what's happening in your here and now.

Improv at its core is listening and responding to the world and the situation around you. Every action has a reaction, right? You're learning how to pay attention to what's going on around you, process that information, and respond to it. You're not flying by the seat of your pants, but with enough practice, it may look like you're doing exactly this while still giving off the impression that you know what you're talking about.

Improv has a long history, much of which isn't important to you or to me, honestly. If you are interested in the nitty-gritty backstory of improv, head down the rabbit holes of commedia dell'arte, Konstantin Stanislavski and Jacques Copeau. Modern improv is thanks to people like John Dewey, Dudley Riggs, Viola Spolin, and Keith Johnstone. Start with those great search terms; I've also included more resources at the end of the book for your interest.

For our intents and purposes, we need to remember that improv has rules, and improv is about listening and responding. The rules are vague yet open enough to build a place for success. You're probably not planning to go on a traditional stage anytime soon, so you don't need to worry about being funny. I repeat: please don't worry about being funny. Improv is not about being funny, or witty, or telling jokes, or doing schtick or anything else. It's about being real.

In improv, you create a reality and live in that reality. All of those scenes you might have seen on "Whose Line Is It Anyway?" are all moments of reality created by the performers. While they perform, they are living in that reality. They also are not flying by the seat of their pants. They are following the rules of improv and listening to one another, collaborating on the creation of that reality. See how it might help in those impromptu moments of speaking that you didn't necessarily plan for?

In 2012, I started what I thought would be a side hustle. I was a museum educator, and I realized that my other educators and coworkers were not as flexible as I was. They couldn't think on their feet when students or adults asked questions they weren't expecting. They often got rattled when plans changed, and they got stuck overthinking things. This isn't to say I didn't get stuck in my head, rattled, or caught off-guard. I simply knew how to recover from it.

At that point, I had been doing improv comedy for years. I also noticed several industries were adapting improv for their day-to-day work. Therapists were using it in sessions with clients, teachers were using it in their classrooms, and sales and marketing professionals were using it to practice for their pitches. So I started The Engaging Educator (EE), with the intention of focusing on improv for educators and museum professionals—I would continue being an educator, and that would be life.

This was true for a few months. Then surprise! Professionals across all industries wanted to learn to use improv "off the stage" and take classes with other professionals, and not with actors or people who wanted to perform.

Since 2012, we've grown and taken our brand of improv-based education and thinking to over 40,000 people in six years. We do not work with actors or people who want to be actors. Our focus is to do exactly why you bought this book: help you think on your feet in professional situations.

Like all good continuing education, you'll have to take some time in real life, when you're not reading this book, to reflect on things you've read. This book contains activities, ideas, schools of thought, research, and examples, but it's ultimately up to you to remember everything you learn from these pages and apply them to real life. This book isn't a cure-all—you won't rock through it and know all of the answers. Improv is something that needs to be practiced and worked on. It's not something you can study, memorize, and be amazing at. As with all continuing education, you have to continually educate yourself about improv.

A few how-to-use this book points:

- **Improv is all about show, don't tell.** You can commit all of this to memory, memorize the ideas and rules, know this book word for word, but that won't improve your communication skills. You've only memorized a book. Take the things you learn here and apply them to your real life. Whether you're an "I need things spelled out for me from the beginning" type or someone who is looking for simple ways to adjust what you're currently doing, improv can offer you something. Remember: Don't just talk about doing it. Do it.

- **Be intentional.** Part of improv is making choices. Not doing something is also a choice, so remember that. The critical part of all of it is knowing that you're making a choice to do something. That intention—the decision around a choice, response, and action—is what makes improv work. You need to be conscious of that intention. More on this throughout the specific chapters.

- **Reflect.** If you want to make a change, you have to start with looking at yourself. Improv won't necessarily change the world. You might, however, change your work environment or work life with improv. The only way to see that change and actually make it happen is to intentionally reflect on what's happening in the situations at work and in your work life, and consider a change. There are many moments for reflection in the book—like right now. Check in with yourself and see what you're looking to work on when communicating. Are you thinking about your current job or a job you want to get? Improvement happens when you're thinking about a specific goal, after you've clearly defined what success means to you. If you don't know what you're working toward—you will 100 percent always be disappointed. So take a moment and look at yourself: What are you looking to work on? Throughout the entire journey, think about what's happening, what's changing, and what you want to work on.

- **Glows and grows.** While you're reflecting, you'll discover amazing new ideas. One tiny thing can change so much so quickly! That will be a *glow*. Glows are also things you do really well. Maybe you are already really great at identifying what you want or keeping a conversation on track. That's great! That's a glow. How about something you need to work on? Maybe you're not the best at flexibility and you really like to take control of the conversation. That would be a *grow*. It's not a failure. It's something you need to work on. I have to give credit here where it's due. The glows-and-grows idea comes from one of our amazing facilitators, Jill Frutkin. I've since co-opted it in all of my workshops and talks. You can use it, too, it's now all yours.

- **Try this and this helps . . . .** You'll notice sections called *Try This* and immediately following, *This Helps*. Try This contains activities you should do. For some activities, you might need a friend, but you can do most by yourself. Do these activities! Improv has to be practiced and you're not going to learn how to adapt it properly simply by reading about it. After you've read through the activity, This Helps explains the point of the activity.

I advise you to read through every section, because even if you think a chapter is not relevant to you right now, it may be useful to you in the future. Or you can adapt it for a current situation. For example, even if you aren't interviewing for a job right now, you might be in the near or distant future. You can adapt this section for a podcast interview or an interview for your company newsletter. You also might read something in the interviewing chapter that helps you with your meeting skills. Improv for professional communication is a funny beast. I could apply just about everything to everything, so throughout the text, I've connected some dots between different ideas and situations. And in other places, I simply had to make a choice about what applied the "best." As you're working your way through, reflecting and actively thinking about the application, as well as your grows and glows, think about where else you can apply each specific tool, besides the situation given in the book.

One reason improv works so well for professional communication is because you're planning for flexibility. Think about it like this: If you have a plan with only one path but you have to be flexible, you're going to struggle. If you have a plan that has a few other possible plans built in, you'll be able to flex when necessary. You're basically stocking up on plans and ideas so when the moment comes where you need to be flexible, you can because you've thought about it.

You're planning for the unexpected. Improv helps you build your "flexibility muscle." So when you ask for a raise, you can do it in the best, most prepared way. You can be ready for anything. Again, improv isn't about flying by the seat of your pants and being spontaneous with all of your choices and decisions. It is about being ready for those moments when your boss says no to your request for a raise, when your coworker is upset with you, when you're trying to meet people at a networking event, and when you have to stand up for yourself.

A few more notes then we'll dive right in. I've given a lot of examples in this book. These examples ground some information in reality. Learning improv from a book is a little like learning how to dance from a book. You're reading about an active skill. It's a little weird. Sometimes, the examples are the best-case scenarios so you can see how something works when it works. It's often the gold standard. Although I've prefaced many examples with "this is the best outcome," I want to make an overarching statement: the examples are here for you to see one way to make something happen in real life. You can take it, improv with it, and make it your own. Really, you should take all of this and make it your own. If it doesn't work, reflect and see what happened. Move along, try again, and make it happen.

Throughout the book, I frequently say *in* the moment versus *at* the moment: this is an important distinction in improv. You are actively part of the moment at hand. You are not a spectator. You are in it, you are part of it, and you are affecting it simply by being there. Your audience is too—no one is just passive at something. Everyone is in it.

Finally, and most important, this book isn't a cure-all. Yes, you will be better, faster, and stronger after this book, if you follow some of the ideas in it, but improvement is relative. If you're currently terrified of public speaking and talking in meetings, and you think after reading this book you're going to be ready to give a viral TED Talk without throwing up, I'm really sorry, you're going to be disappointed. Will you feel a bit better about speaking up in the next meeting in a way that's thoughtful and relevant? Absolutely.

Before every single class, with every single student, we ask: Who are you? Why are you here? What are your expectations for this class? Sometimes, they have no expectations; they are taking the class because they thought it might be fun. Sometimes, they want to be an amazing communicator after the class, sometimes they have something specific like a raise or promotion they are shooting for, and sometimes someone else signed them up for the class.

No matter what your expectations are with this book, take a moment, check in, and write them down. Don't just think about them in your head; really dig in and think what you want out of this. Write it down somewhere, whether that's in your phone, in your journal, in an email to yourself, in a document on your computer. Think about what you want and then dive in. This book is meant to make you better, faster, and stronger. It won't do anything unless you know what you want to work on.

Got your ideas and expectations down?

Let's go.

CHAPTER 1

Attending to Your Audience: *Who, What, When,* and *How*

I still remember a show I did off-Broadway that killed my soul. It was with my improv troop. We got up, put on an "amazing" performance, but the audience never clapped, laughed, or even moved. I'm sure they made an active choice not to clap or laugh. At one point, during an overdramatic western in the style of the old cowboy movies, another performer, pretending to be a tumbleweed, rolled across the stage. There was not a peep, much less a chuckle from the audience. It was as if all the joy was pulled from the room. The rest of the show was in the toilet, and so was the second show that same night because the audience had killed our drive. Instead of responding to their reactions, we kept pushing our brand of "funny" and let them throw more dirt on the holes we dug ourselves into, pushing us into the ground.

Does this performance remind you of a recent talk you gave? Or maybe a meeting you led? Or worse, a meet-up with a potential client, employer, coworker, or collaborator? It's one of the worst feelings in the world when it seems like no one is connecting with anything you're saying. Countless students mentioned having moments just like this during a conversation or presentation at work. Though these situations are not the same as the dictionary definition of "performing," where you are seeking affirmation from people you don't know (although, conferences are kind of like that sometimes), they might be even more nerve-racking because you're talking to people you know and might want to see or work with again.

When I first started The Engaging Educator (EE), I swore up and down I would never, ever train people to perform in front of an audience. It was the big part of improv that didn't apply to what we were trying to do. The affirmation from strangers? No thanks. It wasn't something most of our students wanted either, and if they did, they were referred to one of the improv theaters in New York City. Some came back, never regretting their choice to try something else and realizing performing for a dedicated audience who was looking for a show was very different than professional and personal development. Some performed with the other improvisers and actors in their class and invited the facilitators from EE along.

Until one fall a small group of students really wanted to perform in front of an audience. They came to class one day as a united front and told me that they wanted to put on an improv show together and not with another theater. They wanted to do it together. My immediate reaction was first, "Why?" and second, "You do it every day, why now?" Every time we speak to another person, we're talking to an audience.

Let's take a moment here to define what an audience is. The traditional definition is a group of attentive people at a public event. If you think about this definition, there's a very active-passive relationship between the performers and the audience. You've got people "onstage" actively doing something intentional and a group of people "off-stage" passively watching. The audience generally can't do a lot to influence the people onstage, because those folks will keep doing what they are doing. The passive people, even if they are paying attention, are not necessarily part of the action. Even during interactive plays or improv performances where people are pulled onstage to be part of the action, people can still choose to sit and do nothing. They have no skin in the game.

But this is only the most traditional dictionary definition of the word *audience*. If you've ever been in front of a room full of people during a meeting, attended a networking event, had an interview, or even been involved in conversation, you know the people you're talking to play anything but a passive role during these situations.

If we think of these situations as performances, then your audience is the person or group of people you're communicating with and they play a very active role in your performance. If that's one other person, that's your audience. If it's a crowd of 10 or 10,000 people you're presenting or speaking to, that's your audience. And you, the speaker, are akin to the performer whose goal is to get information across and be heard. You are not just talking for the sake of talking. If you think about it, we are always in front of an audience when we are speaking out loud. The only exceptions perhaps are those silent moments when we read an email out loud to make sure we aren't crazy and we've sufficiently avoided the passive-aggressive tone we've been working on. More on that later.

Before any performance it's important to ask yourself the following four questions: (1) *Who* are you talking to and *Who* are you? (2) *Where* are you? (3) *What* do you and your audience want? and (4) *How* do you feel?

Aside from being identifiers to tap into the moment at hand, these are also the major things that need to be considered in every improv moment. Without these four things, improv moments fall flat, stall out, and go in circles. The same things happen if you don't have these identified in conversations, meetings, presentations, and interviews. Let's take a minute to look at each of these further.

WHO ARE YOU TALKING TO?

An effective way to start thinking about an audience is to ask the very simple question: Who are you talking to? This might seem really basic, but hear me out. If you are talking to a group of people who understand your business, and you're reaching out for collaboration or a partnership, you won't need to get into every single detail about the business. On the flip side, if the audience has never heard of you or your company and you're headed out to "sell" the business, you might want to and definitely need to start from the very beginning. That *who* is really important!

When you identify *who* the audience is, you must define what that term means. Get specific. They aren't just "people." They might be contemporaries you want to impress or coworkers you need to convince. You'd talk to a kindergartener and a high school student differently, right? Same idea.

TRY THIS

Take a moment to think about the last audience you spoke to—remember, this might be one person, or it might be a crowd. Pick a specific communication moment and grab your phone. Set a timer for two minutes, and write down or talk out everything you can remember about that audience. If you're writing, keep writing for the full two minutes. If you're talking, record on your phone and talk for the full two minutes. You're tapping into *everything*: from the largest of details all the way to the tiny minutia. Do not edit, do not overthink, do not stop. You're dumping everything out of your brain about this audience. After you've finished, go back and reread what you've written or listen to what you've recorded and pull out the bits that show the characteristics specific to this audience.

This helps you learn how to quickly identify your audience. We often don't think about our audience before speaking to them. This activity helps you make a habit of checking in.

When you're doing the work to understand the audience, it's important to think about them as more than just generic people. Ultimately, everyone in your life fits into a category within your life. This is something you'll have to do and figure out for yourself, but here are a few to start with:

- **People you want to impress.** This might be an interviewer, interviewee, supervisor, client, coworker, or potential client. You want this someone to see you in the best light.

- **People you want to maintain a relationship with.** This might be a coworker, supervisor, or client. You want this someone to see you in a good to great light. You're going to present a good version of you with the understanding that you might have some "off" days. We aren't robots, which means it's OK to not be OK. You do need to maintain a professional image, regardless of what's happening personally.

- **People you don't care about.** This might be someone who doesn't have an impact on you professionally or personally, so their opinion truly doesn't matter.

These are *my* three categories, and a good place to start when you create your own. The group of people I don't care about is actually a really small group, because so much of my work is word of mouth. That's not to say I communicate to everyone with my agenda in mind or categorize everyone I meet. That's very different. I do want most people to see the best version of my professional self. After you take this inventory of the people in your professional life, start thinking about what version of *who* you are is presented to each of your categories.

. . . AND *WHO* ARE YOU?

Who are you? We're not deep diving into your psyche here. It's safe to say you are a different version of yourself when you talk to your friend at work than you are when you're talking to the CEO. In improv, we tend to start with the *who* as interchangeable—you need to understand both who you're talking to and who you are, and they both have to be clearly defined. People often come into improv thinking we're going to jump immediately into doing scenes and being funny, but the fact is if we started with scenes, or as we call it, moments, I'm not sure people would come back! We tend to forget or not realize that too much creativity is just as crippling as not enough. If you have everything to choose from, you'll get nowhere.

Since the *who* is one of the easiest to quickly identify, even when you're starting out with improv-based thinking, we'll flesh this out before moving on, keeping in mind that both sides of *who* might shift. An example of a *who* might be the version of you that is interviewing for a job you really want. I tell students this is usually that best-self I refer to so often. When you are interviewing for *that job*, you often wear your favorite professional outfit and are usually completely on point when communicating. Take one minute to list those best-self characteristics.

This version of you should be exactly that: a version of you. If you suddenly start using language that isn't authentic to you, you will sound false. Same goes with acting in a certain way.

Here's where improv comes in strong—you get to practice these whos. At one of our Level-Up classes in New York City, a vice president of a well-known communication company and an online talent with a food channel were paired together for an activity. They had one of the longest back-and-forth small-talk conversations either one had probably ever experienced. You know the kind of conversation I'm referring to: those painful ones where everything was about the weather. Their back-and-forth was awkward and superficial at best. It lasted three-plus minutes. I had no clue *who* they were to one another, because their relationship was undefined. The entire class was watching the moment with giant question marks plastered across their faces.

I called time at the end of the painful moment and asked the two students how they felt. My vice president, the amazing sport he always was, said, "I think we need some work on focus and objectives." My online talent looked at me and said, "I have no idea what's going on. That was the worst!" Instead of going into the usual what-happened reflection questions, I asked, "Who are you and how do you know each other?" Blank stares. The VP said, "We know each other," while the online talent said, "We're strangers" over him.

This confusion? This is why the foundational information is critical. Of course, in real life you don't have as many options to choose from: you know who you are and who you're talking to. How often have you clearly defined which *who* you're tapping into before a professional moment? In improv, you get the opportunity to think about the conversation afterward with no regrets and all the reflection. It's just a game, remember? We can have that blank stare "Who are you?" moment, because again, improv is a voyeuristic adventure and you generally have a facilitator calling you out. The audience (other students) is also there to help you with those things that you missed in reflection. In real life, you might walk away feeling like conversations stall out, and afterward, you beat yourself up with the woulda, coulda, shouldas. Instead of feeling the regret, try reflecting on how you can do it better when it goes poorly and plan for next time.

Using the solid decisions you make in improv and improv-based thinking as your guide, you can start defining which version of you will be at that conversation, based on who you are talking to and your relationship with that particular audience. That best version you bring into an interview? You're probably meeting with someone who has some kind of say: maybe it's the decision maker or perhaps the person who will be your direct report. Whoever it is, it's most likely someone you'd want to impress. Boom—you've got your *who* on both ends.

Once you have a handle on that vague *who*—a hiring manager or a coworker—you can refine this further by adding details to your *who*. Is it a hiring manager or *the* hiring manager? Does the person you're talking to report to anyone, or are they in charge? Or are they the person you have to interview with first to get to the person who does the hiring? See how all of this is deeper than the interviewer and the interviewee?

When you're thinking about your personal who, start asking questions about *them* to decide your *who*. If you don't know specifics, do what you can to discover them. We're lucky enough to live in a time with social media at the immediate—you can quickly look up on the internet past events or people who work at a specific place. While it is a nasty rabbit hole, a bit of digging will help. Show the knowledge; don't refer directly to your online research. This "show, don't tell" concept is an improv principle we'll see a lot of through professional communication. We'll dig deeper into it when we work on confidence. For now, it's best summed up as, use the information to inform what you're saying, but don't change your message.

Let's take a moment to bring both of these whos together. At first, this exercise will feel incredibly contrived, and that's OK. The following worksheet will help you work through a few groups and types of people, along with what version of you should come out when talking to them. In improv, we have stock characters. A stock character has clearly defined traits, and each person has a different set of stock characters because they are drawn from characteristics the performer can do well in a moment's notice. This activity works out something similar, but it's more about you than a made-up character you're trying to be.

Category _____

    TRAITS _____

    EXAMPLES _____

    WHO YOU ARE _____

Category _____

    TRAITS _____

    EXAMPLES _____

    WHO YOU ARE _____

Category _____

    TRAITS _____

    EXAMPLES _____

    WHO YOU ARE _____

Category _____

    TRAITS _____

    EXAMPLES _____

    WHO YOU ARE _____

Category _____

    TRAITS _____

    EXAMPLES _____

    WHO YOU ARE _____

WHERE ARE YOU?

The *where* in professional communication can be the physical location and the type of speaking you're doing, whether that's public speaking, a presentation, or a one-on-one conversation. The physical location is important in improv moments, mainly because it helps build the story and situation. In your professional life, the physical location is less of an issue, mainly because it's already categorized as professional. The only exception is perhaps a networking event, which tends to border the line of professional and casual. Thinking about location comes with deciding what type of communication you're about to be part of. Let's think about what this means using an interview as an example. If it's an interview with a panel of interviewers, it might be wise to prep yourself the same way you'd prep for any public-speaking event. If you're in a later phase of an interview for a position that involves presentations, you might want to practice doing a sample talk or a pitch in front of a small group. If it's a one-on-one conversation, it will be simply you and the interviewer. While the number of people involved is one of the easier milestones to determine in a conversation, it's essential for the foundation to be solid.

Presentation, Public Speaking, Communication, Conversation . . . What?

While these are not finite definitions—nor are they *Merriam Webster* approved—they are how we'll think about the terms going forward.

Presentations can be for a large or small audience. They are often planned, sometimes impromptu. Most of the time they are contrived— and that isn't an insult to planning and preparing! The amount of time could be as short as 60 seconds and as long as a few weeks. Presentations are usually not conversations. They generally involve one or more people talking to an audience. While the audience might have questions to ask in a public setting, they also may not have the chance to ask them. Think of a presentation like a theater show. It should be rehearsed, planned, warmed up, edited, and in best-case scenarios, get outside "direction" (coaching).

Public speaking can involve any kind of communication out loud and in public. People are hopefully listening. It could be a conversation, a presentation, an interview, a workshop, a conversation involving small talk, or a networking event—generally any time you are talking, you can consider it public speaking. This doesn't include those moments when you are talking out loud to yourself, to your dog, roommate, mom, or dad, partner, or friend, unless you're doing this in front of a larger audience. You might be leading a meeting, or you might be networking at a social event, or anything in between. When you're talking in a space with other people attending to you, it's public speaking.

One-on-one communication or conversation encompasses communication that doesn't have a passive audience. You might be around other people who are not paying attention to you and the person you're talking to. A small-group conversation among three and four people also falls under this category. Note there is some overlap between this category and public speaking if you are having a conversation in a public space.

Communication is everything that's been mentioned, plus some of the larger ideas around *how* we transfer information verbally to other people.

When we start thinking about presentation skills, we might think about things like the pose, projection, enunciation, cadence (how your voice moves through space), gestures, presence . . . all the "big show" skills we bring when we want to impress and when something matters to us. Public-speaking skills involve much of the same on a slightly lesser scale; if you are talking to two people and you don't have the best and strongest pose, for example, it's less egregious than if you're standing in a less-confident way in front of a conference session. Digging into the definition of communication is when things get a bit more complicated. Communication means focusing on *what* we say and *how* we say it.

My belief hasn't changed in years: you could have an appealing message about the secret behind living a life of happiness and how to make a lot of money, but if you do it poorly, you're going to have quite a few people ignoring you. If you're stammering, apologizing over your stammering, hunched over and presenting an anxious front, very few people will listen to what you have to say, *even if it could change their life*. On the flip side, if you talk about your favorite recipe for lemonade—even if it's the kind you dump into a cup of water and stir until combined—but you do it with confidence, conviction, and care that stimulates action-orientated conversation, you'll have people interested in what you have to say. Even if it's simply lemonade.

Another even more infuriating problem: you plan, prep, and work hard, and you'll still have to figure something out on the fly or pivot in the moment. Nothing will ever go 100 percent the way you planned, and the sooner you learn to roll with it, the easier you can be on yourself. This all? Easier said than done. Even if this is obvious, so many of us don't do this. We don't think about our style and how we present: we focus on content.

So why bother?

Here's the beauty of these skills: you can improve them with a bit of work. Much like going to the gym, you can train yourself to be a better speaker and be confident in your style. Since polish can be so nuanced, it is in a separate section at the end of the book. For now, be sure to identify the kind of communication in your where. Is it a presentation in front of 100 people, public speaking with you and 10 people, or one-on-one communication with you and 3 people at a networking event?

The *where* also determines what version of you should come out. New start-up? Maybe not the time for the ultra-conservative suit. What you wear does tie into your who quite a bit, and they definitely go hand in hand. You add another element when you think about in-person, phone, or video calls. Regardless, the where is usually based on facts versus interpretation, unlike the other three.

TRY THIS

Pick your last not-so-successful conversation. Recall the who and where. Ask yourself, were they both clearly defined? Take a moment to define those aspects as if you were prepping for that conversation for the first time.

This helps you use reflection in your everyday conversation. We don't often realize that by reflecting, we can learn from habits. This activity builds your reflection skills.

WHAT DO YOU AND THEY WANT?

What you want could have an entire chapter—or book—on its own. In improv moments, when people are feeling a bit without direction, it's usually because they don't know exactly what they want. In professional moments, when people are feeling a bit without direction, it's usually because they don't know exactly what they want. In improv, this usually begins with two students. They get up in class to work through a moment. They have their *who* and *where* all figured out, then the conversation stops when they realize they are just going back and forth talking about physical objects around them. Discussing physical things usually leads me to think they have issues dealing with the here and now and I'll dive into that later. But when the students themselves realize that the conversation is going nowhere fast, we usually dig into the wants after the conversation spins for a while.

The same concept applies to a professional setting. If you don't have a focus or something you are working toward, you get trapped in the everyday status quo, spinning your wheels. For every type of communication it's important to define your want for that specific *who* you are in the moment, as well as the wants of your audience. Begin by jotting down your goals first.

TRY THIS

Think about what you want for your career. If this isn't something you've thought about regularly, don't get trapped going too far into what you want for retirement or too stressed about snowballing your "what if." Pick something that could happen in the next year, whether it's a new job, a promotion, or speaking at a conference. Write it down, and brainstorm all the ways you can get what you want. Make sure every step to get what you want comes with an action item. If it's a promotion, maybe your steps are to write down the things you've accomplished, to set up a meeting with your direct report, to practice asking for a raise with friends and specifically define how much money you'd like to ask for, as well as what new title or position you'd like. Each of those steps has a concrete action—be sure yours do, too.

> *This helps* you make your goals more achievable and accessible by breaking them into smaller and actionable steps. We often give up on our goals because they are too big. This activity makes the goal doable.

Ideally, your wants should align with your audience's wants. If you want to sell your product, your audience likely has a problem that can be solved with your product. If you're interviewing for a new job you want, your audience is someone who wants that job filled with the right candidate—you. If you want that promotion, odds are it'll come with more responsibilities that will benefit your company. In theory, getting your wants and understanding your audience's wants are as simple as noting what you want and coming up with one or two ways on how to get it, because they should align, but sometimes other factors are involved. Here comes the hard part: What if Plan A doesn't work? Now how can you get what you want?

In improv, we think about tactics. Whenever I'm teaching wants, I have everyone think of a child who wants candy. That child will try everything: crying, begging, pleading, bargaining, tantruming—you name it. That's why kids are so sneaky! They switch tactics quickly when a particular one isn't working. That pivot and flexibility is a big part of improv, checking in and recognizing something isn't working and trying something new (not easy for adults, no matter what kind of kid they were). While we shouldn't pull out the waterworks to get that job or promotion, we *can* tap into different tactics.

When we think a bit more about getting what we want, we're actually talking about influencing people. You can definitely threaten, demand, cry, beg—much like that child—but those tactics aren't ideal for professional situations and don't necessarily connect with both of you achieving your wants. To get things done and obtain what you want without full-on coercion, understanding influence is important and effective. According to the Center for Creative Leadership (CCL), there are three main types of tactics that can be used to influence people.[1] CCL divides them into The Head, The Heart, and The Hands. The Head taps into rational and intellectual ways: information based. The Heart relies on emotional influencing: values, purpose, and ideals. The Hands involve cooperative influencing: that big goal we're all working toward.

Going back to the improv-based thinking model of determining wants and making it happen in your everyday life, when you're thinking about what you want in public speaking, a presentation, or a one-on-one communication, you need to not only take into account how you'll try to get what you want, but also what the audience needs to be convinced of. This sounds and often feels like a pretty large pile of tangled spaghetti. Let's break it down:

You've got a meeting coming up with other people in your department or at your work. You have an initiative you'd like to accomplish, and you need their help—and simply telling people they have to do something is never a great tactic to get buy-in. You've determined you have to go in prepared and ready to convince a team of people who have been working a bit too hard this time of year. This is a public-speaking moment, with a little presentation thrown in. You can plan what you're going to do and say, and there is space for the team to contribute and ask questions, which means plenty of impromptu moments. The *who* and *where* are clear, and when diving into the *wants*, you think ahead that this initiative will make a few jobs easier and allow for less stress around this time of year next year. Clearly, emotional tactics won't work as well as intellectual or cooperative ones. Appealing with facts and information, as well as a collaborative argument, will probably sit best with the audience in the room and will most likely tie into their wants as well. That's the plan: if convincing needs to happen, that convincing has to happen as far removed from the emotional as possible. By making sure you are effectively using facts and information that connect with what the audience might also want, you're using influence tactics effectively.

Hard stop: this sounds like a lot of work. I completely understand if you're reading this and getting a little crazy thinking and overthinking every single communication you may or may not have had, breaking each one down and assessing them. I'm not going to lie—this will be a lot of work in the beginning. It's going to take some time to develop this habit. Initially, you're going to be catching yourself after the situation, saying either, "Wow! I read that moment correctly," or "Man, I made giant mess of that." The reflective aspect of learning is incredibly helpful. It's another aspect of improv that can move right into reality with a small pivot. Ask yourself how something went, and really think: Did I know what version of me I had to bring into the situation? Do I know my where? Did I try tactics to get what I want, and did I even know what I wanted? If you're hesitating on one of these answers, the communication probably didn't go well.

Since wants are so nuanced, consider this as more of an introduction into wants. The core questions of *what* do you want and *what* do they want should be addressed in each individual moment. Getting what you want is never going to be 100 percent effective—no one gets everything. The more you learn about people in professional communication, the more you can both adjust expectations and ideas moving forward.

TRY THIS

What's something you want? It can be tangible, like nachos, or intangible, like affirmation from the CEO about the new initiative you've been contributing to. Write down what it is, and what tactics you've either tried or can try to influence people into getting what you want. Note: tangible things are *generally easier*. Many times, these things simply require asking and depend on means (money) and availability.

This helps you define your wants in a clear and concise manner. Most of us can't directly voice what we want. This activity gives you an opportunity to define your wants.

HOW DO YOU FEEL?

There's one last element that can make or break the foundation of communication—*how* you feel. Here's where things get a little messy—messier, if you will. This is less about how much information you give out regarding how you feel *in* a situation and more about how you feel *about* a situation. Let's address how you feel *in* a situation first, because you're human. We all are. I've always been a firm believer that it's OK to not be OK: we all have bad days, rough days, days we wish we could just do over. I can't tell you how many times I've said, "My, what a year this week has been"—and that's OK. We can't be bright and sunny all the time. Pretending is exhausting, and we are all going to have bad days that we just can't hide behind the screen.

On the flip side, being more than an open book at work leads to some pretty uncomfortable and awkward situations. Many people talk about specific ways to be and act at work, and many people come into improv hoping to work on professionalism or being taken seriously at work. There are a few polishing tips and warm-ups I'll get into in a later section, but this goes back to what version of you you're bringing into that moment. Quite a few women come into public classes and private workshops wanting to present themselves in a way that earns them respect and helps them be seen in a professional manner. My answer is always the same: be the best version of *you*. Whatever that version is, that's who should show up when you need to be taken seriously. When it comes to showing emotions at work in communication, keep the best version of you in mind at all times.

At the same time, it's important to be honest with whatever specific feeling you have. You have to be honest with yourself above all things. When you enter a situation and you're having an awful day, be mindful of your emotions and how they may impact your reactions. That lens is crucial to how you're taking in information. If you have any control on when you can give a presentation or host a meeting, you might want to do whatever you can to make sure it's on a day you know you're going to be feeling pretty great. Scheduling it after a long flight, a big move, or another big change in your personal life might be a poor choice. The awareness of your emotions prior to entering a speaking situation will only be more information in your control. Since we can't control everything, controlling whatever you can gives you structure for greater flexibility. If you can't adjust the day and you know you're having a bad one, take a moment to focus on what you can control in and for that moment. Can you acknowledge you're not feeling the best and do what you can to help it work out in the best way possible?

The *how* also pertains to your perception of the situation. Do you care? Hopefully yes! We both know it's not always yes.

The idea of caring about what you're talking about is *huge*. If you don't care, why should the people you're talking to care or listen to you? This is where the *how* gets a little difficult. If you don't care about what you're talking about, everyone in the room can see it. They might not know why they feel a little funny about what you're saying or why things feel a little off. We re-create the energy we put out. If that energy is happy and excited, people are also going to feel happy and excited. If that energy is apathetic or annoyed, that bounces into your audience and right back at you, which leaves you more apathetic or annoyed, which sends that energy right back at the audience, and that is going to bounce right back . . . see the vicious cycle? It's one that leaves a lot of people annoyed with their public-speaking skills. If the only energy you get back is apathy, annoyance, fear, nervousness—or whatever negative emotion you are projecting out at your audience—your feelings won't be positive toward speaking in public. Make sense?

When you're thinking about how you feel about a public-speaking situation, presentation, or one-on-one communication, the best thing to do is immediately swing positive. This isn't about faking it or being false—authenticity is one of the most important things when you are communicating. It's about taking reality and looking at the positive side, not the doom and gloom.

For example, say you aren't thrilled about a new initiative at work. You've been asked to give a presentation about it during a meeting. You can present it as a negative, or worse, do it in a way that seems false. Or . . . you can present it as a change, highlighting the positive *and* negative, giving it thoughtful discourse, and leaving it open to discussion. You can bring up some of your concerns, or you can comment on those concerns from the perspective of someone who might find it positive and someone who might find it negative. Pivoting to the positive—or in this case, neutral—view of the situation lets you come across as educational instead of negative. You're not going to go completely into optimism mode if that's not you—there's no need! You are just not going to go full-on negative with your thoughts and what the outcome can be. If you want to be catastrophic in real life, that's up to you. It's not effective to be there at work.

It's a strange and touchy space discussing feelings and showing feelings in the workplace. At the end of the day, you want to keep your best self in mind. An extra part of this equation that complicates things even further: the way you show and express emotion at work doesn't need to be the same way someone else shows and expresses information at work.

It sounds obvious, but to so many of us, it isn't. Often we want people to care as much as we do about a situation. If we don't care, we want people not to care either.

At one of our classes, a director of public programs and an educator were in a moment together. The director was very set on a high-stakes situation between the two of them. He set up the situation and wasn't getting a lot of help from the educator. His character was putting up a fence between his yard and the neighbor's yard. The educator was the neighbor and didn't see the issue with the fence. The director kept pushing for what he wanted, while the educator pushed to sit and relax. There was bargaining, pleading, bribing—everything the director could think of, and the educator just kept sitting and relaxing. The moment hit an impasse and I called time.

During the reflection they had two very different responses as well.

The director: "I couldn't get her to care about anything I cared about. I knew she wanted to sit and relax, so I tried to make things as annoying as possible and nothing happened."

The educator: "All I wanted to do was relax and I was sitting and relaxing. I thought his neurosis was part of his character."

While this seems pretty funny from the reflection, the difference in their care was stark. This happens in real life all the time. Quick, think of the last time you cared about something, even remotely. Did everyone care at the same level as you did? There were probably people who cared much, much more than you did and people who cared much less. How frustrating was it on either end of the spectrum?

Emotional intelligence (EQ) is something that improv develops at a high level. EQ is the awareness, control, and expression of our emotions, and the ability to connect with others in an empathetic manner.[2] The "how you feel" balanced with "how they feel" heightens. One of the best lessons we teach regarding emotional intelligence: you don't have to feel the same as other people. You also shouldn't force them to feel the same way you do, to show their emotions in the same manner that you do. You should try to understand how others feel.

Using improv-based thinking, there are a few ways to better understand how someone else is feeling. Reflection is a nice way to start. Asking yourself how you felt, and then the additional question of how you think the other person (people) felt. That why question that gets deeper into issues? That's a good question to pose right now. Why do you think they felt the way you think they feel? Here's an example:

Going back to a previous instance, you finish up that meeting about the new initiative, and you feel it went pretty well. It seems like most people want what you want: for it not to happen because it would take resources away from ongoing projects. There was one person who sat silently during the dissent, and that person has quite a bit of pull in the office. How do you think they felt?

You could go on the defense: they hated everything you were saying and thought you were an idiot. That's probably not true, because they aren't that petty kind of person. They might think the initiative is a great idea. That might be true because that's a pretty logical explanation of their silence during the dissent. Why do you think they might think the initiative is a great idea? And why do you think they were silent when everyone else was talking? If they disliked the idea, why might they be silent?

While it might feel as though the whys will make you a little crazy, they are actually a pretty helpful technique when you're working on your EQ. If you're truly working on your EQ, you need to not only work on your awareness of others' emotions, but also understand how you define and express yours.

There's an improv activity called Viewpoints that feels silly when you're going through it, but it forces you to get in touch with your emotions. Traditionally, the activity is conducted by a facilitator calling out emotions one after another, and the participants adjust their face and body positioning to show that emotion. I'm not suggesting that you call out, "Angry! Excited! Scared!" in your office, but I do think it's a good idea to think about what your body does when you feel different emotions.

In psychology, there are quite a few different schools of thought when it comes to what emotions exist. Ask psychologist Robert Plutchik, and he'll tell you that there are eight basic emotions.[3] Book Two of Aristotle's *Rhetoric* gives nine and Darwin will insist there are eight, and those eight are slightly different than Plutchik's.[4] Let's experiment with a few. This is by no means an exhaustive list of emotions, but it's a good place to start. With each of the following emotions, think about what happens with your face, your body, and your voice:

Happy

    FACE _____

    BODY _____

    VOICE _____

Sad

    FACE _____

    BODY _____

    VOICE _____

Mad

    FACE _____

    BODY _____

    VOICE _____

Afraid

    FACE _____

    BODY _____

    VOICE _____

Excited

    FACE _____

    BODY _____

    VOICE _____

Disgusted

FACE _____

BODY _____

VOICE _____

Admiring

FACE _____

BODY _____

VOICE _____

Frustrated

FACE _____

BODY _____

VOICE _____

Proud

FACE _____

BODY _____

VOICE _____

Nervous

FACE _____

BODY _____

VOICE _____

Go through each emotion, and think about how you show that emotion and then show it. Really dig in—how do you show things on your face? Is it more in your body? In your voice? Let's look at happy first. What happens to your face when you feel happy? What happens to your body? How do you move when you're happy? What happens to your voice? Or your responses to things going awry? You don't have to get this deep into every emotion, but it's a good idea to dive in more than, "I smile when I'm happy." Look at one or two more, and think about how your face and body changes. For example, if I'm frustrated, my whole body is tense and I'm not the best to talk to. I don't listen well when I'm frustrated. Take an inventory of how you interact with the world in the emotions mentioned earlier.

Viewpoints is the starting-off point for an improv activity that shows how much emotions truly affect our communication. Changing Emotions is the next step. A moment is played out with all of the other components—who, where, want—and starts in whatever emotional state makes sense in the conversation. Throughout the conversation, a facilitator calls out emotions and the people in the moment change their emotions based on what is called out. That emotion carries the moment forward, and the people involved let the emotion change the direction or heighten that moment.

For example, one moment in a workshop involved a man who was playing the husband. He came into the house and asked his wife what happened to the car because it was missing. She responded that she had finally sold the car because she was upset he hadn't cleaned it in months. Simple enough—they were husband and wife, they were at home, specifically in the kitchen, she wanted him to clean the car prior to the moment and now wanted him to pull his weight, and he wanted to know where the car went. Clearly, the emotions were tense moving forward, and as soon as the conversation stalled a bit, I started calling out emotions like, "joy, rage, fear, love." The moment could have very easily been tense the whole way through, but through Changing Emotions, the couple ended up realizing they no longer needed a car, because there were too many fumes in the air and they could change the world together through their loving relationship. Weird, huh?

When the reflection started, they commented on how much they enjoyed the change of emotions. "It made reactions so easy, holding on to emotion and letting the emotion do the work for me," the wife said. The husband looked troubled.

I see this "processing face" all too often in workshops. We don't always pay attention to how we communicate. It's not really something we learned in school. We learned how to write, give a presentation, do research, and at some point during a job or college class, we learned how to professionally communicate. When it's suddenly a focus, especially on emotions when you aren't a person who often shows emotions, things might feel a bit strange.

Never one to let a learning moment go by, I immediately asked him why he had a processing face. His response? "I usually don't show my emotions that much, am I supposed to?"

No, absolutely not, if that's not who you are. This is not about using emotions to make decisions and drive communication forward faster. When you let your emotions lead, you make huge decisions, have a lot of initiative for everything, and react instead of respond. The purpose of Viewpoints and Changing Emotions is to show how much your emotions *do* drive what you do and say. They also help you better understand that if you are unaware of how much your emotions play into what you're doing when you speak, present, or communicate, you need to check in to make sure your emotions aren't leading everything you do.

Too often, we are so caught up in whatever emotion that is driving us, we don't take a breath and sit and reflect. If you are reflecting hours or days afterward, think about why you made the decisions you made and how they might be different based on a different emotion. Simple example: A colleague asks you a question and you snap at them for asking the question. Was it a question you had already answered a dozen times so your irritation was (kinda) warranted, or did the irritation come because you were upset all day?

That's a very basic example of checking in with your emotions and seeing how often you let those emotions drive your conversation. Sometimes, this is a good thing. If your emotions are excitement, happiness, joy, or motivation and you end up pushing harder, getting things done with efficiency, and overlooking communication issues you might have with other people on "off days," great! What happens when you have those negative emotions? Do people get the best version of you in communication?

Understanding your own emotions ties into learning empathy for others. By developing an awareness of your own emotions and how they drive your communication and decision making, you're seeing people in a different way. This awareness might cause you to pause before making a judgment of another individual and how they communicate, and it definitely will give you a completely different lens on how others might make their decisions with respect to communication. The idea of excelling at EQ is to not only understand your own emotions but also to be aware of other people's emotions. By understanding how *you* show frustration, for example, you might see similar things in *others* when they are experiencing frustration, and that may change the tactics you use to communicate with that individual. Think about this:

If someone is frustrated, and you *knew* they were frustrated, how would that alter your communication with that person? How might you change how you work through what you want versus how it might be different when you are dealing with someone who is feeling joy or fear?

YOUR CHEAT SHEET

A quick note before moving forward: the best-laid plans often go awry. That is OK. You might prep for all of the upcoming situations and know exactly who you are, what version of you needs to come out for that meeting, who you are meeting with, and what they want. You've read their situation emotionally and developed your emotional intelligence to its highest point, and things might still go poorly or simply meh. Reflection is still key in these situations where you've planned and prepped, as is understanding that sometimes it isn't you, it's the other person. Toxic work environments are going to be touched on in a later chapter. They are real and they do exist. Keep that in mind when you are reflecting on your communication practices.

- Think about who you are and what version of you serves the situation best.

- What kind of situation are you in? Presentation, public speaking, one-on-one?

- What do you want out of this? What do they want? How do they connect? How can you get it?

- How do you feel? How do they feel?

- Reflect—how did it go?

Interpersonal Communication—the Everyday Professional Communication

Effective communication is crucial to a healthy workplace and to success at work. It doesn't matter if you work behind a desk or computer screen, or if you are the front-facing person in your company. If you can't communicate well, your job will be that much harder. Studies show we spend between 70 and 80 percent of our days communicating.[1]

Everyday professional conversations is the hardest form of communication. Doing a presentation can be learned with a structure; leading a meeting also has its dos and don'ts. Interpersonal communication? It's all improv! You can plan and plan and plan, and you'll still have no clue how the person you're talking to will respond to anything you're saying. There are ways to practice and prep for this type of communication, especially when you spend time working on active listening. If you haven't tapped into a basic foundational element like listening, you can't get into the back and forth of exchanging information, giving feedback, or asking questions.

Conversation is so much more than what you say—it's about how you say it. When you're talking to another person at work, you're not only balancing the content, you're attending to status. We'll deep dive into the ideas behind "Yes, and" versus "Yes, but" shortly, but it's important to note that something as simple as a three-letter word you've probably used in the last 24 hours can completely change the dynamic of a conversation—and the substitution of that three-letter word for another three-letter word can change everything.

When it comes down to the environment where we do the communicating, a celebratory culture expedites effective and supportive communication . . . but what happens when both people aren't on board with the conversation?

While interpersonal communication is one of the most unexpected parts of professional communication, it can be the most rewarding. It's not every day you give massive presentations or lead group meetings. Chances are, it *is* every day you talk to people in your office. That makes it something you can almost immediately work on and improve, with just a little nudge.

ACTIVE LISTENING

Think about the last conversation you had. How much of it do you remember? Did you stay focused on what they were saying, or did you drift off thinking about something or someone else? When I started teaching, I worked with kids. Kids are great—they'll let you know immediately when they aren't listening to you. They'll actually show you because they'll start fidgeting, talking, humming, or straight up say, "This is boring!"

Adults are terrible. Adults will feign interest. They'll smile, nod, and look like they are paying attention, all while thinking about their emails, work, things that are happening at home, their date, or breakfast. I'm guilty of this, as we all are. It happens and usually we can all get away with it in many situations. The problems come when you need to remember something you just heard, or if a person just gave information that is imperative to your job. Then you have to guess or you go back and ask, or you do it wrong based on what you thought you heard.

Hearing and listening are two *very* different things. We hear things all the time. I still remember one of my first cubical jobs. I was in a cube next to someone who breathed very loudly through their mouth. It made me crazy and I couldn't concentrate until I got headphones. All I would think about was his breathing, so that's all I could focus on. When I started focusing on it, it was all I heard.

Active listening is making that conscious choice to hear what someone is saying *and* understanding the message being conveyed, usually by thinking about it. Essentially, you're digesting what's being said. This is a critical skill in improv—and life. When two people come together to create a moment, they have to actively listen to what the other person is saying to create reality in that moment. One of the activities I use to develop active listening is called Three-Line Conversations, or ABA. Two people face one another and in three "lines" they establish *who* they are and *where* they are (sound familiar?). Lines can be one-sentence or one-word long, or they can go on for five minutes. There's no catch. Essentially one person talks, another responds, and the first person responds to that response. For example:

> Person A: Mom, I really want to use the car tonight.
>
> Person B: Only if you come here and dry these dishes.
>
> Person A: OK.

Simple, right?

It's actually one of the hardest activities we teach. It's taught before the longer improv moments because it creates the necessary foundation for using improv as a professional development tool with any kind of focus. In the previous example, Person A is the "child" of driving age, Person B is the "mom" and they are in the "kitchen." The importance of listening comes in and is best shown with an example where listening was done poorly.

This example comes from a longer improv moment. In a private workshop for an engineering firm, one of the things they wanted to work on was listening skills. In most workshops, I start with listening skills anyway because it's the foundation of all communication. A man and woman stood up to start their conversation. The woman started dancing, and the man sat down to pantomime reading the newspaper. She said, "Dad, do you think I'm good enough for *American Bandstand*?" to which he replied "Sure, sure." The conversation kept going, and finally she asked him to pay attention to her, to which he replied, "This is the weirdest strip club I've ever been to!" I am uncomfortable just recalling this situation.

I called for the conversation to end, we gave them a round of applause, and then I followed up with, "How was that?" and "What made you make those choices?" He answered first and said, "You told me that any choice was a good choice as long as we make it." This is really true, I do say this often. But this guy's choices simply didn't fit the situation and probably broke a few human resources (HR) rules. I replied, "Sure, but in the conversation, she was your daughter." His reply, "No she wasn't," and immediately looked at his moment partner, who said, "Yeah, I was."

Dead silence. He didn't hear her because he wasn't listening. He looked mortified that he missed that bit of information and kept moving the conversation along with his original premise. This happens a lot in real life. People are so focused and fixated on what they want to say and their next thought or agenda that they miss what other people say.

While it could have been all agenda-focused thinking, which we'll discuss, it was most likely a combination of agenda, looking forward to making his "funny" comment, and not listening to what his partner was saying. Fortunately, listening is a skill that can be learned over time, and unfortunately, it is a conscious choice. While a person hears between 20,000 and 30,000 words during a 24-hour period, most people remember only about 17 to 25 percent of what they listen to.[2]

This happens because you have the choice to decide to actively listen or to simply hear what people are talking about. When you choose to listen to someone, you're really hearing what they have to say, making sense of it in your brain, and working on the meaning behind it. Simply hearing is exactly what it sounds like: hearing something but not processing it. In active listening, the listener also shows that they are listening. The head nods, smiles, and mmm-hmms, and we do all that we have politely learned to do. The comprehension usually follows. The unfortunate part of this: it's really easy to learn these signs of "listening" and use them when you're not actually listening. The engineer in the conversation between the dad and daughter said, "Yep," and nodded a few times while she was talking to him. He was exhibiting those things he had learned to do to show he was listening, but he was not actually listening at all.

TRY THIS

How do you show you're listening? Take a moment and think about a recent conversation. If you can't remember one, immediately following your next conversation, note the ways that you show that you're listening. Maybe it's smiling and nodding—or maybe it's another away. Jot a few physical and mental actions down before you forget—and don't spend so much time paying attention to yourself that you forget to listen!

This helps you identify how you demonstrate active listening. If you're not doing it well, you can easily increase the intensity or frequency of what you're already doing as a start. This activity draws focus to specific skills you might be using to show listening.

To improve, we need to understand how we listen. Taking note of the ways you show your active listening forces you to pay closer attention to how well you listen. If you find you are in fact not actively listening and simply nodding along, by all means, try to tune in more.

There are ways to show active listening that are better than the yeses, nods, and mmm-hmms. While those are ways to show you are listening, there are several ways to demonstrate your understanding, and improv enhances many of them. First, let's dig into how improv helps with the act of listening.

When you're creating a moment in improv, you know you need to clearly define *who* you are, *where* you are, *what* you want, and *how* you feel. When you're working with one or two other people, you have to create the moment together and the *who, where, what,* and *how* have to agree. I think one of the biggest things people misunderstand about improv is this part: you work together to create the world around you. Think about that earlier example in the Three-Line Conversation of mom and child. They didn't discuss what the conversation was going to be about. One person came up with a premise, and instead of fighting for their own idea (if they had one,) they took the suggestion and went on to the next moment. Now think about the dad in the strip club. He didn't attend to that small bit of information of "Dad" that his conversation partner dropped.

In improv, these bits of information are called *gifts*. A gift is any detail that adds to the world creation, which your partner or partners can then affirm and use to further the conversation. Tina Fey actually presents this idea perfectly in her book *Bossypants*, so I'm adapting her explanation for your understanding.[3]

Say you're in an improv conversation with your partner, and they point their fingers at you like a pair of scissors and say, "Time for a haircut!" and you reply, "That's your hand, not scissors!" You haven't accepted the information and you've actually negated the gift. (And you're probably really difficult to work with, but we'll get to that later.) Now the same situation happens, your partner points their fingers at you like scissors and says, "Time for a haircut!" and you reply, "Oh, OK!" This time, you've taken their gift and affirmed it. Finally, the same situation happens again, your partner points their fingers at you like scissors, and says "Time for a haircut!" and you reply, "Um, didn't you just start cosmetology school yesterday, Mom?"

This last situation? You've not only accepted, you've added more: the scissors, the relationship, cosmetology school, yesterday.

When you connect this idea back, it's not enough to just offer or accept gifts. They have to be taken and used to move the conversation along. In improv, two or more people are making something out of nothing, creating a vibrant world that didn't exist when they started talking. When creating that reality with another person, you have to hang on to every word to know where they are going and drive the conversation forward with this new information. If you're not listening, you end up with a daughter in the strip club. The same with conversation—if you aren't paying attention to one another, you're simply talking *at* each other with no sense of grounded conversation.

There are many different ways to listen, and the most common types of listening in professional communication are informational listening (listening to learn), critical listening (listening to evaluate and analyze), and therapeutic or empathetic listening (listening to understand feeling and emotion).[4] Informational listening is what we might do in a meeting that we don't really care about. We're just attending to the information, taking it in, and often taking notes we might look at later. Critical listening involves thinking about what the person is trying to say—you're thinking beyond just the words you're hearing. You're digesting the information and digging into it, whether with verbal reflection or internal thought. Empathetic listening happens more in your home and personal life. You're thinking about feelings and emotions. While empathy is an important skill in leadership, usually professional situations don't require tapping into the emotional side of things too much. Empathetic listening should be used to understand how the speaker might feel or the circumstances around what they are saying.

TRY THIS

Turn on the TV, a podcast, or a video. First, listen for three gifts. Write them down.

Now listen to learn for two minutes; then listen to evaluate and analyze for another two. How did your listening change or stay the same? Write down a few similarities and differences.

This helps you practice in a safe and controlled environment. You can build this skill at home first, where the stakes are low. This activity gives you a failure-free option.

Jumping back to verbal ways to show that you are actively listening, people generally know a lot of these tactics. The big intentionality happens when you incorporate them into your everyday work conversations. First, remember you want to tap into that improv rule of "show, don't tell." Telling someone "I'm listening" is not as effective or affirming as actually listening to them. Keep in mind that a lot of us have a terrible memory. It's OK! If you struggling with listening and know you have a terrible memory, write things down. Better to write it down than to not remember, right? Even if all you remember is the name of the person you're talking to and one thing they said, you're making a point to connect the words coming out of their mouth to the information those words carry.

TRY THIS

If you want to work on your memory, there is an improv game called Rumor Mill that helps. You can play this game with people you know or with yourself. You start with a statement about someone—maybe it's "Did you hear that Jen has a dog!" The next person says, "Did you hear that Jen has a dog and his name is Drumstick!" The first person (or next, if you're playing with more than two people) says, "Did you hear that Jen has a dog and his name is Drumstick and he's really silly when he's tired?" and so on and so forth. Each person must remember the original rumor and add to it.

If you're playing with yourself, it's the same premise. Say a statement out loud to yourself. Take a breath and add on to it as though you were another person. The key here whether you're playing with a partner or yourself, is focusing on information that is being established and what was said, and not changing the meaning of what's being said. The quick way of doing it would be "Jen's silly dog's name is Drumstick." Sure, that's kind of what was originally said, but not the point.

This helps you develop your listening and summarization skills. We often summarize a lot of information incorrectly because you tune in and tune out of conversations and miss key information. This activity forces you to focus in on the previous statement because you need to repeat it before you add on to it.

Summarization and Reflection

One verbal tactic to show you're listening is summarization. You're taking the key points of what's been said and relaying them back to the speaker. The important part of summarization is making sure you give the speaker a moment to correct if necessary. This is similar to reflection, which is closely paraphrasing what the person just said. Both are foundational skills in the rudimentary part of "Yes, and," which is one of the strongest ways to show you're listening—and a key principle in improv.

When I start teaching "Yes, and" to groups, it's crucial to scaffold the information because it's complicated, nuanced, and when used correctly, magical. We usually start with the simple I See, You See activity. One person starts and says, "I see [something they see in the room]," and the next person will say, "Yes, you see [that something that person one sees in the room] and I see [something else in the room]." It might sound something like this:

Person A: I see a wall.

Person B: Yes, you see a wall and I see a chair.

This is like reflection. You're repeating or closely paraphrasing what the other person just said. Consider this real-life example: I was working on communication skills development for a new group of junior vice presidents at a cable station. Part of my job was to sit in the room and "watch" interactions: mostly take notes about interactions and culture. Listening skills were often lacking. It was infuriating to hear so many people just repeat what the last person said and present it like a totally new idea. You all know what I'm talking about—when you say something and someone says that exact thing a few minutes later, proud of themselves for thinking of the same thing you just thought of. Rage inducing.

I brought up that the team didn't seem to be listening to one another, and suggested they try to use "Yes, and" as part of the solution. This made two things happen: first, everyone had to listen to everyone else. They had to because they weren't sure when they would want to—or could—jump in with an idea. Second, to add their own opinion to the conversation, they had to affirm the person who spoke before them. Notice how they didn't have to agree with one another. What we have essentially done is replace *but* with *and*. The word *but* is contradictory and has a more negative connotation. When we are trying to convey we are actively listening, it may come off as defensive and argumentative. However, by replacing *but* with *and*, we show the other person that we have heard what they are saying, even though we may have a different opinion.

Think about how it feels for a person to listen to you. Great, right? Now think about how it feels when you know they are trying to understand you, and they are vocal about it. "Yes, and" helps you convey exactly this. Boom, magic.

TRY THIS

The next time you're in a professional setting, try to "Yes, and" to someone in conversation. How did it feel? A little contrived at first? That's OK! How did they respond? Keep going with the "Yes, and" and see what happens! "Yes, and" takes time to understand and more time to be natural.

This helps make Yes, and a habit.

Clarification and Questioning

The last two verbal tactics to show active listening are also related: clarification and questioning. Clarification helps you make sure you understand the information the speaker is trying to relay, and uses an open question to let the speaker expand on their points. Questioning involves getting more information from the speaker and often shows interest, as long as the questions are relevant. The two go hand in hand, so we'll address them together as one. There are several different kinds of questions, some are more effective than others for showing that you are listening.

Open-Ended and Closed-Ended Questions

Open-ended and closed-ended questions are some of the most common questions we encounter in our everyday life. Closed-ended questions can be answered with a yes or no. Some examples of closed-ended questions are:

- May I go to the bathroom?

- Do we have salad?

- Can I delete all of my emails?

Open-ended questions, on the other hand, require more than a one-word answer. It might be a list or a paragraph. Some examples of open-ended questions are:

- How should we renovate the bathroom?

- What are your favorite salad add-ons?

- How did all of your emails get deleted?

Open-ended and closed-ended questions are both used when you simply need a response. While open-ended questions are used when you want to evoke conversation, closed-ended questions often end or cut off conversation, since they are answered with one word.

Leading and Loaded Questions

Leading and loaded questions often contain a gift. Leading questions *lead* people to answer in a specific way based on a phrase. They subtly push a person to think and believe in a manner determined by the question asker. Some examples of leading questions are:

- Do you love your beautiful new desk?

- Isn't the boss the greatest?

- How do you feel about our amazing customer service?

In all of those questions, something is quantified, and they are pushing the answerer to be positive.

A loaded question is similar in that it pushes a person to a response. It assumes something about the question answerer and pushes them toward one kind of answer. Some examples of loaded questions are:

- What do you love about the space?

- What do you hate about the nachos?

- What do you like about our customer service?

These questions assume that the person loves, hates, or likes the things they are being questioned about.

Repeated Questions
The final kind of question is a repeated question—this doesn't add information or request more. It usually happens when someone doesn't know what to say next and is simply repeating back something that someone just said. If one person says, "I'm tired of all this noise," the repeated question might be, "Oh, you're tired of all this noise?" You're regurgitating the information in the form of a question.

The only types of questions you should be using in a professional setting are open- and closed-ended questions. Remember, you're having a conversation, and you want there to be a back-and-forth rapport between you and the other person. I tell students, you want to trade off between the driver role and the passenger role. If you're the only one talking or doing most of the talking, you're probably driving and should give someone else a turn. By asking those open-ended questions, you're looking for additional information, and you're letting the other person "lead" the conversation. The argument can also be made that you're actually lead-ing the conversation because the questions you're asking are resulting in the other person giving additional information. This is actually the perfect scenario because you are going back and forth, conveying that you are listening.

If you ask a question, you're driving: you're influencing what gets said next. The person who's expected to answer the question gets to choose what they respond with. They don't have to answer your question, and if they do, they can choose to answer your question in any way possible. On the flip side, if someone is asking you a lot of questions in a conver-sation, you can ascertain that they want to (1) know more and (2) show that they're listening. Closed-ended questions can also be used to "show" listening, although because they aren't very detailed, they can be answered in an autopilot mode. Leading and loaded questions are usually asked when someone is focused on what they want out of the conversation. This can be good or bad, depending on how you look at it. If you want to get to the point of something, and you're providing context to the person you are asking a question to, this is direct. Using the information that already exists in the reality you're in (in this case, the office) places that question in context for the person you're talking to—which sets up the conversa-tion in a way that you can *actually* get to the point.

TRY THIS

In the next conversation you have, allow yourself to use different types of questions. Let the questions lead the conversation and see what happens!

This helps train your brain to recognize different types of ques-tions. Too often we question on autopilot, and this activity allows you to be more intentional with your questioning.

Questions might seem out of place when discussing listening, but they're actually very connected to active listening. If you aren't actively listening, you can't show it by asking questions. If you can't show it, the person talking to you might stop, because you become the person who doesn't listen. If people aren't talking to you because you're the person who doesn't listen (or fixates on your own issues more than anything else), your job becomes exponentially more difficult to do, unless you work alone in a lighthouse and never need to talk to anyone to get anything done.

People tell me all the time—I don't need to work on my listening skills. I'm a great listener. Once we start doing any kind of listening activity, they realize very quickly that listening is a lot of work, and they aren't as good as they think they are. I know that I have to work on listening better, as well. We all have room for improvement. I started becoming a much better listener when I realized how much work goes into listening. I used to be *exhausted* after performing. And now I'm exhausted after teaching one class.

A lot goes into being "on" for any duration of time—active listening and presence is a hard world. It should tire you out. I tend to laugh a little when someone says, "Wow, my brain is tired and all I was doing was practicing my listening!" Listening is focusing and digesting information while paying attention to the words coming out of someone else's mouth, all while you're thinking about how to show you're listening, and on top of that, continuing the conversation and considering the words coming out of your mouth, plus remembering what you want out of the conversation.

When you admit and realize how much work goes into active listening, you learn something else very important. You learn that you have to turn your listening on. It's almost like flipping a switch to pay attention and listen to someone. When you decide to turn it on, you also make a decision to turn your focus on. Remember that mouth-breathing cubemate I had? I made a decision to listen to his breathing because I kept thinking about it. It held my focus because I let it. Even right now: think of all the sounds happening in the background while you read. Maybe there is buzzing, talking in a coffee shop, even a train or a radio. At any moment, you could attend to and choose to listen to any one of those things, and your focus will be on that until you focus on something else or enter a meditative space.

Valuable communication does not exist without active listening, and active listening means asking questions to keep the conversation going.

WORK CONVERSATIONS:
ADVICE AND FEEDBACK

If your active listening is the foundation for professional communication, the back-and-forth conversation and its content would be the building blocks.

If you aren't in the moment and if you're thinking about a bunch of other things, you won't be able to have any rapport. When you're in a conversation with someone after you've adjusted yourself so you aren't putting out negative energy (or nervous energy), make an effort to see if you need to be an informational listener or a critical listener. If it's an informational listening situation like when a coworker is telling you about a client, or a problem, or maybe even something they are excited about and they aren't looking for an opinion in return, your presence can be established just by smiling, nodding, and simply paying attention. Don't start thinking about lunch, or your date later, or how many emails are in your inbox. Just listen and show you are paying attention.

A solid way to be sure you are listening for information is an activity we do in our beginning improv classes. While someone is talking, listen carefully and note two points. This balances your informational listening skills. Then practice critical listening: note one question you can follow up on. For example, say I'm talking about my morning and I say I toasted some bread and used some honey to make it a full breakfast, and then I walked my dog. Maybe your two points are (1) I toasted bread and (2) I used honey. The question might be, "What kind of dog do you have?" Simple as that. And it works because if you have a task while listening, you can focus easily on the objective, which is simply to take in information. This gives you content to respond with.

If you are in a conversation where critical listening is necessary such as when your colleague asks for your opinion on a new client, project, or issue, you need to analyze, then respond to the information. It's a good idea to watch *how* you present that response. Essentially, you're giving feedback and possibly internally groaning about the idea of giving feedback because it isn't easy. Giving feedback is one of those skills that often gets lumped into leadership skills. While the ability to give feedback *is* a skill often associated with leadership, it's also part of everyday professional conversation.

Since feedback isn't easy, we as a company use a Glows and Grows concept. A "glow" is something you do well, while a "grow" is something you need to improve on. It's less about focusing on the negative and more about changing for the better. We're constantly modeling this idea of Glows and Grows in workshops, keeping in mind that everyone can benefit from getting solid feedback and learning how to give it. Most people expect feedback when they ask for it, even if they are asking for it in a critical listening situation. Giving it in a way that is effective and actionable allows for the best results. I generally run my feedback through three markers.

The first marker to feedback is safety. If a person gets feedback and they don't feel comfortable in a situation, they won't apply it. Feedback isn't meant to make someone feel foolish or stupid in a situation—it's meant to help them grow. In our improv classes, we're all looking a little silly. That vulnerability lends itself to a safe situation.

Here's an example of that first marker: a new manager started taking our improv classes to learn how to give feedback. His staff would constantly ask him for his opinion, and he was always very nervous about giving it because he thought he was overly critical. Our classes are a lot of fun. I don't mean to brag on this moment, but most people leave our classes sad they're over, and a few students converted into teachers because they loved it so much. We do a lot of laughing, and you bond with people pretty quickly when you're allowing for fun and vulnerability. The manager who wanted to learn feedback took about three classes with us. Each time he talked about how he wanted to be "better" at giving feedback for his team, and each class, he'd come back with another story of someone he offended a bit along the way. Finally, I think he hit his frustration threshold. He approached me after a class and asked how I managed to give tough feedback to people and still keep everyone happy. The first thing I said was, "Well, this is a safe space."

Creating a "safe space" has been a bit of a throwaway and buzz phrase in recent years. It's talked about a lot in leadership and customer service conversations in the workplace. If a workplace is safe, there generally won't be retaliation if someone is upset with feedback or a change, and there is fairly open and good communication and little fear for speaking up. It's also why in improv class I can tell someone that they didn't connect with their partner without worrying too much about someone getting upset with me.

The manager saw the fun, games, and reflection, and then the really solid feedback that was happening. He immediately tried to apply some of it at work—minus the fun and games that helped everyone feel comfortable around one another. While you probably can't play games at work, you can get to know one another through conversation, small talk, and repetitive behaviors. The more you get to know one another, the closer you become and the safer the space. This isn't getting to know one another on a personal social level. You can (and should) keep this professional. What this does is start to create patterns of behavior that lead to a perception of safety. If someone makes a mistake that isn't simply a creative attempt that didn't work out perfectly, for example, try encouraging them to be more careful rather than chiding, or worse, calling them out. The more open conversation and learning are discussed and put into action, the safer the space.

The second marker is specificity. Telling someone that what they just did or said was good is pretty similar to just nodding your head and smiling when they are talking and you're thinking about email. What was good? What needed work? Do you have a suggestion to improve the work? Be as specific as possible. I rarely say, "Oh that was great," and have nothing more to offer—same thing with, "Wow that didn't work." There is always the *why*, which is for you to identify if you want to give effective feedback that they can actually connect with something tangible to work on.

The third marker is immediacy. The feedback has to be immediate, or as immediate as possible. You need to tie it to the action that recently happened, not the action that happened two months ago. If you can't do something in the here and now, then wait for it to happen again. If too much time passes, you're going to end up with a warped history of what happened and everyone is going to be a little confused.

If a conversation starts with a critical listening moment, you better believe you're going to be giving feedback—or at least expected to give feedback. By running your feedback through these three markers, you can give effective and clear information that will be helpful, instead of a polite smile and nod.

QUICK TRY THIS!

Recall the last time you left a conversation and thought, "I wish I would have said this!" What happened? What would you say if you got a do-over with what you know now?

This helps you reflect on past conversations to see if you have habits in the woulda, coulda, shouldas. We often have that regretful moment when we think of something "perfect" after the moment has passed. This activity lets you account for this feeling.

I Wish I Would Have . . .

Being present in the moment will eventually allow you the time to say what you'd like, but at first, there will be a lot of, "Oh, I wish I would have thought of this" that hits you later on. When you start being present, you are usually too busy paying attention to think of things on the spot that you want to say, which leads to more frustration that the skill isn't developing fast enough. This cycle will happen for a while. When we learn a new skill, there is a learning curve, and we experience something called Going Against the Grain. This causes a temporary decline in execution before jumping forward in performance. Essentially, you get as far as you can, then you have a learning opportunity, then you have stress because "it's not working yet," then you leap forward with performance recovery and growth, and the whole process repeats itself.

Going Against the Grain is a learning moment, especially working on responding in the here and now. But this is what practicing improv is about. Being present *is* improv. You're responding and reacting to the world and situation around you. You're not thinking or regretting; you're simply doing. When you're having that conversation and you're working on a response that might be feedback or a reaction, or simply showing that you are paying attention, give yourself some grace and silence to think about what you will say next, as well as some grace in your reflection afterward.

I can't tell you how many students say, "I'm just not good at this." This is new territory for many of us. We're used to planning what we want to say or thinking about our response before the other person even finishes talking. It's new, so there will be some stress and discomfort. While you're working past those moments of stress and discomfort, you can slowly start responding in the here and now with one trusty phrase we touched on earlier: "Yes, and."

Let's return to that new manager and his feedback problem. After we worked out the foundation of feedback, we thought about his style of presenting the information. He was giving feedback and using a lot of language that made his staff defensive. Expressions like "but" and "if only" and "well actually" elevated his status when he gave feedback, and immediately put them on the defense to "fight" for their worth. Substitute the phrase "Yes, and" for "but," and you have one of the best improv rules for conversation, feedback, and conflict.

One of the items of feedback he had for his team involved their social media accounts. They were a new start-up, and he was tasked with making the millennial staff be less millennial. The founder was upset at how much social media posting not related to work was happening during the workday. Instead of saying, "But we told you not to be on your phone unless you're also contributing to our social presence," we substituted "Yes, and": "Yes, we know that you're on the phone during the day, and we told you not to be unless you're contributing to the social presence of the company."

The difference between the "But" and the "Yes, and" seems simple enough at first. *But* tends to pit two things against one another. *But* often elevates one thing above another. *But* is a word that we think we need to immediately argue against. The word *And* is an equal sign. You're putting two things together and framing them as equals. In the manager example, it's more about eliminating the "But" to eliminate the argument. It got a bit more complicated when he came back to the next class and told us that he used "Yes, and," and his staff came back with, "You don't trust us. We feel like you're micromanaging us by telling us to post about the company."

My response to him again? "Yes, and": "Yes, you feel like I don't trust you. And I'm sorry. I would like to fix this—how can we?"

Yes, this sounds contrived. Think of what it does, though. You're affirming what the other person is saying and feeling. This is a great way to make sure you understand what is happening with the other person. You're forcing yourself to listen and be present. It also lets you think a bit more about what you're going to say next. Affirming an emotion or a statement from someone is an excellent way to make them feel validated. Yes, you feel this, Yes, you feel that—it doesn't start an argument with that person by trying to make them feel something else. It simply takes what they are feeling and confirms you understand it.

The point of "Yes, and" isn't to agree with someone—you aren't a doormat that says Yes to everything. "Yes, and" enables you to have that open conversation with a colleague, one that is a real back-and-forth exchange of ideas and information. Consider this example:

You're having a talk with a colleague about something they feel very strongly about—and you feel strongly about it too. For this example, let's say we're talking about a new initiative or program. They present the information:

> Them: I think we need to start this program next week.

> You: Yes, you think we need to start this program next week, and I think we need to wait a bit first.

You've affirmed what they think and linked your idea with that *and*, making them equal. You're not necessarily agreeing with what they said. In this case, you aren't agreeing at all, you're presenting a completely different viewpoint. You are allowing the two opinions to be equal because they are. You aren't saying, "but we need more time," which would elevate your thought over theirs.

TRY THIS

Strike up a conversation with someone about any topic at all. It could be about something that is actually happening at work or something superficial, like nachos. Tell them you are trying a new communication tactic for this conversation, so you are going to be saying "Yes, and" a lot. Afterward, ask them how it felt, or simply reflect yourself. How did the conversation go? Was it helpful? Aside from contrived, how did it feel?

> *This helps* you start to use "Yes, and" in everyday conversation. Often times we learn it in a clinical or professional development setting and have a hard time applying it to day-to-day conversations. This activity helps you use it immediately.

Status

A big part of the elevation of one phrase above another and why "Yes, and" works so much better than "But" in conversations is because of status. Status is a tricky thing in the workplace, especially in communication. Understanding your status and your coworker's status—as well as how they perceive your status and their status—is critical to effective communication.

In improv, status is always considered. If you have two high-status individuals in a moment—maybe two kings, two CEOs, two billionaires—that moment might be marked with arguing and fighting to keep the higher status or might be amazing because two motivated people are working to a common goal. At the same time, two low-status characters might end up with a battle of no-decisions—how much responsibility can two court jesters pass to one another? Or the two might work together to overthrow something else, which turns into a battle of statuses. Similar statuses can be effective or challenging. When you have two vastly different statuses, things often get a little awkward because one person is clearly above another. This is true in real life, as well.

Many times when I go in for company consulting, we end up diagnosing companies with some communication issues. Sometimes it's the culture, and sometimes it's one or two people who have communication issues. Many times, it's either an empathy issue (not understanding emotions) or a status issue.

One venture capital firm we worked with in the first years of EE had a lot of status problems. A few members of the staff had the old guard mentality—that is, they were there the longest and felt they should be treated as if they had the most authority. One woman in particular felt she could never be wrong, had the most authority in the group, and no one should question her. She had a PhD and often said that it was exhausting "being the smartest person in the room." She even said that out loud, around coworkers. The director was at a loss because when this woman was questioned on her self-described authority, she blew up at whoever questioned her—including him.

This was all a moment of perceived status. Because she was part of the company longer than everyone else, including the executive director, she thought she should have unquestioned authority. She saw herself as high status and everyone else as lower status. This was a difficult situation because we aren't HR experts. EE usually gets brought in as a softer option, something to try before larger measures are taken. Our plan? We did a few improv moments that played with status. Even in those improv moments, she had to be the higher-status character. Whenever anyone else tried to take the higher status in the conversation—even ones that involved kings and queens talking to servants, the ultimate stereotypical status conversation—she would fight to have it back.

In this particular situation, we discussed status and what we preferred: high or low. Surprise, this woman talked about how she preferred the higher-status characters. It gave her a sense of control, she admitted, and also a sense of responsibility. If she got the thing done that needed to be done, she could relax. Waiting for someone else to get the same thing done was really stressful for her. See, sometimes people who like higher-status characters aren't complete sociopathic control freaks. Sometimes, they like control and responsibility, which comes with higher status, but it's much less about being the "highest in command" and more about being the one who gets things done.

As improv moments often do, we continued to dig in her behavior, and one coworker brought up her smartest-person-in-the-room comment, to which she said, "Oh, I wasn't insulting. None of you have PhDs." Here's where that lack of empathy comes in. She was so shortsighted that she couldn't see how her comment was bothering her coworkers. She only thought about her own accomplishments. As the conversation continued, people started to discuss her behavior. We were pretty lucky she didn't feel attacked. She was just oblivious to how her comments were bothering and offending her coworkers. While this was a joint issue, a lot of this connects to status, both actual and perceived.

How do you connect this to your experiences? Start by thinking about how you see yourself and how you see others. If you see yourself above others, you very well might be treating them the same way this woman was treating her colleagues. If you see yourself below others, you might be lacking some of the confidence required for people to see you as equal. You get the energy you put out, remember?

Think of situations at work and people you interact with. Write out three different people or groups of people, and assign high or low status. You can also look at them like a deck of cards. A 2 will have a lower status than a K or an A. Now look at your own status with these people, and rate it on the same 2–A card scale. How does this affect your relationships and communication?

This helps you start considering status when you're talking to people. It's often something we either ignore completely or use subconsciously. This activity draws your attention to it.

There is an improv activity called Mirroring that I love for status work that immediately connects to real life. In Mirroring, one person leads and you follow the leader. The leader isn't predetermined. Two people face one another, and someone just starts moving. What ends up happening is one person will start and the other will follow along, then the other will take the lead, and the first person will follow along. The leader and follower positions are fluid. Maybe one person chooses to lift their arm and the other decides to move their head at the same time. The activities, if done slowly enough, will blend into one another instead of seeing one obvious leader.

> *This helps* you connect with status in a physical world. We often forget that status is not just expressed verbally; it's also very physical. This activity draws attention to the physical.

The problem with the woman in the example with the venture capital firm is that she kept making comments that established her status over her colleagues. She may not have intentionally been trying to one-up her colleagues, but that's exactly what she was doing, and her colleagues did not like it one bit. If you are constantly trying to one-up someone with status, you're probably not going to be perceived as the best coworker or conversation partner.

On the flip side of the woman in our venture capital example, what happens when someone is constantly taking the lower status in conversations? Please note this behavior, and don't be the person who constantly takes the lower status in conversations because you think that self-deprecation is a good strategy. Again, you get the energy you put out. If you are constantly the lower-status person because you think you deserve to be or you feel it's easier to be the lower status, you're always going to get the lower status, and with that comes lower respect.

We are all equal and should be treated as equal. Therefore, the best way to establish your status in a company is to match or complement the statuses and the energy of the people you're talking to in everyday conversations. Say you're speaking to a coworker and they are really excited about a project they have coming up—you can totally be excited for them and not get jealous or lash out with microaggressions. You're both pretty amazing, I'm sure. If you are talking to someone who is really upset that something didn't work out well, you probably should hold off the #Humblebrag (more on that soon) on your project until there is a better moment. You shouldn't feel less about your successful project; just maybe wait to celebrate with them. That's not to say you should undercut what you've done in your workweek for someone else to feel better.

It's a bit like reading the room. Try to figure out the status and energy of the person you're talking to, and have your status match theirs. This, of course, doesn't mean you should talk down to your boss or the CEO—in fact, you shouldn't be talking down to anyone. It means you should try to match their presence and confidence. Speak with authority, be positive, and communicate in a way that lifts others up.

Autopilot On

What about those times in conversation when we can't help but zone out? It happens to everyone. In improv class, it's right there in plain sight. Remember the daughter at the strip club? That might have been zoning out. If you find yourself doing this, especially in that 3 p.m. hour of sleepiness during the workday, you can go into a bit of autopilot *and* pay attention at the same time. Mirroring also works well for this; if you find yourself unable to remember details while someone is talking to you, it's helpful to repeat in your head the words they are saying to store the information and think about it in multiple ways. You're getting the information through them saying it, you thinking about it, and you repeating it in your head.

You're also practicing the concept of mindful listening. While this is often seen as an alternative in some workplaces, mindfulness, according to Jon Kabat-Zinn, professor of medicine emeritus at the University of Massachusetts Medical School, is simply "paying attention in a particular way, on purpose, in the present moment, and nonjudgmentally."[5] Making a choice to mirror or actively listen *is* mindful listening. Improv is mindful listening as well: that choice to listen is yours and yours alone.

Aside from active listening and status, one of the biggest issues I see in conversation in the workplace happens when people formulate answers before the question has even been asked. A few things happen: the first, people go into that checked-out autopilot with answers. I bet you've done it too: Think of the last time you took a flight. You're going past the person who is checking tickets, and they say, "Enjoy your flight!" and you respond without missing a beat, "You too!" Wait, that person is not flying, they check tickets.

This automatic response happens a lot, and it's a bit of not listening and a bit of speaking before you think. You hear the beginning of the comment or question, and you go immediately into your canned response. This also happens with, "Hey how are you?" someone will ask, you'll say, "I'm fine, how are you?" and that person will say, "I'm fine, how are you?" If someone notices, there is usually a big question mark blank face.

When someone asks the same thing twice, they are probably distracted by something else and not remaining completely present in the situation. Presence is really exhausting, remember? This autopilot and lack of active listening happen often when we are too busy to take time to attend to the person in front of us.

TRY THIS

A great improv activity for this issue is called Last Word. Try this with a coworker or partner. You say a statement, anything at all. It could be as simple as "Nachos are good." The person you're talking to has to use the last word of your sentence as the first word of their next sentence. They could reply with, "Good food is hard to find," and then you'd start your next sentence with the word "find," and it would carry on as such. Aside from getting a great laugh out of this activity, you are forced to wait until the person is done talking—until their thought is completely out of their mouth before you can even start to formulate your answer. Since you have to use that last word to start your sentence, you have to wait until that last word happens, and when it does, you have to take the time to process the information to formulate your next sentence.

Even better and harder: Try to make as much sense of the conversation as possible. Give yourself time to pause, time to think, and really make the dialogue make sense. It won't always make sense, and that's why I don't recommend using this activity as is in the workplace for conversation if the other person doesn't know what you're doing. You're going to look a little crazy and sound a little like Yoda if you're constantly using the last word of the previous sentence to start your next sentence.

This helps you listen and respond with care. We often formulate an answer before the question is even finished. This activity forces you to listen, process, and respond.

In your next conversation, take a moment when the person is done speaking to think about what you're going to say next based on their last word. By doing this, you'll be attending to the person and having a conversation that won't have those drifting-off moments. On top of that, pauses are confident. Don't rush a person when they are speaking, and be comfortable with silence in your speech pattern as well as in the speech patterns of who you're listening to.

CELEBRATE THE UNHUMBLE MOMENTS!

This next area of professional interpersonal communication is a tough one for a lot of people; it's why we started a class on it. Think of your last professional accomplishment. It might be speaking at a conference, or maybe landing a great client, or accomplishing a goal you have been working on for a while. Now think about how you talked about that accomplishment. Did you tell your coworkers? Did you just tell your friends and family? Did you tell no one?

We spend a lot of time *working* at work and when something "bad" happens, we might spend a lot of time trying to fix what happened or making sure that doesn't happen again. We don't spend nearly enough time celebrating accomplishments. It's one of the reasons we talk about Grows and *Glows*—what are you doing well?

There is a lot to unpack when it comes to why we don't celebrate accomplishments in the workplace, why we should, and why we have such a hard time talking about the things we're proud of. Let's first start internally with celebrating our own accomplishments. Talk to any number of individuals, and you'll hear how we all need to be humble to succeed as well as how we need to work on being less humble to succeed. I'm willing to bet the group you ask will be divided, probably right in half.

Yes, I absolutely believe you should have some sense of humility, and I also believe we do ourselves a disservice when we are too humble, so we need to work on UnHumbling ourselves.

EE actually started our UnHumble class in 2017. One of the things people, specifically women, needed to work on was their confidence in talking about accomplishments. These ideas of humility and humbleness go too far when people can't even discuss what they are proud of. Look up how to be humble at work, and every other entry, from big sites to small blogs, dive into things like "6 Ways Humility Can Make You a Better Leader." (*Fast Company*) to "8 Reasons Why You Shouldn't Be

Too Humble at Work" (LifeHack). Sometimes, being humble is associated with being a doormat, letting other people take credit for your work, being walked on in meetings and in the office, being a pushover. On the other hand, being humble can also be seen as a positive. Humble people listen well. They put others first, they use "we" and "us" more than "I."

So what's your definition of *humble*? I think the best definition of *humble* is our own, and it's important to be humble. At the same time, I believe that it's a struggle to talk about our accomplishments. It's even hard for some people in an improv moment to talk about accomplishments! In life and improv, we use qualifiers like, "Oh, it was just . . ." or "It wasn't a big deal . . . ," which temper the responses toward our success. We don't want our accomplishments to come across like bragging, so we soften them with statements that make them sound like they're "no big deal."

TRY THIS

Define *humble*. My own definition of *humble* involves caring as much about other people as you do yourself, and not looking for a parade when you recycle, but a mutual celebration when something really amazing happens.

Now list your last big accomplishment—something *that* you are proud of.

How long did it take you to think of that accomplishment?

This helps you understand what humble means to you, as well as how difficult (or easy) it might be for you to talk about your accomplishments. While this isn't a public talk on your accomplishments, it might still make you uncomfortable.

The issue with these qualifiers is that they are statements that qualify what you're saying. You want to eliminate all of the half-hearted lead-up to something; you don't talk about doing it, you simply do it. Remember the "show, don't tell" idea? It's like that—stop talking around it, just do it or say it. Qualifiers aren't completely weak and evil. They can be a good thing, especially when you're uncertain of something. Ask yourself, are you sure about what you're going to say? If yes, say it! If not, then it's OK to use a qualifier. And make sure your answer isn't, "well, I think I'm sure, but I don't know what they will think." Here's an example:

In one of our UnHumble classes, one woman wanted to learn how to talk about her sales goals with her coworkers. She was a realtor who had set personal goals every year. This year, she had surpassed her goal of a million dollars in sales. It was something she personally set for herself and wasn't requested by a boss. Sure, the company itself had individual goals, but this particular one was all hers. She was so excited she had accomplished it but couldn't bring herself to talk about it with her co-workers without saying something like, "Oh, it was just this little thing I do," or "It's not a big deal, I just set a goal for myself, so it doesn't mean anything." Sound familiar?

In class, I asked her to get to the point of her statement: be specific, be simple, and eliminate the qualifiers if she meant what she was about to say. She looked at me and said, of course, she meant it, she just didn't know if anyone else cared.

Know what? They might not. No one might care you made your goal. No one might want to hear about how you made your goal. No one might want to celebrate with you. And no one might say congrats when you say it—they might not even fake it.

Know what else? You don't know how anyone will respond, because an everyday conversation is always improv. Even if you've had the exact same conversation several times with different people, you aren't in this person's brain to see what they want to say and what they actually will say. Thinking you know that they won't care or that they'll judge you is thinking you can predict the future. And you can't.

I asked this realtor if other people could change how proud she was. Did it matter what others thought? At this point, even if she said no, I knew it was a lie. We all, to some extent, care what other people think of us. It's a higher or lower degree of importance in people, but we all have some kind of concern for the opinions of others. The best and worst part about that? We can't change them—they have to be changed by the person who has the opinion.

That's one of the reasons I asked her to remove the "oh, it's just this little thing I've done"—if they were going to hate it or make fun of her for having goals, they would regardless of the qualifier. All the qualifier did was lessen the information and make it weak—and no matter who is listening, it was a true statement. She hit her personal sales goal and was excited about it.

Being specific and getting to the point are great ways to balance the worry we might have about bragging about our accomplishments. Remove the qualifiers and focus on the facts. This includes removing words like *very*, *too*, *so* and anything that adds an amount to what you're going to talk about. Keeping the emphasis on your accomplishment, you should also remove things like, "Oh, it was easy," or "It's really no big deal." Stick to the facts of what you're proud of.

TRY THIS

Go back to that accomplishment you thought of earlier and say it out loud, without any qualifiers. Remember, qualifiers add some kind of amount or emotion to the accomplishment. How did it feel?

This helps you get comfortable talking about your accomplishments. We often know what we're proud of and can't express it well. This activity starts to build comfort in talking about accomplishments.

Celebrate Your Accomplishments and Your Coworkers

Another way to talk about accomplishments in a way that doesn't make you feel like you're bragging is the magic improv rule yet again: "Yes, and." The *idea* behind "Yes, and" is present here, rather than the actual words. You are more than welcome to use the words, but they aren't necessary. If you're proud of something you did, and you're about to talk about your accomplishments, make a point to not compare your accomplishments to another person—either in a positive and negative manner.

Say you're talking about a client goal. You want to serve a certain number of clients this month. When you're talking about that goal and how good you feel about potentially accomplishing it, you have no reason to talk about someone else's performance. Why pit yourself against another person and their goals? We often go to the deprecation strategy—

either for ourselves or for someone else. Does that person have anything to do with your personal accomplishment? No. So don't bring someone else down by lifting yourself up. At the same time, if you're excited about your goal or accomplishment, you don't need to bring up someone else's to belittle yours.

Here are examples of both, starting with the negative. Back to those client goals for the month: if you say, "No one even got close to how many clients I've gotten this month!" you're belittling others to elevate yourself. What do they have to do with your success? Now the positive (ultimately negative) way of comparing: "Well, Kelly brought in more clients than me this month, so no big deal." Why bother to bring up Kelly? I'm sure she's nice and all, but what does her goal have to do with yours? Is she even there?

Talking about other people when they aren't in the room brings up a can of worms we'll discuss in further detail later.

Celebrate Together to Build Your Team

While it may seem like I'm going off the rails talking about celebrating, I bring it up because celebration is a key workplace conversation we should all have with our colleagues. Celebrating with others helps us not only learn to talk about our own accomplishments but also allows us to bond with our coworkers, so we may connect with them better for future conversations. While celebration might be a far cry from the norm of your office, you can start it simply by celebrating your own accomplishments.

Talk about your accomplishments, don't self-deprecate, don't compare, don't belittle someone else by talking about your accomplishments. And let other people talk about theirs while you are genuinely listening and excited for them. It's incredibly powerful to listen to someone. By celebrating your accomplishments with your coworkers and celebrating theirs *just as much*, you eliminate the braggart part that everyone worries about, because you're genuinely happy for other people. And they will be genuinely happy for you. We get the energy we put out. Sharing your accomplishments not only models successful behavior for everyone, it also inspires everyone.

Sharing celebrations with your coworkers are great conversation moments and help foster team building. Now I'm not suggesting we should have a party for every success or take time out to tell everyone you answered an email. I just think we need to celebrate more often and get excited about accomplishments.

When you're thinking about how to share your accomplishments, think in specifics and tell a story. What happened? Why are you excited? Who cares? Keep those things in mind when you're talking to a coworker. Remember not to compare, and keep it about you, not belittling someone else or even belittling yourself.

Relationships, even professional ones, are all about the ups and downs. You have to share both the successes and the low points. Too often, conversations with coworkers can default to complaining. In improv conversations, the go-to is arguing. It's really easy to argue. The problem with an argue-based moment is the loop you end up with. You said this, he said that, you think this, no I don't, yes you do ... all of the back and forth that happens in an argument is similar to the complaining route of coworkers. When you start complaining, you keep going down the route of complaining, and getting out of it needs a full stop. The balance is healthy. As difficult as it might be to share complaints *and* accomplishments, both make for a strong team.

If you manage people, it's crucial to celebrate their successes just as much as your own. A recent study from OC Tanner, an organization focused on engagement and culture in the workplace, shows that almost 80 percent of people who quit their jobs do so because of a lack of appreciation.[6] In improv, we do something called world building where all of those gifts add to the who, where, what, and how, and build the world. If you manage or are part of a larger team, you have to make sure the world you're creating is one that celebrates. By celebrating the success of your employees, you enhance the team connection. If someone feels their success contributes to a bigger picture of success, and they know you appreciate that and understand they contribute to those larger successes, they feel that sense of belonging.

This culture can be built regardless of whether you manage people or are managed. Even the small gestures add to the greater feeling. Saying "Great job," and "Thank you!" contribute to an appreciative work culture. What doesn't work is thinking the "Thank you" is implied or that gratitude should be used to soften a blow of feedback. The latter is a qualifier. If you're using positive feedback simply to soften criticism, you're lessening both items by not being intentional. If you mean both and are intentional with both, it works. Both are critical to building a strong team in the office, and improv lends itself to strong teams.

Team building is a natural side effect of improv. You see, improv in the office usually results in people doing an activity together for a common goal and often laughing together. Research by American neuroscientist Robert Provine states that "laughter is the quintessential human social signal. Laughter is about relationships."[7] While we have very specific relationships when we're thinking about professional situations, they are still relationships. That human connection brings people closer together and lets them work together on a common goal, instead of working side by side on the same thing. A few years ago, we worked with a group of summer interns and their focus was team building. Our contact really wanted us to help the interns feel connected to the rest of the company. Sounds great, right?

The problem: no one else from the company was there. It was only the summer interns. Don't get me wrong—they definitely connected with each other. Improv for team building not only lets you see how other people work, but laughing together, celebrating, and having fun together is a great way to get to know one another better. They even took an activity back to the larger group and emailed me about it later, telling me how well it worked to get folks excited about accomplishments in the workplace.

The activity is called Yes, Let's!. It starts with the group either standing in a circle or in some way so they can all see one another. One person calls out, "Hey! Let's [insert an activity]!" to which everyone in the group answers, "Yes, let's!" and then starts doing it. It might sound like:

> Person A: Hey! Let's yell as loud as we can!
>
> Group: Yes, let's!
>
> (Everyone yells as loud as they can.)
>
> Person B: Hey! Let's sneak around the room!
>
> Group: Yes, let's!
>
> (Everyone sneaks around the room.)

And so on and so forth.

The reason the intern (Morgan) said it worked to celebrate? They all did a thing together, and because they got to let their guard down and play, they trusted one another. In 2011, Google conducted a study they monikered "Project Aristotle," a play on the famous philosopher's quote, "The whole is greater than the sum of its parts."[8]

This study indicated that the best teams—the most effective and highest performing ones had "high psychological safety." These teams could to take a risk without worrying about embarrassment or punishments for their mistakes.

Sounds a lot like improv, and sounds exactly like what happened with the interns.

When they saw one another let their guards down, they connected to each other. When they all did the same thing together, they felt closer. When they felt closer, they trusted one another and worked better as a team, and they could celebrate with one another.

TRY THIS

Tomorrow at work, tell someone you're proud of something they did. Don't pretend. Look at the things that have been accomplished in the last few months, and pick something you really are impressed with. Don't say it just to say it. Mean it, and don't qualify it. If you need a script, you can say: "Hey [name of person], I wanted to tell you how proud I am of you for doing [this thing]." If this feels weird, you can also say: "Hey [name of person], great job with [specific thing]." See what happens, and how they react.

This helps you talk about accomplishments and pride, even if it starts with someone other than you. Building a culture of celebration takes time, and this activity starts that journey.

WHAT HAPPENS WHEN NOTHING WORKS?

You're not pizza: not everyone will like you.

I read that quote years ago, from a Post-It on a friend's desk. I don't know if it was the hot pink, the fun handwriting, the fact that pizza is the best, or the sheer honesty of that quote, but it's stuck with me. So true, right? We're always going to have one or two (or more) people we just don't click with. Sometimes, this happens in a very obvious manner and you can just ignore that person. Sometimes, it's a little less obvious.

We've had multiple students come to classes with us and stick around after to chat with the facilitator about personal things. A lot of the time, it's work conflict. They have been trying and trying to "click" with someone at work. Sometimes it's their boss, and sometimes it's a coworker. All of the time, they have tried everything they have thought of, and they just can't find that common ground. They have tried to be serious and dedicated to the job and to be friendly, and nothing is working.

Sometimes the reality is that no matter what we try, it just doesn't work, and you just can't communicate with some people. If this happens, this is a nice time to check in on your own communication: Do you feel like you need to hold back information at work? Why? When you share information, do you feel like people are listening to you? Are you listening to them when they share information, or are you distracted by the outside influence? In an improv moment between two people, this distraction often happens in the form of talking about a third person who isn't in the room. This person is a distraction from what's happening in front of you, and the conversation might be making you feel uncomfortable. Instead of leaning into the discomfort, you talk about something else that isn't right there. Are you letting people get to know *you*, or are you keeping everyone so far away they can't connect with you?

If you've done a quick diagnostic, and you're using "Yes, and," adjusting your status, trying to celebrate, paying attention when they talk, asking questions—and you *still* can't connect, this might be one of those people you simply can't connect with. Because remember, you aren't pizza.

We can try and try and try—and sometimes, you just might not connect with the person in front of you. *This is OK.* You cannot please everyone, and you can't actually change how anyone communicates. Even if you're modeling the best communication, celebration, and clarity, you can't change how someone else communicates. You can only change how you respond to their communication.

That's it.

YOUR CHEAT SHEET

Professional communication can be a bit tricky at times—you're balancing the line between professional and friendly, confident and cocky, serious and everyday. The tightrope isn't an easy one: it can be easier if you keep the foundation in mind—actively listen to people. Put down your phone, your thoughts about dinner, or your inbox, and when someone is talking to you, pay attention, show you're listening, and respond to what's happening in front of you. If you focus in on what that person is saying and respond to *that*, you've got a conversation. Your qualifiers will take time, as will your ability to be UnHumble, and that's OK. Those are things you can work toward. Today, just listen.

- Focus on the words coming out of *their* mouth.

- Respond to the words and the meaning.

- Celebrate accomplishments.

- Be specific with feedback.

- Attend to status.

- Remember: not everyone communicates like you.

Networking and Small Talk

I am a closeted introvert. I love to create situations where people have a wonderful time or teach people a new skill, and then go hide in the back.

I really, desperately, wholly, completely hate networking situations. You know what I'm talking about: those big lead-generating moments where everyone needs your one-liner and wants to know how you can help them, only to be talked over when they decide you aren't the lead they are looking for. Those big parties or social situations where you're meant to find more business, get a new job, or connect with new people. You're attempting to expand your network, but your brain becomes fried with small-talk situations that feel a little bit like torture.

Did I mention I'm a closeted introvert? Many people don't believe me when I tell them that—that I hate big social situations and would rather just quietly sit at home or talk to one or two other people.

It might be because networking often feels fake, transactional, and focused on results. As a self-described process over product person, I think that being around people so focused on products makes me mental. It might be that networking feels cold and calculated. It might be because it feels cliquish; some people network only with people they like, and people who know people they know, which changes the dynamic quite a bit.

While I agree with the cold sentiment, I don't always think you have to network with people you like. Sure! Networking with folks you like makes it easier. It also creates this incestuous bubble of connection. Know the same 10 people you see talking to one another at every networking event in your field? They are their own network. You have to meet new people to actually take advantage of networking.

Taking a class—like one in improv—is a great way to network because when you are in class together you are creating a bond over a shared hobby. However, if you want to meet people outside of those who share your interests, you will have to prepare for those impromptu situations. Before we move into any new tips, let's take a minute to refresh what we learned in the previous two chapters, because you'll need to use them in a networking situation:

- **Pay attention to your audience.** What kind of situation are you going into? What do they want? What do you want? Do a brief identification of who they are.

- **What version of you needs to show up?** When I'm doing work for EE and networking on behalf of EE, I need to show up as a certain version of me depending on the audience. College students and professors? I need to be a bit fun and funky. Learning and development crowd in the South? I'm pulling out a pair of heels and covering my shoulders—no F-bombs to be seen. New York City? Usually donned in my professional end of attire and very little filter in my workshops—straight to the point with no fluff.

- **Listening is crucial.** You have a very short time (usually) to get to know people in a networking situation. Pay attention. Stop thinking about your email or what you're doing next. Be present.

Now that we've recapped those skills, let's move on. A necessary evil to professional and personal development, networking can make or break your next career move. Studies estimate 70 to 80 percent of jobs are not published online, which makes networking even more crucial.[1]

A DIFFERENT KIND OF WHAT YOU WANT

Once you've thought about your audience and what version of you is coming out for this audience (and if you haven't, do it now), dive deeper into what they want. What kind of people might be at this event? What are their objectives? Are they there for the food or for the people? Are they going because they have to or because they want to? "Have to" versus "want to" changes how people feel about a situation. If someone has to be there, they don't want to be immediately hit by your résumé. If they want to be there, is it because of the potential of meeting someone, or because of the food, location, drinks? These would all require a different approach and direction in conversation. A quick overarching note for all networking and small talk: you don't want to treat this as simply transactional. You also don't want this to be completely wide open and spontaneous, especially if this is the first time you've thought about a networking event in advance and didn't just go on a whim.

Who could be there and why are you going? This is a little like how you feel in a conversation, and if you don't care, why bother? If you don't care who is going to be there and you're going because you have to, that energy is going to come right back to you, and apathy isn't pretty. Once you figure out who might be in the room and why you're going, think about those wants and what you want out of an ideal situation. What would be the best-case scenario with the best results?

One of my favorite things to work on with people is networking, which is hilarious because I hate it so much. To be clear, while I personally don't like it, I do find it fascinating and I enjoy helping people feel comfortable doing it. Recently, I was working with a man who was trying to get a new job in tech. He was in a bit of a toxic workplace, and every time he went out networking, he desperately hoped to get a new job out of it. You know where this is going.

Clearly, his desperation was showing. He never walked into a situation with the best case in mind; he just kept thinking, "If I don't get a job here, I'm going to be stuck there for this much longer." That's not a pretty thing to come across in networking, and it definitely doesn't help the situation when all you're looking for is the next opportunity. Yes, he understood his want, but that's all he focused on. He didn't think about who might be there and how he felt about the overall event, which led to an agenda-oriented mind-set.

We worked on some other wants. He wanted a new job, and he also wanted to be introduced to more people because it widened the chances of the job he wanted with a company that wouldn't necessarily be at any of his networking opportunities. He ultimately wanted any kind of in to connect with his dream company. Aside from his workload, he was also exhausted dealing with the toxic people on his team, and he simply wanted to meet more people who weren't toxic. After digging into these other wants, we thought about the best-case scenario. Turns out, it wasn't him getting a "You are hired!" on the spot, it was an introduction to someone at this dream company because he felt that he could get the job if he got the chance. So his goal wasn't to talk about getting a new job, it was to meet as many people as possible.

Usually, I would say this isn't the best networking goal. I don't think it does a service to people to throw business cards at each other or go around collecting as many as possible. We tempered this goal: in a two-hour networking situation, he would try to have at least five conversations—more than, "Oh the food is good," or "What do you do?" with five different people he hadn't met yet. He couldn't go up to people he had previously met, and he couldn't just approach a group of people he recognized from another event. He had to find new people to connect to the people he was looking for.

At his next networking event, he connected with five people. Same thing at the one after that, and the one after that. It was helpful for him to have a finite number because he, too, wasn't the biggest fan of networking, so once he was done with the five, he gave himself permission to leave. After a few weeks of meeting his five people per event, he finally met someone who had worked for the company he was looking for. He followed up with the connection, continued the conversation, and got a new job—and away from the toxic workplace.

This was an ideal situation. He saw his want, set up his action items, and accomplished what he wanted. As perfect as this outcome was, he set himself up for success by making his goal achievable. Will every goal happen like this with networking? No, because again, like so much of impromptu communication, you have no idea what the other person will say or do. You can plan your side, and only to a certain extent will it help. Connecting this back to improv, only so much in networking can be planned—the rest has to be figured out as you go. By planning and prepping for what you can and focusing on what can be affected by planning, you have freedom in the moment and you're less uptight about doing it right.

Identify a local networking situation. It could be a meet-up of like-minded professionals or a gathering specifically for networking. Why do you think people are going to this? If you were to go to this, what would your goals be?

This helps you identify your audience prior to networking situations. We often think one size fits all for networking, which is not true. This activity helps you think about your specific audience and needs prior to the moment.

ELEVATOR PITCH: AND GO!

Let's get planning! After you've determined your want and what version of you needs to be out there, you should make sure you know how to introduce that version of you to other people.

This trips up many people. In improv, we start in the middle. You don't start from the beginning. You go to the point where the stakes are the highest. In networking, you have to start at the beginning, and that's often with your elevator pitch. The original idea behind an elevator pitch is pretty simple: you're taking an elevator with another person and you have that amount of time to introduce yourself. It is not long. This isn't a pre-war crank elevator. Elevator pitches are meant to start a conversation. They are intended to get another person interested in hearing more about the person who is doing the pitch. Think of it as a really great movie trailer. It makes you want to learn more. You don't want to give off the impression that everything that needs to be said is already out there. This is why they need to be **short**, **specific**, **interesting**, and **authentic**. Many people will suggest solving problems and defining your brand promise with your elevator pitch. I think it might work for some people but not necessarily everyone. The only must-haves for all elevator pitches—brand or personal—are the four characteristics just mentioned.

Before you work on refining your pitch, you need to have a group to focus on. Pick a basic audience and a simple goal. This is the **specific** part: you're tailoring it to one audience, not every audience. Maybe it's a local group of professionals who you want to collaborate with. Keep your goals simple. Just like with wants in improv moments, they can definitely be something you're striving toward and they shouldn't be something so far-fetched that you will never be successful. Once you've got your goals, start to construct that elevator pitch. *You need to cover who you are, what you do, and why they should care.* Spend some time working those three things out, and get it to a place where you feel comfortable encompassing those three points together in one sentence.

You might have a very long sentence. A client I'm working with on networking had a full paragraph. It started with: "Hi, my name is Kate, and I work in financial analysis for a local hardware company, and I try to make sure things stay in a place where people both understand and can process . . . ," and went on for a while. If you can't stick to simple in the beginning, be ready to edit. She could have simply said, "Hi, my name is Kate and I work in finance with a local company."

TRY THIS

Let's break down the building blocks of your elevator pitch. Ask yourself the following questions:

Who is your audience:

Who are you:

What do you do:

Why do they care:

This helps you attack an elevator pitch one step at a time. Since it is such a concise statement, you don't want to miss a single piece. This activity makes the daunting elevator pitch accessible.

For some people, I suggest staying away from scripting elevator pitches word for word. Our writing voice is often very different from our speaking voice. Try talking it out. Pull out your cell phone and answer the questions in the previous Try This activity a few times. Record it, listen to it, then refine it to make it sound more like what you want it to say. Continue to do this until you end up with words and phrases that you feel comfortable working with for the next part of this activity.

Before you start this next part, time yourself. See how long it is. It's important to note that you don't want to memorize any of this. You want to know the main points, and it might sound similar from time to time. You don't want to memorize the word order. Aside from forgetting the pitch, because you're only concerned with the order, you'll sound disconnected from those words. You're losing a lot of the authenticity of conversation if you over-rehearse or memorize. If you're stuck, just answer those three questions, and make sure you know those answers backward and forward, left and right. Take the answers to the questions and put them together in something that runs between 60 and 90 seconds.

Now say it out loud. It's not going to sound perfect; as long as it works with the audience you're thinking about and sounds like you, it's a good start. Something I always remind myself and my clients—you can always edit something but you cannot edit blank pages. Once you have something down, edit, edit, edit. Record yourself speaking and pay close attention to places where you trip up, stumble, or become repetitive. These are all things you can cut out or trim. It'll be uncomfortable to hear yourself speak, but this is the best way to practice your pitch and pick out what works and what doesn't. Listen to your pitch from the perspective of your audience, and you'll be able to finesse it in a way that will gear it toward them.

TRY THIS

Remember how you timed your pitch? Take that time and half it—and try to say the necessary elements that you can in that halved time. Now take that second time, and half it again—and again, say the elements you think are necessary to fit in that amount of time. This doesn't mean you talk as though you've had a pot of extra-strength coffee. This means you take out the fluff. Charge yourself to condense it as much as possible.

> *This helps* you cut the fat. A clear and concise elevator pitch is far more effective than one that goes on forever. This activity lets you get to what needs to be there and lets you remove what doesn't.

Practice your pitch on as many people as possible to see where the meat lies in your info. What are the essential parts that make you *you*? Those bits are the important ones, and when you know those, you can improvise your pitch depending on the person. That's where the **authentic** part comes in. Since you want your pitch to sound conversational and like *you*, having a few different versions is a great strategy, because then you can pick and choose different elements from different versions. You'll also never directly say why you care. It's not natural to say, "I care about the work I do in communication because people need to do a better job connecting with one another to not sound like robots." I might say instead, "I'm Jen and I run a communications consultancy that helps people connect through their verbal communication."

See the difference? Now refine yours: think about what needs to be there, how you're showing you care, and why they should also care.

My secret hack to being so flexible in these conversational situations that are often super awkward? Overprepare. Yes, you heard me right—plan for all the extremes—know the extra-long version of your pitch and the fast version. By understanding both ends, you can be flexible in the center. If your creative box is small, you can't be flexible in the same way you can be if you have a big box of options. If you have a lot to play with, you can pivot whenever you need to.

Once you've got a basic outline down, you can work on expanding it for different audiences and situations. You're going to be using the same core information, and it will still be in your style. You're just changing or adjusting the important information.

One client was looking to add more speaking engagements for the year. She ran a gym and wanted to be seen as an authority on self-care for female entrepreneurs. We worked on her pitch, and the biggest issue she kept running into was trying to get out all of the information that she thought was important. We ended up taking a five-minute intro and bringing it down to about two minutes. Every time we tried to get shorter, she ended up speaking faster and faster.

Pro tip: don't exhaust your audience if you want them to do something for you. Or work with you. Or ever listen to you again.

Her biggest problem wasn't that she was rambling about nothing. She felt everything she was saying was crucial to tell people she was meeting. There were so many points and accomplishments that she felt needed to be brought up, and no matter what I said, it was always the same, "What if they just needed one more bit of information?"

This is usually not the case. That one more bit of information is usually on the far end of too much. You want your pitch to be evocative, and that's what makes it **interesting**. The people you're networking with should always want to learn more. They shouldn't feel like they know everything about you already. Stay focused: if you want to be the CEO of a Fortune 500 company, great. Is that the next step? Probably not. Take steps to what you want, remember? If you're simply going through all the steps at once, you get overwhelmed. If you focus on what's next, things become doable, actionable steps. You don't go from entry level to CEO. Don't worry about what comes after the first "next"; just focus on what is directly next. The people you're meeting right now might not be the same people who will help you or who you need to connect with down the road. Focus on that immediate audience, and think: How much of this do they need to know and what do you want them to ask about? If they didn't ask, would you be upset? Would it matter?

With my self-care for girl bosses client, we trimmed the pitch to about 90 seconds—this is a pretty long time for one person to be talking to another with no breaks. It feels even longer if you're talking at them. Since she was pretty high energy and loved to ask questions, the compromise was this longer pitch allowed her to feel comfortable getting her information out, knowing she'd take the backseat for much of the rest of the conversation and let the other person drive.

People often ask, how long is long enough? Personally, I think pitches that are one sentence are the strongest. You're often remembered more for the conversation than that one line, so spending time being a great listener and having a back and forth is so much more effective than a rambling elevator pitch. Keep it simple and short.

Once you've got your pitch to a place where you're ready to work it out with an audience, get yourself to a networking situation and go for it. Ready, right?

I wouldn't throw you to the wolves like that—I'm a planner, re-member?

TRY THIS

Run your reworked pitch through the diagnostic. Is it specifically defined to an audience? Is it short? Does it feel like you, authentically so? Is it interesting? Since the last question can get difficult sometimes, be sure to find your own interest in what you're saying. If you don't find it interesting, your audience won't either.

This helps you reflect after creating something. When you're too close to anything, you can't see what is possibly missing. This activity runs your elevator pitch through a quick checklist.

AFTER THE PITCH, LET THEM DRIVE

When you are ready to start getting that pitch out there, you need to simply get out there. If you're overthinking things too much, this isn't going to progress. Remember the idea of "going against the grain"? If you're plateauing, you need something to shake things up so you can continue to grow. When you're looking around a networking situation with a new pitch, aim for the low-hanging fruit. Go to people who look approachable. Maybe they are turned out with shoulders and feet facing the larger audience, or standing by themselves, looking around for people to meet: get the positive reinforcement to go in and introduce yourself. Shake hands (and not like a dead fish), look them right in the eyes, and go for it . . . and let them talk first.

Trust me on this. Taking the initiative to go up to someone and say, "Hi, I'm Jen," and asking them what they do does a few things:

- **You get to find out why they might be interested in you.** By hearing what they do, you can quickly edit your intro to be relevant to what they do.

- **You get a moment to quell your racing heart** from walking up to someone you don't know. The first few times you do this will feel incredibly awkward. You're going to overthink, it's going to be nerve-racking, you might actually shock another person by going up to them and straight up introducing yourself.

- **You look confident.** How many people come up to you at networking situations? Not many, I'm willing to bet. A nice way to stand out, mostly because of the next point . . . .

- **People love to talk about themselves.** A 2013 study from the Harvard University Social Cognitive and Affective Neuroscience Lab showed that when participants talked about themselves, their opinions, and personality traits, brain areas associated with reward, pleasurable feelings, and motivation showed high levels of activation. Essentially, the same areas that activate with sex, cocaine, and good food lit up when people talked about themselves.[2] If you make a person feel good during that small-talk conversation they had with you, they will associate you with those great feelings.

This isn't to say you should just let someone talk and wait for your turn to talk. As I mentioned, you should be listening to what they do and what they are talking about, to adjust your intro to them specifically. A great example of this is a woman we were working with in our Small Talk and Networking class. We actually started this class in 2017 because so many people expressed a lot of anxiety in meeting people. Tara was no exception. She felt as though she had the same feeling after every single interaction at a networking event: "I wish I would have told them that I [insert fact about herself]."

She had a great elevator pitch about her love of customer service, experience in sales, and her next set of goals. Here it is: "Hi, I'm Tara! I'm working to connect companies with customers who know their worth."[3] Really nice for her: specific, straight and to the point, evocative to ask more questions . . . the problem happened when she was talking to someone else who was a bit more nuanced, so she couldn't pivot after she made that very specific and concise statement. Once she said who she was, she got so caught up with that definition she couldn't see outside of that box. Think about your elevator pitch like your umbrella: this simple statement is the connector of all of your parts. Tara saw her elevator pitch as her defining factor, rather than the start of a longer conversation.

Tara struggled with the pivot. She started conversations in a confident and comfortable manner. The moment the person she was talking to
said something she would need to add on to, she couldn't find the confidence to add that information, because she panicked that it went against
her elevator pitch statement. We simply flipped the script. She started to
go up to people and introduce herself, and then immediately ask what
they did. During that time, she worked on listening to them (don't skip
that step) and reworking her intro to fit what she wanted this specific
person to know about her.

This is difficult. Plenty of studies show our brains can't multitask and
the truth is, you're not completely present and attentive while you're doing
this. You are thinking about something else while you're listening. It's a
balancing act between really processing what the person in front of you
is saying and thinking about your next move and waiting for your turn to
talk or thinking of a question that inserts your opinion and agenda. This
sounds like a lot, because it is. Start by listening more than thinking about
your next move. The more you practice this, the easier it will get. Again,
the more prework you do, the more flexible you can be.

TRY THIS WITH A FRIEND

There's a great activity that specifically works the skill of attention and processing. While it's best done with a partner or friend,
you can also still do this yourself.

What Are You Doing? starts with two people next to one
another. One person starts doing an activity, and the other asks,
"What are you doing?" The first person replies with any activity that is not what they are actually doing, and the other person starts doing it. The first person then asks the second person,
"What are you doing?" and that second person replies with any
activity that is not what they are actually doing and that first person starts doing it. It might look and sound like this:

Person A: (Pantomiming making a sandwich)

Person B: What are you doing?

Person A: Skiing on a mountain.

Person B: (Pantomimes skiing on a mountain)

Person A: What are you doing?

Person B: Knitting a sweater.

This goes back and forth, with people saying one thing and doing another. Since active listening is that willingness and ability to hear, connect, and understand information, you're doing all of this in the activity and thinking on your feet. There isn't a lot of time for overthinking what you're going to say, and like all improv, it's reality on steroids. You're learning that processing skill that shortens the time you spend with the feeling of going blank. This activity can be done without the pantomiming, as well. You can go back and forth with another person, no motion required (my husband and I do this in the car when we want to up our creativity or reaction time), or you can play with yourself (no motion required) and try to do as many creative jumps as you can, as fast as possible. Playing with yourself might sound like:

Out loud: I'm running around in circles

[Internal: What's the farthest thing from running in circles? Maybe safari hunting?]

Out loud: OK, now I'm safari hunting!

You're concentrating on those creative jumps and not getting stuck on running in circles. If you get stuck on things related to running—running a marathon, running to the store, running after my dog—you're not pushing that flexible creativity that can be gained from this specific activity. You have to concentrate on what's happening *now* and what's about to happen *next*. When you're playing with no motions, you go through the activity verbally, keeping away from fixating on a subject, just like when you're playing with yourself.

This helps you practice dealing with brain locks and blanks. When people get caught in a brain lock, they usually give up or convince themselves that they just aren't quick enough. This activity lets you practice and shorten the time you are lost in the blank stare.

PROCEED WITH CAUTION

A few warnings before we move along to the actual small-talk part of networking.

1. Do not make things up.

I repeat, do not make things up. Lying in your elevator pitch is a terrible idea.

If you don't know something or realize you have nothing in common with this person, have a pleasant conversation and move along to another person. Don't pretend to understand something; don't nod and say, "yes, of course," if you have no idea whatsoever. Don't get trapped in a lie, because there are only two ways out of a lie: admit you lied or lie more. Both are terrible options. It's better to tell the truth, admit you don't know something, ask a question. There is *nothing* wrong with saying, "I don't know that," or "Tell me more about this," or "I'm not familiar with that." Admitting you don't know something is confident.

Students fight me a little on this one—isn't improv one big lie? *No.* It's a reality that's created for that moment. Sure, you can create whatever reality you want to in the moment in real life. In real life, you have to deal with that one moment in the next moment. In improv, that created reality ends in about three to four minutes, and you never have to deal with it again. You reflect on it and move on. If you lie or even fib a bit in your elevator pitch, you're going to end up having to lie or fib more just to get out of it.

There is a big, big, big exception here: you can spin to positive. If you stick to the facts, you don't need to spin, but if you find yourself using a statement you feel fraudulent with, either stop using it or lead with the positive aspect of it, not the negative. There will be a lot more on the pivot and spin in the chapter on interviewing.

2. Don't make split judgments on worth during that opening time.

If they are talking and you are thinking, "Wow, I have nothing in common with this person," or "This person has nothing to do with my goals," please, for the love of all things, have a conversation and then excuse yourself.

The moment you start thinking of disappointment or that you are wasting your time talking to this person, you're going to give that energy out, and that's the impression they will get of you. You never know who they know, who they might be connected with, and how your life might move along to need this person in the future. Everything doesn't need to be an opportunistic moment with an immediate selfish result; sometimes you can simply have great conversations with people you don't need anything from. I hear from clients and see situations at networking events where people shut off when they are done talking to someone—and you can see that glazed-over look. Stop doing that, or stay home. Your want in the conversation is to have a nice conversation. Full stop.

3. Don't be so agenda-oriented that you don't let a person finish their thoughts.

Imagine this scenario: you're in front of the person who you've been waiting to meet. It's them. It's the person you know you can impress if you could just get in front of them, and now you are and you just keep talking—for an excessive amount of time.

This is just as bad as the glazed-over look, if not worse. If you are in front of that amazing person who simply needs to hear you talk and they will be impressed, simply talk. Do your perfect elevator pitch and have a conversation. Do not suddenly forget the practiced pitch and tell them everything about yourself, or decide you're going to interrupt them while they are talking to tell them the awesome thing you've been waiting to tell them. Use a variation of the Last Word activity we looked at earlier if you have to. Use the last word of their previous sentence to *inspire* the first word of your sentence. Do not repeat the last word of their sentence as your first word, unless it makes sense or you'll end up sounding like Tarzan. Let yourself be thoughtful, instead of rude.

Diving further into agenda-orientated thinking, don't ask questions to another person simply because you want to talk about your answer. That's agenda-oriented thinking at its worst. This happens often during improv workshops, and most recently, in a class for an insurance company. One of the agents got up to do a longer improv moment with another agent. He started the conversation with an evocative statement about robbing a bank. Expecting the person to go along with him, he phrased his statement and gift in a way that allowed for choice: "Are you all set for today's job? I think we can walk away with a big payout—I've already got the place staked out."

Now, in the world of "Yes, and," beginners would think, "Oh, I have to do this!" and would respond accordingly with a "Yes, I'm ready to rob the bank!" or something with a similar meaning. In this particular workshop, we dug into the nuances of "Yes, and"—and his partner accepted the reality of the situation. She acknowledged they had a history of robbing places, but she decided this would be the moment that she gave up her life of crime. Instead of following her on what might have been an interesting journey, he kept bringing up all of these instances where she apparently just said she was ready to rob today, and she batted all of them down.

We wrapped up the moment and started reflecting. Neither was terribly pleased with how the moment went, and he complained that she didn't follow his idea. She replied back that she didn't want to go along with the bank robbery premise, so she made herself a recovering bank robber. It was a "Yes, and": she didn't negate; she made the moment about making a different choice in the same reality. The problem came when *he* kept pushing the decision he made in the beginning, and *she* didn't recognize that he wasn't giving in, so she didn't change her goals. He wanted the moment to be about robbing a bank—she wanted it to be about getting out of a life of crime.

The conversation didn't end up going anywhere, because they both kept fighting for what they wanted, and neither would give in. Maybe if he let her out of the life of crime after one more job, or she offered to do this last job and then they were done. Neither offered that up as a solution, so it kept bouncing back and forth in the inactivity.

I bring up this moment because you can have something similar happen at a networking event when you're talking to someone so agenda-oriented that you have no idea how to proceed without offering them what they want. I spend a lot of time at local small-business meet-ups, and I'm thinking of one person in particular. No matter what you say, he ties in his business and how his business helps small businesses to every single conversation. Talk about food? His business helps food-based businesses. Talk about women-centric spaces? His business could be an ally to women-run spaces. You know this kind of person. If you are this kind of person, let's work on this.

Both people in that earlier moment were pushing their agenda. There's a possibility they are both like this in real life, to some extent. Part of improv is being able to make a strong choice that builds on another strong choice, and part of it is being a follower. That's one of the reasons why it's so great for communication: you need to learn when to drive and when to be a passenger.

If you realize that the other person is pushing their agenda, you can do a few things. You can go along for the ride. This is always a choice—and while it might be a little frustrating, sometimes these people simply need to drive the conversation. Let them: react, respond, have a great conversation, and then next time you see them at a networking event, find someone else to talk to.

Or you can try to drive the conversation: keep in mind this might very well be an incredibly frustrating effort. You can't change the way that other people communicate—you can only change the way you respond to it. You might hit the moment when they want to have a real conversation or they might be completely oblivious to what they do. You can't change them.

If they are someone close to you, you can always bring it up to them. A simple, "Hey, every time we talk, it feels like you're always talking about [insert thing here]." This might not be well received. Transparency is confidence; it's also intimidating.

If it's you: make a point to learn something about everyone you talk to. Don't always teach them about you. Ask them questions about what they do, why they do it—open-ended questions that have more than a yes or no answer. Brainstorming a few before attending events is a great idea. Stick with it. If you've been doing most of the talking in networking conversations, it's a good idea to pull back and do some listening. People won't think less of you if you're doing more listening than talking—remember people love to talk about themselves. You have that in your favor, as long as you are focusing on asking questions and listening to the response. If you ask a question, you need to attend to that response.

4. Don't self-deprecate.

People often use self-deprecation as a tactic to jokingly fib about their insecurities. Self-deprecation is not attractive when you're meeting people—

and I'm willing to argue it is never attractive. That's another discussion I have often with students: *but many funny people are self-deprecating.* Are they though? Think of the people who use it as a strategy to make people laugh: Are you laughing because it's funny, or are you laughing because it's a little awkward? And while awkward is funny, I doubt anyone wants to be associated with awkward. If you're seeing someone you've met before, keep your hello and handshake. Remind the person where you met—not in a self-deprecating way. None of this "You probably don't remember me, but . . ." nonsense—stick to the facts. A simple "We met last month at this event . . ." will suffice before reminding them of your name. If you don't remember their name, that's OK. Ask them.

Since these warnings start to tap into small talk, now is a great time to dig into the part everyone loves.

THE MEAT: SMALL TALK

We dislike small talk because of its very definition and our experiences with it. Small talk is a nice conversation about trivial things. When I think small talk, I think about the weather immediately—and often find myself talking about it. The first thing to do: check in to see how you feel about small talk. Do you love it, hate it, feel indifferent toward it? Are you good at it? Find your starting point, and let's improve it.

There are a few routes you can go with small talk. For initial interactions, using improv at its basic core is usually the best bet. Let the other person talk first, then listen and respond with the active listening points from earlier, and let that be the conversation. If it gets deeper than that, great. If it stays on the surface, connecting with what that person does and the questions you have about it, and then moves on to what you do and the questions they might have about it, great. Let the conversation flow naturally and see where you end up. Don't try to force it. Especially if you're meeting for the first time, you can let the newness of the situation allow for questions.

So when it's past the introduction and into the meat of the conversation, how do you get away from the "That weather!" that so many of us default to? Core principles of improv are still at play here. You need to listen and respond. Use active listening. That much is easy and should almost always be able to keep a conversation going, once it's started. Getting the conversation started might be a bit more difficult, so thinking about ways "in" to the conversation is a crucial homework assignment to complete prior to the conversation.

Think of a few topics that might be useful in the situation. You can also implement some of our active listening strategies there. Talking about the setting is always a great in (as well as digging into information the two of you talked about last time, if you've met before). Tapping into the psychology mentioned earlier, you can always ask the person about themselves. Asking questions like, "Are you planning any trips this year?" is a pretty safe option. It doesn't make others feel bad if they aren't, because then you can have a laugh about how busy you are, how much travel costs, how it's hard to decide on one place. It opens up a conversation that people are excited about if they are—where are you going, why there, what are you most looking forward to.

You can also discuss current events, but be careful. Not because you're going to offend the person you're talking to or get into a weird conversation when it comes to NPR-type conversations (although, given the current political state of the nation, you might). It's more about that you can't unring a bell. If you introduce a topic, it's difficult for you to unintroduce it, especially if the person you're talking to wants to talk about it. Think back to listening for gifts in improv moments: you can't take back a gift that's been given. If you say it, it's all fair game and continues to be until the moment or the conversation is over. As a general rule of thumb, don't bring up things or ask questions you aren't comfortable with answering yourself. If you're going to ask a question, be fully prepared someone might ask you the exact same thing. You don't have to prep your answer as if you've been waiting for them to ask that question your entire life. If you bring something up, chances are you're going to also have to discuss it unless the people you're talking to just like to hear themselves talk.

In general, maintaining a conversation is a two-way street. You can do as much work as possible and the other person might be checked out or agenda-oriented. One of the things people bring up in our classes as another concern: what to do with topics you don't want to address. What if the person you're talking to starts to talk about uncomfortable topics that might lead to arguments or simply things you don't want to talk about? Remember, you can't unring the bell, so you just have to deal with it.

Improv moments in class tap into this discomfort. Occasionally, people use that space to have the conversations they wanted to have as well as conversations they are testing out. Conversations like the break-up talk, the wedding proposal, the "I want a raise," and the "I quit" moments are only a few that I've seen in class and in workshops. The difference here: usually you have these conversations with people you know, so there is a bit of a relationship that you can not only build on but also connect to. When you are meeting someone for the first time, then you have to deal with that awkward moment of not knowing how someone might respond to you not wanting to talk about those sticky subjects.

Planning in this situation, like so many impromptu moments, is helpful. What are the topics you want to avoid? Any topic might be fair game for me; if I'm in a situation where I'm not quite sure how someone might respond and it matters what they think of me, I will probably avoid "hot topics" like politics. Also, it's not just avoiding this topic, it's also asking the question of, "Do I need to know what this person thinks about this sensitive topic? Does it matter?" Only you can answer that one.

TRY THIS

Brainstorm a list of topics and possible questions, and rate them however you'd like.

Here's my list:

Weather (boring but easy)

Setting and visual cues in the room (great and easy)

Hobbies (great and easy)

News (could be dicey, especially in this day and age)

Entertainment (good and kind of easy)

Your day (great and easy—don't worry about entertaining)

Traveling (great and easy)

Food and cooking (my favorite actually)

This helps you prep a list of potential topics for the moments you get stuck. Anyone can get stuck in the moment. This activity allows for the grace you might not give yourself if you "mess up" in the moment.

Awkward Silence

What happens when nothing works, and you hit the perceived death knoll of communication: silence?

Repeat after me: "Silences are OK. Silences are good things." Silences in conversations are perfectly normal and could be happening for a number of reasons. There is nothing wrong with a small lull in the conversation. Things get weird when we try to fill silences with chatter or awkward comments about the silence. Silences can be thoughtful; they are also necessary for us to think about what we want to say next or what was just said. Silences are also powerful: remember Obama's manner of taking silences?

If the silence gets too long and you see that everyone is uncomfortable, feel free to bring up one of those items that you've brainstormed as openers. This is where that list comes in handy.

THE EXIT STRATEGY

After you've thought about the topics you'd rather not discuss and those you are comfortable discussing, you now have to think about your exit strategy. You should have an exit strategy no matter what, even if you're in a "fine" conversation and you'd rather not be in the same conversation all night. Using the word *need* in your exit, "I need to get food," or "I need to go to the bathroom," is usually a surefire way to get out of the conversation. Shake hands with the person you're leaving, tell them it was a pleasure to talk to them (or whatever words express that you had a nice conversation), and then state your reason for exiting. You can exchange a business card at this time, and then go do what you were planning on doing. Simple, clear and direct. It's a lot easier having a reason to leave rather than waiting for a conversation that might never end. Another great strategy is bringing up those gifts they dropped in your time as the listener! You can comment how nice it was talking to them about [insert gift here] and you'd love to hear more, and set up coffee or a call for next week. Simple, straightforward, and clear—and the added bonus of showing that you're listening!

This exit strategy can be used when someone brings up a topic you'd rather not discuss as well. If you're in a conversation, you can always exit that conversation. Another way to deal with a topic you don't want to talk about is changing that topic. Again, transparency is often a good strategy here, but if you'd rather not state that the person you're talking to is bringing up a topic that you'd rather not discuss, you can comment on one of the topics you've brought up prior, ask a question about something that's either happening in the room or that person's job or family/life. Students often ask about the smoothness of this conversation switch, and I have to say, this isn't usually a smooth moment. You clearly are getting upset or nervous because a topic came up that you'd rather not talk about. The person you're talking to either has no issue with that topic *or* they like to cause waves in conversation. Chances are they have no issue with the topic, so that issue is your issue. You're going to feel a little stressed at that moment, so simply change the subject if the conversation is worth it, and move along. You'll probably also notice this discomfort more than the other person. We often think things are much worse than they actually are. Take a breath and give yourself some grace.

There is a time and a place when you need to cut your losses in a conversation and move on to another person—even if this person was "the one" who you wanted to talk to. What happens when they won't let you go? This is something I feel folks deal with all the time—you have a conversation, you realize you need your exit strategy, you execute that strategy, and boom! There they are again, outside the bathroom, at the food table, or in your next conversation. To be clear, this isn't the creepy and possibly-bad-for-your-well-being kind of person who won't let you go. If a person is following you and you feel unsafe, please immediately find someone that you do feel safe with and tell them, or get out of the situation.

In all of the other situations where a person just won't stop talking to you—there are ways out of that moment that don't involve excessive awkwardness. Once again, you need to find your exit line, practice it so it's confident, and use it. An easy one that just about anyone can use: "This has been such a great conversation, I really want to keep talking, and I know I need to chat with a few other people tonight—can I get your card to make an appointment to talk more?" You've got the need statement that gives you something to do, you have an action item for them in giving a card, and you can now (or not) set time to follow up with them.

In networking workshops, I really like to do an activity called Trigger Word. Essentially, each person is assigned a normal, everyday word that might come up in conversation. It won't be something like *and* or *it* or *or*—those are too commonly used and often missed even when you're actively listening. Think more of words like *orange* or *often* or *common*. These words aren't out of the ordinary but won't be in every sentence. Maybe there are three people in the moment, and Person A gets the word *orange*, Person B gets the word *often*, and Person C gets the word *common*. They start an improv moment, having a conversation and paying attention to that who, where, what, how—always, always pay attention to the driving factors—and whenever one of those trigger words get said, the person who has that word has to immediately leave or immediately return. For example:

> Person A: Wow, it's an absolutely beautiful day for our anniversary picnic!
>
> Person B: I'm so glad we get to have it in the same park where we met.
>
> Person A: I know! Remember last year? All of that rain! Not common for this time of year.
>
> Person C: (enters) I can't believe you are here with her. You're cheating! I knew that orange sweater wasn't mine!
>
> Person A: Oh . . . I have to run . . . I forgot the basket. (leaves)

The trick to this activity is not only to pay attention, but it's also to find a quick way in and out. You could always just leave; the higher-level skills happen when you're focused on making your entrances and exits consistent with what's happening in the conversation. While this is a far departure from real life—you're definitely entering and exiting way more often than you would in an actual conversation, and on a specific word, which isn't a normal thing you're working on—those quick moments and solid exit and entrances can be adapted to real life.

The application in this involves a little bit of split thinking—think about a conversation you just had that you wished you could have gotten out of faster. Was there something they kept saying that made you want to leave? What was it? Now, in hindsight, how could you have left? This isn't about a woulda, coulda, shoulda situation—this is about learning from past moments that might repeat themselves.

This ties into another reason that improv is key practice for communication skills—situations often repeat themselves, and they are almost always mash-ups of past situations. Reflect on this past week or last week, and break down moments to their core parts: What did people want? Who were you talking to? There will probably be a lot of overlap when you start looking at these situations as a whole.

TRY THIS

Looking back on those past moments, think about:

1. **Your trigger:** What's the moment when you know you want to leave a conversation? Is it a word? Is it a feeling? Really flesh them out.

2. **Your exit line:** What could you have said, and what can you say moving forward to get out of the situation? If you've been leaving them with absolutely no problem, is there any place you can improve? This helps brainstorm a word bank of sorts to help get you through similar situations. If you have a number of exit lines, you can pull the appropriate one out in the moment. Remember, too much creativity is just as bad as not enough. If you have a long list or even a medium list of five or six lines that will get you out of or into a situation, you can pluck one from that grouping, instead of plucking one out of thin air.

This helps you reflect on past situations and helps you prepare for the future. Professional conversations, especially in networking situations, tend to be variations of one another. This activity helps you see those patterns.

FINDING YOUR GROUP

This might feel a little backward—why did we think and work on everything first? Don't you need a group to approach to practice these skills?

Taking the initiative to approach a group or a person is the hardest part of all of this. Reading the room and conversation is a skill that gets easier with time. Start paying attention to how a room feels. This might sound more intuition than quantitative based, and some of it is—much of it is further developing that empathy. Remember all the work thinking about emotions and recognizing how people show emotion? This is an applicable place. When you walk into a new space with people you don't know (or even one you do!), take a breath and spend some time looking around. You don't have to stare at people, just look at their body language and pay attention to the sounds in the room. Are people laughing? Is there a lot of chatter? Is it silent? Does it feel like everyone got there and no one is talking? These are all ways you can start to read the room.

With individual conversation, you do much of the same. What does their body language look like? Are they all hovering around the food? Are people crossed arms and legs, not because it's cold but because they are uncomfortable? Are they standing and whispering in a tight circle or intimately talking in a corner, or are they in the middle of the room in a loose cluster? When you're approaching a conversation that is already in progress, aim for the loose clusters and not the intimate conversations. They often will be easier to walk into and more open to another person than the tight conversations will be. They might be talking about something more private, which are conversations you don't necessarily want to walk into cold with your cheery introduction.

This is a great time to think about your own body language during a conversation. Are you welcoming other people into the conversation? Are you trying to keep it more private? How is your distance to another person? What status are you showing? Tap into the elements of pose—what body part are you leading with?

Distance is a huge factor in conversation, as is the space you take up. Tackling distance first—if you're hosting a conversation, you want to be sure you're setting the tone for other people to join in. You aren't standing too close to the person or people you're talking to, you aren't closed off, you're not giving off tension or whispering to the person you're talking to—you're also not constantly scanning around for someone better to join the conversation.

There's a hilarious improv activity related to personal space I've done with groups that are open to something like a person possibly invading their personal space. You're doing an improv moment, and you start off with your usual checkboxes and then you either move closer to the person you're talking to or move farther away. You could even move across the room. It's an interesting one to try at home with someone you know to see what happens with the conversation and the feeling between the two of you. Usually, when it's farther away, you feel a bit more impersonal with the person—this can even happen when you're in "normal" talking distance. Many of us also tend to backpedal when we talk or move around because of the nervous energy we hold in our hips, so the farther away you are, the more impersonal you will be in that conversation. There's also a possibility you'll end up getting farther away from another person because of nervous energy about the subject. *Don't try this at work.* It's too weird to get so close to your coworker.

On the other side of this, if you're standing very close in a closed-off group, you're giving the impression that no one else is welcome in that group. This might completely fit your intentions—make sure it does if that's what you're doing. If you want that private conversation with another person, fantastic—stand close (not too close so you invade their space and comfort), speak softly, and have the conversation you want to have. If you would rather leave the conversation a bit more open for others to join, be sure your body language is reflecting this. If you've gotten closer or farther away from someone, pay attention to how they are reacting to this change. Did they mirror you? Did they move away? Respond to their nonverbal cues as you would to their words. If they move away, stop getting closer just like you'd get softer if they asked you to stop talking so loud.

When it comes to taking up space in a conversation, bigger is usually better, and that's not always easy for women. Amy Cuddy, professor and researcher at Harvard Business School, states that space equals power. Men generally take up more space than women because they are physically bigger. Women often make themselves smaller because of a number of reasons, ranging from weight and size all the way to worries of arrogance. According to Cuddy, women still "feel looking strong is risky." While Cuddy doesn't advocate for men to take up less space, she does believe through building relationships and establishing trust, confidence can be built for women to exhibit comparable strength and power.

Cuddy also talks about faking it till you become it when it comes to body language. We touched on this with Viewpoints, and faking the smile until you felt the good vibes that come with smiling. Her Power Pose—a powerful stance like Wonder Woman or Superman[4]—can possibly change the chemistry in your brain, making you feel more confident. If like energy attracts like energy, clearly you want to be surrounded by confident people, right?

TRY THIS

Check in, and assess how you feel. Now power pose for 90 seconds. Did anything change?

This helps you find your center. We get the energy we put out, and by standing in a confident way, we can *feel* confident. This activity gives you the extra jolt you might need.

Think about how you do something like power posing in a conversation, especially in networking. While I encourage bathroom pep talks and getting rid of tensions, you can work on taking up more space in the moment if you know what that looks like in practice. Have a conversation today with someone with your feet close together, maybe even crossed in front of you. Keep your shoulders tight, and your stomach and butt clenched. Maybe even cross your arms and see what that person says or how they behave. They might ask you what's wrong or how you're feeling because you're giving out all of that nervous energy.

Now try the opposite, even if it's in the same conversation. Stand open, feet under your knees, under your hips, under your shoulders. Release tension. When you're making gestures, don't lock your arms at your side. Take note of how you feel here versus how you felt with the closed stance.

That open stance will also welcome others into your conversation or allow others to feel comfortable walking up to *you* in a networking situation. By practicing an open versus closed stance, you're getting comfortable with what both of those feel like. You'll probably end up somewhere in between both of them, but to know when you are open or closed, you'll have to know what your thresholds for both are.

YOUR CHEAT SHEET

Networking can be a nightmare but it doesn't have to be. Small talk for some people is akin to fears of the dentist or snakes. With a bit of prep, you can lower the nerves and expectations of the moment and focus on the person in front of you and the goals at hand. Keep in mind that it's helpful to plan for the things you can plan for, and let the other things simply happen. Since you can't change how another person communicates, your prep lies in how you get ready for that conversation.

- Have a purpose and know your goals.

- Know your pitch—and which one is appropriate.

- Practice entrance and exit lines, and have a list of potential conversation topics.

- Listen more than talk.

- Watch your body language, and start to spend time paying attention to how a room feels when you enter.

CHAPTER 4

Leading a Meeting and Leading in a Meeting

I remember when I worked in an office and had the worst meeting of my life—I'm not even exaggerating. I had a pretty tough deadline for a report. Even before this last-minute meeting, I was staying *very* late at work and leaving home *very* early—12- to 14-hour days and a lot of grocery store sushi—so I had brought up to everyone that I had to make this a quick one. This was a creative job; we dealt with a lot of New York City museums and colleges, as well as their interns and students, so nothing could prepare me for the hour-long meeting on . . . Post-Its, specifically the color of Post-Its we used in meetings.

I still remember cursing that I went to school for theater, dance, and art. "People in *real* offices don't go through meetings like this!" I raged to my roommate. "They have efficient meetings!" I'll wait until you stop grimacing and laughing.

Through the work I've done with EE, I have yet to participate in another meeting about Post-Its, thankfully. I have learned quite a lot about meeting etiquette (or lack thereof), and our students often either are leading meetings or want to have a voice in those meetings. All too many times the student feels they lack authority or respect and don't know how to be heard. Unfortunately, as mentioned earlier, we do get the energy we put out, and without that confidence, we won't get respect.

This chapter focuses on that very specific time at work: meetings. It could be with one or many people, at a standing time each week, or a fun surprise—we have a meeting! This is less about those casual water cooler chats and more along the lines of a conversation that is a dedicated meeting. Meetings often balance a fine line between authoritative and assertive—and occasionally, you ask yourself the question if a meeting could have been resolved by an email. Using things like charismatic leadership tactics can help those assertive moments come across as confident, and storytelling techniques like hooks and buttons can start and finish a meeting with ease. Meetings happen often enough, so it's a good idea to improve in both conducting meetings as well as speaking during a meeting. As you move through the activities and ideas in this chapter, reflect on your glows and grows. You'll get the most bang for your buck this way.

REFLECT ON THIS

How do you feel about your in-meeting skills? This can be when you've led a meeting or when you've been a participant. While active listening, it's important to not repeat everything that has just been said. Do you feel like you've gotten your point across and been heard, or do you feel like you're simply another warm body in the room? Take a few moments to reflect on your current style and what happens when you're either in charge of the meeting or taking part of it.

CHARISMATIC LEADERSHIP TACTICS

Have you ever gone to see a show in a theater, and you just couldn't take your eyes off of an actor? Have you ever felt that way watching a public speaker? Maybe you've seen someone keep the audience's attention, and you can't quite put your finger on why. Charisma is often hard to define. That charming quality that keeps your attention and inspires action— that's charisma. It's part of the presence and confidence that draws attention. It's also a really nice way to get or keep focus in a meeting.

Think about the kind of people you want to pay attention to at work. They often exhibit some type of charisma. Like confidence, it can be taught and enhanced. Research by John Antonakis, Marika Fenley, and Sue Liechti from 2012 showed that people could be trained in charismatic leadership tactics (CLTs).[1] These tactics connect directly to quite a few improv principles, and like improv, these can be practiced much like training for a marathon. Charisma is occasionally looked down upon in business; leaders choose to focus on other leadership tactics. While we need to master all types of skills, when we are specifically working on meeting skills, charismatic leadership tactics can be easily employed whether you are running it or taking part in one and want to be heard.

Quite a few CLTs could be used to inspire meeting room confidence at work. The effective CLTs are:

Stories and anecdotes*

Contrasts

Rhetorical questions

Three-part lists

Express moral conviction

Reflection of the group's sentiments*

Set high goals*

Convey confidence that goals can be achieved*

Animated voice (nonverbal)*

Facial expressions (nonverbal)*

Gestures (nonverbal)*

And less effective by research:

Creating a sense of urgency

Invoking history

Using repetition

Talking about sacrifice

Using humor

The tactics with asterisks can be grown and enhanced with improv.

Notice how I *did not* asterisk "using humor"? This is very intentional. Improv doesn't make people funny. No matter how many improv books you read or classes you take, if you want improv to make you funny, it won't happen. When humor exists within an improv moment, it's often not because some*one* is funny, it's because the group has made strong choices and created a reality that is interesting. They exist in it, and it's so real that it's funny. There's truth in comedy, and that's why we laugh.

Another public service announcement: please don't use humor if your friends and coworkers wouldn't call you a funny person. It's simply awkward for you, feels terrible, and just makes the audience feel weird.

Stories

Let's focus on the first CLT that improv *can* enhance: improv is all about the story, and using stories and anecdotes are great ways to exhibit charisma—if the story is told well. Unfortunately, so many stories when used in a work environment go wrong. One of my clients was leading a meeting on a new initiative he needed buy-in for. He wanted to use humor as an in for the story, and the story he wanted to use was the idea origin story. His opening line was, "I never thought I was idealistic while I was in grad school, and that I would be sitting in this boring boardroom with people like you, wearing a tie."

He wasn't a jerk. He just thought that a joke would be a fun way to start the story and his meeting. An attention getter, he called it. The problem: he was forgetting a major part of the story—the audience. He was more focused on how great his idea was, thinking they would love it even more if he made a joke to start off his ask for help. He didn't stop to think about how his lead-in would undoubtedly offend the audience.

His story also wasn't well developed. Sure, it had this "great" beginning, but it was meandering at best and more focused on the jokes (all terrible) than the idea and reason for the story. The point he wanted to get across was ultimately a team effort, hence his asking for team support. To restructure the story, we used a very simple improv activity, Sit-Prob-Sol. With Sit-Prob-Sol, you first establish the situation: specifically who is there and where there is. Then you introduce a problem. Something has to happen to our who, and it has to have high-enough stakes to make it worthwhile. Finally, you have to solve the problem—there doesn't need to be a happy ending, but things do need to come to an end. As I tell people when they are looking to incorporate storytelling into their professional lives, the audience needs to know when to clap.

> ### TRY THIS
>
> Think about a story you use as a go-to. We can even move away from work in this moment, and it could be a story you tell friends or strangers in your Lyft ride. What was the situation? How about the problem? Finally, what was the solution?
>
> *This helps* you refine your go-to story for the best results. If you're telling a bad story over and over, it's never going to get better. This activity refines and gives you a structure for future stories.

I believe in the most concise story possible, specifically when talking to an audience versus writing a novel. If the audience wants to know more, great. It's always better to leave them curious than to make them bored. Boredom is a hard bell to unring, especially when you have very few minutes to win someone's attention. When you focus on keeping the story specific to the needs and concerns of the audience, again centering it on their cares and experiences, you're going to have a clean and clear story that will do what it needs to do. If you aren't thinking about the action items you want the audience to take, and you waste your time with details that only you care about, you're not going to accomplish the goal you sought out by telling the story. Ask yourself: Are you telling it for *you* or *them*? Exactly.

Sit-Prob-Sol takes all of the fluff that occasionally gets tacked on to stories and focuses that story to essential parts. In the case of my client, the situation involved work and his coworkers, the problem directly affected each and every one of them, and the solution? You guessed it, his idea. The fat-trimmed and revised story that he didn't think was bold enough was the perfect way to show his confidence in a group project through simplicity, and the rest of the meeting let him tell the story of the idea moving forward to an audience who was incredibly interested. He could play to the audience and flex where he needed to.

In the same way this worked for leading a meeting, this can work for contributing to a meeting—keep it simple. The moment a story gets too long, aside from being boring, your voice can turn into white noise. When you contribute something like a story to a meeting, you definitely don't want it to take away from the focus of the meeting or waste time. If your contribution can be best made by using a story, then keeping it clear, concise, and specific is in your best interest.

In improv, stories can get bogged down in the details. It's one of the reasons I adapt the half-the-time activity (do it in half the time, then half again, then half again) so often. This is an improv game that actually is very performative—doing a moment several times and hitting those guide posts each time, speeding up and cutting the fat. Too many details can kill a story, bore your audience, and in meetings, you become the person who tells too many stories. Use them when they can make things better and stronger, not because you "have" to.

While it's important to trim the fat, don't get too caught up on the length of time it takes to tell the story. There is no perfect amount of time for a story. Cutting the fat is about trimming out the unnecessary details rather than keeping your story within a certain time frame. If a story is interesting, told in an interesting way, and appropriate for the audience, and has some kind of action item for them to take away or some knowledge that helps them move along, it can go on for a long time without people losing interest. It goes back to the ideas on talking about how to live a happy life, and if it's done in a boring manner, no one will listen. This is why I err and tell clients to err on the side of short and sweet. You'd rather leave them wanting more and asking questions, than overwhelm the audience.

TRY THIS

Think of that first story we recalled as a go-to. Time yourself, then tell the same story in half the time. Now half the time again—you don't necessarily need to make it a beautifully woven bedtime tale. You're looking for the point, and from there, you can expand on it depending on the audience.

This helps you cut the fat for an effective story. A clear and concise story that taps into the interest of the audience is more effective than one that never ends. This activity finds the necessary components for the most concise story.

Emotional Intelligence

Being able to reflect on the group's sentiment is understanding emotional intelligence. This one has already been discussed, specifically when thinking about how the audience feels and tapping into empathy. The more you understand how people show emotions, the more you can understand how they may be feeling. This reflection takes that understanding and uses one of my favorite confidence boosters: transparency.

As you work to understand yourself, you can learn to recognize emotions in other people. Next time you're in a meeting (either leading or taking part in), try to notice how everyone feels. If you notice everyone looks a little uncomfortable, instead of sitting there quietly, say, "I think we are all feeling uncomfortable about X." By showing empathy (understanding and recognizing the emotion) and calling out the literal elephant in the room (what's making them uncomfortable), you're exhibiting confidence. Confidence is charisma.

Diving a bit deeper into emotional intelligence when it comes to leading a meeting and demonstrating confidence, we'll have to dive into research by Daniel Goleman, the codirector of the Consortium for Research on Emotional Intelligence in Organizations at Rutgers University.[2] Goleman breaks emotional intelligence into four domains: self-awareness, self-management, social awareness, and relationship management. Under these domains are 12 competencies: emotional self-awareness, emotional self-control, adaptability, achievement orientation, positive outlook, empathy, organizational awareness, influence, coach and mentor, conflict management, teamwork, and inspiration leadership. Hopefully, at this point you're already seeing connections between earlier chapters and these 12 competencies. Since there is a wealth of information on emotional intelligence, we'll dive only briefly into the 12 as they pertain to improv-based thinking and action.

Self-Awareness: Emotional Self-Awareness

As we've discussed, understanding how you feel is integral in improv moments and in life. If you don't quite understand how you feel when you're entering a situation, you very well might go in and make choices that seriously change the outcomes. Meetings are no exception: say you're having a rough day, and you haven't quite pinpointed the cause of you being tired. If you go into a meeting with the emotion of tired and you're unaware of that emotion—just focusing on your meeting, you might snap at attendees or not listen carefully enough.

If you are aware of your tired emotion, you can prep yourself for the meeting: maybe take notes because you might forget, or give your coworker a little grace for coming in late.

Self-Management: Emotional Self-Control, Adaptability, Achievement Orientation, Positive Outlook

Self-management involves self-control, ability to adapt, a focus on achievement, and a positive outlook, which are all critical to leading in a meeting. Tapping back into our tired emotion from the previous example, your self-control is exercised by not letting it affect your ability to conduct the meeting. Adaptability, achievement orientation, and positive outlook can all be accessed by using "Yes, and."

Here are a few more details on using "Yes, and" in self-management. Adaptability is the flexibility so many people seek when they take improv: they want to be able to roll with it and go with the flow. By affirming the reality with *yes* and going along with it with an *and* instead of fighting it with a *but*, you have a mind-set that is more focused on adaptability. Since Yes is a *positive* and affirmative word, simply by using it you're not just starting with a positive outlook, you're also inspiring listeners and meeting attendees that Yes, you all can make this happen.

Social Awareness: Empathy, Organizational Awareness

Empathy is often thrown around in the professional world, and while it hasn't been reduced to a buzzword quite yet, it's getting a bit close. Make sure you're actually developing your empathy and awareness, specifically regarding the emotions and feelings of others around you.

Tapping back into our tired emotion, what if it's not *you* who's tired, what if it's everyone else? Knowing people are feeling a certain emotion and not just being aware of it, but also adjusting and adapting to how they might interpret you and your actions, is critical to holding constructive meetings. If you know everyone is tired, you might speak a bit slower or not throw too much information at a tired group that might not retain that information. On top of that, if you can not only see individual emotion, but also develop an awareness of the organization as a whole, you'll be able to adjust your approach in a meeting, both as a leader and a listener, based on what the organization needs at that moment. Remember, you can't change how others communicate; you can only change how you respond to them.

Relationship Management: Influence, Coach and Mentor, Conflict Management, Teamwork, Inspirational Leadership

Since relationship management involves a large swath of subjects, we'll look at these in pairs. When you're thinking about influence and coach/mentor, you're really tapping into leadership. Recall that we discussed influence tactics in Chapter 1: when you're coaching and mentoring, you need to not only understand what the other person wants, but also motivate them to get it. Since meetings comprise goals and should not be purely status updates (because that can be an email), you're thinking about how to get others to see the importance of the "ask" and reason for the meeting, and to motivate them to do it.

Teamwork and inspirational leadership draw on my favorite improv idea: you always seek to make your partner look good. If you're in a moment with another person in improv, you don't just want to make yourself look amazing, you want to make them amazing. By making your partner look good, and them making you look good with the same understanding, you both are elevating each other. Draw this into a meeting: you're all working together to elevate one another, which taps into teamwork, and by elevating one another, you're leading by example.

Conflict management is the final area of relationship management and possibly the hardest. As we'll discuss in Chapter 6, conflict is something that quite a few people have issues with. For our purposes here, when conflict arises in a meeting, you can "Yes, and" the situation: *Yes,* we're disagreeing, *and* we might need to take a moment to collect ourselves. Or you can discuss it head on, being sure you've checked in with the other areas of emotional intelligence (specifically, make sure everyone isn't tired, the organization didn't just go through a lot of change or something equally as disruptive).

Emotional intelligence is critical to attend to the matter at hand as well as the other people in the meeting. While you can consider yourself competent in all of these areas of emotional intelligence, it's a space that can have consistent improvement and learning, and one that is best served by our active listening and attention skills.

Gotta Have Goals

Meetings should be about an objective that the group is working toward together. While it might not be as big as "change the world," the group should focus on something that they are all working toward. Meetings that are simply about recaps usually yield the groans and blank faces that happen when everything in the meeting could have easily been an email. When your meeting as a whole is focused around a goal, even if it's something like, "stay open" or "make money," they have an actionable item that the entire group is working toward, which is effective to motivation!

People like things that can be accomplished. If you suggest even a smaller goal, you're taking initiative (just like making a solid choice in a moment), and you're giving the group something to work toward. If there is too much open-ended interpretation about success, even self-determined, you'll never be satisfied. Because you'll never achieve what you're looking for if you don't know what it is!

This means you need to set high goals that can be achieved. Remember the wants we focused on? A goal is very similar to a want. It's something that has a clear end point and something you need to work to achieve. Much like wants, many people don't put a fine point on a professional goal. Goals should be clearly defined, and you should be able to state it in one simple sentence. A goal like, "We want to serve our customer better," is difficult to achieve, because what is "better"? Rephrasing it to, "We want 30 percent more customers to participate in our referral program," is much more effective, because it's specific.

For a goal to be achievable, it needs a solid finish line. We often recommend our students also look at the SMART[3] mnemonic when setting their goals:

S: Specific

M: Measurable

A: Attainable

R: Relevant

T: Time-bound

These can all be considered through the improv mind-set—specific decisions are critical to progress a moment forward. If you don't know what you're measuring, how will you achieve it? Attainability is less about the confidence you have in yourself and more about how you can achieve it. And it's about doing it, not talking about doing it. If a goal isn't relevant because you don't actually care about it, then why do it? Finally, if you have all the time in the world to wrap something up, where are the stakes? When does the audience clap?

TRY THIS

Apply the concept of wants in a conversation, and tie it to a recent work meeting. Can you think of something that everyone wanted? Something everyone would be satisfied getting? Is it attainable, realistic, something you could do if everyone worked together? Use that as the example for the rest of this section.

This helps you figure out what your team is working toward. Meetings happen because people are working toward a common goal. This activity draws your attention to that goal.

When you're thinking during the preceding activity, try an easy goal suggestion first. See how that goes. One of the most important parts about goal suggestion and setting is expressing the confidence that it can happen. This is a tricky part for a lot of professionals, probably quite a few of you reading this book. While I can't teach you confidence in a book, I can offer bits of advice along the way, specifically for confidence in goal completion. When you break something down into smaller, bite-sized pieces and think like that toddler trying to get what they want, you'll make it happen. Try everything. If you suggest you all work together and break it into smaller pieces, and everyone takes a separate piece, you'll all be in this together.

Another thing to consider when setting group goals is bringing in an outside person to help, especially in instances when you're having a hard time motivating your team toward reaching your ultimate goal. While it *is* easier to see the forest when you aren't stuck in the trees, an outside voice valuably offers a different perspective. An outside person likely won't have any skin in the game and could provide rational feedback you might miss being too close to the situation. This is also why I won't coach my husband professionally—sometimes you are just too close to a situation to offer feedback on it and sometimes too connected for people to take seriously.

Here's a recent professional work example. We were hired to work with a major real-estate firm in New York City. They wanted to reach a younger audience and appeal to them in a way they hadn't before. We were tasked with motivating the group to work together to accomplish this goal set forth by the founder.

Everyone on staff wanted to connect with younger people. But they were having a difficult time doing so and the founder was getting frustrated. The team was getting frustrated because they felt as though they were trying and nothing was enough. In addition to the issues with how vague the goal itself was, the team members weren't splitting up the tasks. In fact, they had no clue what tasks were needed to achieve this goal. To get the goal moving forward, we first asked the founder to define it. He knew it: he simply had not made it specific or put it into words for the team. He wanted to increase their millennial audience by 15 percent by the end of 2019. After we clearly defined the goal, we had a creative brainstorming session using the improv principle of "Yes, and."

"Yes, and" in the case of creative brainstorming, specifically with goal setting, isn't about agreement. It's simply about adding information. We start with a small action and keep building on that action until we reach the end goal. In the case of the real estate company, we started with an action offered by a team member: "Let's use more social media." Using the idea of "Yes, and," the next person said, "Yes, let's use more social media and post on a regular basis." The person after that added, "Yes, we'll post on a regular basis and test out other platforms to see what gets the most engagement."

See the power of "Yes, and" here? Not only does everyone get to contribute a part of the whole, but they are also affirming the prior person, listening to what they say. This makes sure they don't say the same thing as the last person—a consistent annoyance during meetings. And most important, everything becomes possible, because you're simply ideating without thinking about the parameters. This is why "Yes, and" works for brainstorming—you're not putting a budget on the brainstorm or a staff, you're removing the realities that often stagnate ideas. This isn't to say that we're suddenly without restriction: it is a way to jump-start your creativity to a time before budgets. A reminder of one of the biggest rules with "Yes, and": you can't say no and you can't say *but*. No one could say, "But we don't have time to post on a regular basis," or "No, that won't work." They have to build on one another and believe they are indeed capable of coming up with a solution.

TRY THIS

Think of a company goal. For my own, it might be to develop a new class in the next year. If I was using "Yes, and" with my team, we might say:

Person A: I want to develop a new class.

Person B: Yes, and this new class will be on how to say no.

Person C: Yes, and it will be wildly popular.

Person D: Yes, and we'll conduct it with women and men.

And so on. The idea here is to eliminate the concept of failure, get rid of the "blocks" (we don't have time, money, resources), and exhibit confidence that it *can* be achieved. By suggesting a goal in a meeting and displaying confidence that it can be achieved, you're showing those two CLTs.

This helps you see if you're limiting yourself. We use a lot of typical things to act as road blocks—time, cost, resources—and we often don't realize that those go-to excuses are just that: excuses. This activity removes them and opens you up to possibilities.

Be More Interesting

The next three CLTs that can be elevated by improv connect to one another. When you're thinking about Animated Voices, Facial Expressions, and Gestures, you're thinking a lot about your presence and focus. Presence has a lot to do with confidence in how you move around "onstage." It's also directly connected to how you carry yourself and interact with the space around you. Remember the basic definition of improv? It's simply listening and responding to the world around you.

Let's start with speaking in an animated voice: I'm a huge proponent of moving your voice around. This is the cadence of your voice; the regular beat or rhythm of how your voice moves through space. Think about the last person you talked to. What was the scenario like? Where were you? Were you fully listening to them, or did a lot of background noise distract you? Were you fully processing the information they were trying to get to you? And now, how interesting were they to listen to? Why?

Great speakers are often called dynamic. The dynamism often isn't because they do something unexpected or something that exists for sheer shock value. I'm willing to bet much of the time the dynamism is due to the speaker's voice. They show emotion through their voice, and it's not sitting at the apathy end of emotion. By showing different emotions in your voice, you're changing your cadence. Remember Viewpoints and Changing Emotions? Both activities let you think about how you show emotion on your body—and if you didn't try to show emotion in your voice, think about that now. How about that last person you spoke to? Did they have an interesting cadence, one that you wanted to keep listening to or kept your attention? Or was it a cadence that made you start to think about what you had to do later or what you were eating for dinner? Did the cadence move because they got excited about what they were talking about, or did it stagnate because they were simply relaying information to you? Now pull it back to yourself. How do you show emotion in your voice? When you get excited, does your voice speed up or does your voice sound brighter when you smile?

But wait! Didn't I say it's important to check some emotions at the door? Why would you ever want to show anger or sadness in your voice when you're trying to lead a meeting? Isn't that worth the stress? Aren't your words enough? Nope.

Aside from showing one of those amazing CLTs, exhibiting passion and connection in your voice not only shows that you care about what you're talking about, but it also changes up that cadence. You're not expressing everything you're feeling. You're using emotion to your advantage to make your voice more interesting.

How can you start to think about incorporating cadence changes as a deliberate choice? The first thing I warn all of my students and clients: you have to understand any exercises that work on cadence will feel very contrived, and they should. I really would rather not teach you to think, "Oh, I see this person getting bored, I should change my cadence right now to get their attention back!" It's much easier when you automatically change your cadence because it goes with the flow of what you're saying. Like everything, that skill needs to be scaffolded.

TRY THIS

Think about how your voice currently moves through space. Do people tell you to speak faster? Slower? Repeat things because you mumble? Cover their ears because you're a bit too loud (I get this, and it's soul crushing). Do a quick diagnostic on your own voice. If you're stuck, you can ask someone or record yourself and listen to it. Either way, jot down a few words that describe how you normally speak.

Now, think about different ways to move your voice through space. This activity is a little difficult to do in an impromptu manner, because right now, you're probably stressing about your voice. I would like you to read the following paragraph out loud, and while you're reading, I want you to speak *faster* than normal, *slower* than normal; *higher* than normal, *lower* than normal; in a *happy* voice, in a *sad* voice; as if you are *convincing* someone and finally as if you could care less, or in an *apathetic* voice. Ready?

Let's begin.

> Moving your voice around might seem easy, but it's actually a lot of work. People tend to think they are not animated speakers and that's just the way it is. I believe speakers can learn to be animated. It takes time and that's usually what throws people off. Because it doesn't happen immediately and it takes some work. Many people simply assume this just isn't their style, so they give up and resign themselves to being "not that great of a speaker."

How did you do? If you missed one or two, go back and try it again with the others.

This helps you understand the limits and depth of your voice. If you don't know where your voice can go, you're never going to use it to its full ability. This activity lets you play with your voice with direction.

While this activity is extremely contrived, reflect on how it felt to move your voice through space in a way that was probably very different than you are used to. What worked? What didn't? What was uncomfortable just because it was new, and what felt like it might work to make your voice more dynamic?

Developing an animated voice when you're speaking takes quite a bit of multitasking during your thought process. We don't normally think about cadence when we speak. So you need to consciously think about it in the beginning until it becomes a normal practice.

The preceding activity is one we do in almost all of our presentation skill classes, and in just about every class, we have one or two people who ask, "What does this have to do with improv?" *A lot.* When you get to a level of comfort where you can adjust your cadence naturally to connect what you're saying with what the audience needs, you need to multitask and also be aware that you are not overly contrived when you change your voice. For example, if you're trying to get a point across, you might want to slow down every time and enunciate your words a bit more. But if you decide you're going to do that every single time you try to get a point across, you'll be the person who sounds condescending when they are teaching something. That's where the improv comes in. Based on what you're seeing in the audience, what you're feeling at the moment, and what the words coming out of your mouth need, you need to decide in a very split second what your cadence is going to do.

A few professions struggle more with this than others, and it's usually the professions that spend a lot of time talking, like academics or people in sales. I spent a lot of time with museum educators at New York City museums like the Guggenheim and MoMA (Museum of Modern Art) when I first started EE. When some of them got into teacher mode, their voices would take on a certain cadence that, for lack of a better comparison, made them sound like the adults in Charlie Brown (Wah wah, wah wah. Wah.). They would sound perfectly friendly and then, *bam*! Right into boring teacher mode.

We started out with some baseline reflection exercises that let them figure out on their own that they were falling into this voice, which almost always was preempted by a "Well, actually . . . ." Their next step was breaking the bad habits and keeping the good ones. When relaying important information, they started to slow down, but not to the point of condescension—this was something they needed to keep. Getting into a pattern of "starting a sentence down in a low tone and *then* going *up* like you're asking a *question*," sounds incredibly condescending, and makes us shut off any capability we have to listen and retain information. No one wants to be talked down to—especially not people already somewhat confused in a museum. When the educators dug into their tonality, they realized a more casual and conversational tone helped with dealing with the public. This led to less telling and more discovering together.

At the same time, a lot of educators use storytelling when they are teaching about the art and they often think the story would be good enough. The story is *never* good enough, unless the reader gets to hear it in their own head with their own imagination. When you're telling a story or delivering a message, you get to play with tonality. Your voice can build tension with a long pause, it can elicit excitement with speed, and it can show emphasis.

Your voice is part of the story. This connects to any profession that uses storytelling to make a point. From sales pitches to mission statements, storytelling is better when your voice is engaged.

Think of a very exciting moment in your life. What happened leading up to it? What happened when it happened? What change did it cause in your life? Now tell the story of that moment out loud.

Now tell the story of that moment out loud again, and instead of your normal excitement level, bump it up to be the *most exciting moment on the face of the planet and you're sweating when you're done telling it* because it was so awesome.

This helps you take the experimental previous activity into your reality. By taking a story you actually use, you're learning how to use your voice to its highest ability to help your story. This activity takes the play and makes it real.

The point of the preceding exercise is to understand yourself and your excitement level. Knowing our own abilities is a strength. If you don't know how excited you can get, if you don't go over the top, it's hard to tone things down and refine them to work for you. You can't tone down low energy, but you can go over the top.

When I started doing this activity with museum professionals, and then later with professionals, I finally tapped into playing with cadence in a way that made sense. Some people can do the first cadence activity and understand how important it is to slide your voice around to keep attention. It's far too contrived for many of us, so the storytelling focus works best. Either way, there is no perfect cadence for anyone. Moving your voice around takes work and leads to a greater presence when you're speaking.

Your facial expressions go along with your voice—it's really difficult to keep a straight face when you're moving your cadence. Go back to either of the cadence exercises, and think about what was happening to your face when you were getting excited about what you were talking about or making a larger point to your audience. Was it deadpan the entire time? Probably not.

The advice I'm going to give next is one that has been given often. Many women reading this might hate me for this, but hear me out. I think everyone should smile more when we talk. My biggest argument for this? We get the energy we put out. Your energy bounces from you to the person you're talking to, and then back to you again. If that energy is apathetic, that's what you get. Awkward? Right back at you. A smile? Well, that's a good thing to get back!

TRY THIS

A smile also changes your cadence. Read this next sentence out loud, without a smile: Smiling makes your cadence brighter. Now read it again, with a huge grin. Hear the difference? That change is another tool in your tool kit when you need to swap your cadence or notice that your audience is slipping.

This helps you use an idea immediately. There is a lot of negativity around smiling as a tactic. This activity shows you that it does more than improve your looks.

There's actually quite a bit of psychology behind smiling. In 1988, Martin Stack and company conducted a study, "Inhibiting and Facilitating Conditions of the Human Smile"[4] and it's one you've probably contributed to and shook off: put a pencil or pen in between your teeth, and hold it there. How are you feeling? Holding a pencil between your teeth actually works the same muscles as smiling.

They hypothesized and proved that when you are led to smile, you perceive the world around you as "funnier" than people who were led to frown, which backs up my mantra that you get the energy you put out. If you're putting out joy, you're going to get the joy back! Wouldn't you want to stack the deck in your favor? Newer (2002) studies by PhD student Tara Kraft and Sarah Pressman, PhD[5] of the University of Kansas, showed that smiling is *actually* good for your health in stressful situations. Simplifying the study to not include several types of smiling and their definitions, Pressman stated, "The next time you are stuck in traffic or are experiencing some other type of stress, you might try to hold your face in a smile for a moment. Not only will it help you grin and bear it psychologically, but it might actually help your heart health as well!" The research found that, after a stressful situation, participants who were told to smile had a lower heart rate.

Showing emotion is showing confidence. This *isn't* leaving yourself open and airing all of your drama out for the world and office to see. This *is* allowing yourself to have emotions on your face and be a human. Tap back into Viewpoints or Changing Emotions—what emotions might be helpful to show at work? And which emotions support your communication style and the information you're trying to get across.

Another part of facial expressions: eye contact. I hear *a lot* in classes and workshops that eye contact is hard. I agree—eye contact is incredibly vulnerable and leaves you very open to the person (or people) you are connecting with. But if you want to be a better speaker, you should make it a habit. Idiap Research Institute writes that "eye contact shows a person's social hierarchy and dominance in a conversation."[6] This same study shows people with high status make more eye contact *and* receive more eye contact in return. This means that displaying eye contact also increases your status in the conversation, making you more credible and relatable.

Eye contact is an excellent way to show confidence, work those CLTs, and show status. How much is enough though? According to Quantified Impressions, a communications-analytics company, adults make eye contact between 30 and 60 percent of the time in an average conversation. The same company suggests 60 to 70 percent to create an emotional connection.[7] Many of us could be doing up to twice as much eye contact.

What does that translate to in real life? First, you have to make meaningful eye contact. We use an activity called Zip, Zap, Zop in every improv program. It's a tried-and-true improv activity that everyone can benefit from. The activity starts off with a group of people standing in a circle, and one person points to another, makes clear eye contact, and says "Zip." That person points to another person, makes clear eye contact, and says "Zap." That person points to another person, again makes clear eye contact, and says "Zop." The process repeats, with people pointing and keeping the order of Zip, Zap, Zop, all while making clear eye contact with the person they are pointing to. Sounds a little wacky, I know.

Zip, Zap, Zop is a fun activity that builds several skills, but for our purposes of thinking about a meeting, we'll emphasize the eye contact. Whenever I first start teaching this game, we find the flow and then take away pointing, so the message has to be sent via eye contact. No matter what kind of group it is, there are always people who will attempt to point with their body, jutting their head forward, leaning into the person they are sending information to, and making things incredibly obvious. I always stop them, then ask them to take a moment and send the information using *only* eye contact.

A few moments go by. We're back to the weird head thrusting.

Why is eye contact so difficult? The vulnerability of looking at someone in the eyes feels very intimate. In fact, in a study by psychologist Arthur Aron intended to force intimacy on two people, the pair was required to stare into each other's eyes for four whole minutes.[8] This makes the sharing of information with Zip, Zap, Zop a lot easier, doesn't it?

I'm not suggesting you stare people down in the audience to the point where they fall in love with you during every single meeting—that goes pretty far against my "don't date at work" life rule—but you should look long enough to send a message. What's too much though? Often students say they make a lot of eye contact, and it makes people uncomfortable. And I agree, too much can be creepy and not enough is avoidant. Where do we draw the line? Unfortunately, the research jury is out on that one, with studies ranging from two to nine seconds. Think back to sending those three little words, Zip, Zap, Zop. If you truly send it by making the eye contact, you're taking the time to say the word with meaning and really look someone in the eyes, and not at their eyebrows or forehead. Use the basics of that game to manage your length of consistent eye contact.

Eye contact is not just confident, it's meaningful, and you should use your words to connect with your eye contact. This isn't "use eye contact because it works!" The intentionality of improv-based thinking should be employed with eye contact—do it because you mean it, and don't talk about doing it or kind of do it. Do it or don't. In a group, try saying a few words or sentences to one person, making very clear eye contact and sending a message to them. Then move your gaze to another person for a few more words, maybe even a sentence this time. Keep with this process: move the gaze, say a few words or a sentence or two, and then move to another person. Wash, rinse, repeat.

Stay away from scanning. This is where you're looking at everyone and not connecting with anyone. You're moving your gaze so quickly through the audience that no one feels attended to. The other bad thing that happens with eye contact is a fixation on one or two people on one side of the room or table and completely ignoring everyone on the other side. Share the love!

TRY THIS

Really, though, trying to make eye contact for that extended amount of time? Find your partner, friend, parent, or kid, and try it for two and a half minutes. Two is just enough to start going crazy! It's a closeness that's hard to describe.

This helps you consciously use eye contact to its fullest potential. Since eye contact is so personal, it's difficult to experiment with it. This activity gives you an opportunity to see how powerful eye contact is.

With one on one, eye contact is a little different. This is where I hear the most uncertainty; everything from, "I feel like I make people uncomfortable when I make eye contact," all the way to, "People make me uncomfortable when they make eye contact!" The same rules apply: make it intentional. While I acknowledge studies show that looking up or down make a person seem less confident and more uncertain, think about how threatening consistent eye contact can be perceived. This one goes back to the audience. Who are you talking to? Are you trying to display some kind of dominance over that person? Are you asserting yourself or trying to? There's nothing wrong with it if you are. It's understanding that if you are not, you need to acknowledge holding that eye contact will up your status, and might lead to a confrontation if the person you're talking to thinks there could be one.

Play with longevity to see what works best for you and your audience. Specifically, if you are meeting with one other person, think about status. Who holds it? Who needs to show it? The same process should happen with a larger meeting. Are you holding the meeting or attending?

You don't want to make a ton of eye contact with a person who isn't talking; you need to pay attention to the person who is speaking, and make intentional eye contact. If you're making eye contact and thinking about sandwiches, your eyes will look blank. You know that faraway stare people get when they are thinking about leaving the meeting about Post-Its and taking a break to Thailand from it all? You really don't want that gaze to be attributed to you in any way possible.

The intentionality of improv needs to be evoked by the last CLT: gestures.

TRY THIS

Quick! How would someone describe your gestures? How would you describe them? If you answered "I don't know" to either of those two questions, you're not alone.

This helps you think about your gestures. When it comes down to it, we often ignore our hands until we are overthinking them. This activity starts to draw attention to gestures.

Defining gestures first—we're thinking about those nonverbal body-language bits that we don't often pay attention to enough. Specifically, we're going to deal with hand and arm gestures, as well as some head gestures. Several studies show that gestures can increase the value of messages by as much as 60 percent—but how much of our message is taken away if our hands are too busy?[9]

One specific study analyzed TED Talks and found that *least* popular TED Talks used an average of 272 hand gestures during their 18-minute talk—and the *most* popular TED Talks used an average of 465 hand gestures during the same time.[10] We use gestures because we are animated. We are animated because we are passionate. When we care, they do too!

While we can agree that gestures can help a message, what gestures matter the most? How can we cling to our authenticity as a speaker while using the right gestures?

The first gesture-based improv activity I immediately default to involves pantomime.

> ### *TRY THIS*
>
> Hold up an imaginary phone. Yes, right now, hold up an imaginary phone.
>
> Did you make your hand into the shape of a phone, or did you pretend to hold up an invisible phone?
>
> *This helps* develop your pantomime skills. Most people pantomime incorrectly. This activity develops the skill that helps with the awareness of our gestures.

When you're thinking about pantomime, you want to hold imaginary things. There's no science behind this next premise, simply something we've learned working with so many students: pantomime lets you be more aware of what your arms and hands are doing, lending itself to helping with your gesture work.

Think about it: with true pantomime, which is pretending you are doing or holding something, you have to be so connected with what your hands and arms are doing at all times. If you're holding an imaginary cup of water, and you see a friend, you need to hold on to that cup when you go to hug them or shake their hand. You can't just "forget" you're holding it, or your water and cup are suddenly on the floor.

That connection between your hands, arms, and brain is important when you're thinking about nervous gestures. A lot of times, people do repetitive gestures. They stir the air in front of them; they move their hands so much it looks like they are voguing, Madonna-style. There isn't a single repetitive gesture that *adds* to what someone is saying. That's the key to a *good* gesture—it needs to enhance what you're already saying, not distract from it and not just be a way to get out your nervous energy. The awareness that comes from pantomime helps you attend to what your hands are doing and start to use gestures with intentionality. If you're not paying attention to them, and you're not actively aware of the gestures you might be making, you're going to end up making repetitive gestures that don't help anyone. Repetitive gestures can be any gesture that is used consistently. Sometimes it punctuates the end of the sentence, and other times it's just a constant flow of movement.

How do you practice pantomime? First, pretend to be doing something that doesn't involve talking. Things that involve verbal communication won't help with your arms. Let's run through a few scenarios together: pick up that phone again. What kind of phone is it? Where are the buttons? Is it a house phone or a smartphone? How heavy is it? Pretend to dial—and when you do, really try to see the numbers and tap where they are.

Next, and slightly harder: pick up an imaginary toothbrush. Put some toothpaste on it. Start brushing your teeth. *Now stop.* Look at your hand and how you're holding that toothbrush—is there space for a toothbrush, or are you clenching your fist so tightly there's no way a toothbrush could *ever* fit in there? Or is your finger pretending to be a toothbrush?

One more: pretend you're standing in front of a fridge. Open up the fridge, take out a beverage, and take a drink. Suddenly, you see a friend of yours who you haven't seen in a long time. Go give them a hug or a high five. Now reflect: did you close the fridge? Did the beverage you took out have a cap? Did you need to pour something? Did you just magic a glass or cup out of nowhere? When you saw your friend, did you set the drink down? Were you still holding it? Did it fly through the air and hit the ground when you hugged or high-fived your friend?

This is a slightly longer way to help gestures than the traditional "record yourself and watch." The first step in improving and making a change is getting a baseline understanding. If you don't know where you are, you won't know where you're going. After you've played with pantomime a bit, take some time after your next meeting to reflect on your gestures. Did you feel stiff or over the top? Neither are good places to be. Your ideal place for gestures is personal to you. Developing what that looks like goes a bit like this: develop awareness, assess how you feel, add or subtract gestures, get comfortable with change, develop awareness . . . wash, rinse, repeat. Practice your gestures so they look natural. Because gestures are so personal, you need to understand who *you* are first before you simply emulate someone else's gestures.

Whenever I'm giving a talk on gestures, I always see one or two people doing the exact gestures that I'm doing, trying them on to see if they fit. This is actually a pretty great technique as long as you make it your own. Just like you try on clothes, you can try on styles of gestures. Think about why you're making the gesture, and focus on being intentional. Either make a gesture or don't.

CLTs are quick ways to demonstrate charisma when you're leading or participating in a meeting. Incorporating one or a few of these into your next one has the potential to show you in a different and more confident light. Presence isn't everything, though.

THE BEGINNINGS AND THE ENDS

Reflection moment: how are you starting your meetings and how are you ending them? If you start in a mildly awkward and uncertain manner, you're going to get that mildly awkward and uncertain energy right back at you. If you end without conviction or with a meek "I hope you all know what to do . . . ," then you will have an unsuccessful meeting. The Story Spine is a nice way to tap into the flow of a meeting. The Story Spine is often attributed to Pixar Studios, arguably one of the best storytellers of our time. It was actually created by Kenn Adams, a teacher, author, and the artistic director of the Synergy Theatre Project.[11] While the spine itself is excellent for creating stories within presentations, we often use parts of it for creating improv moments, and in this case, thinking about a meeting as a whole.

The Story Spine starts with the traditional "Once upon a time . . . ." Think about what that phrase does to you: are you immediately ready to pay attention and see what's coming next? You know a story is about to happen when you hear those words, so you tune in. While I'm not suggesting you start your meetings with Once upon a time (although that would certainly get attention), it's the *hook* of that statement that lends itself to real-life application. You need to tell people you are getting started. Capturing their energy and interest is important.

One client was getting ready to lead a multipurpose meeting. She was a new employee in a new position and she not only had to introduce herself, she also had to talk about her vision for the new position and initiative. It was part of a regular meeting that she would be leading, and she wasn't a very outgoing person, even though she took many improv classes with EE. We were working on the meeting structure, and she wanted to start with something that was more than, "Thanks for coming today." That is an excellent "Once upon a time," but she wanted something a little more here. So we brainstormed her purpose for a big start. Since this was her first meeting, we first discussed what tone she was bringing—how was this different than what had been happening at meetings? Her goal was to get the team thinking creatively, because not only was she brought in to "change" the culture, her position was created to get people moving in a completely different direction, and her experience spoke to the new direction.

Meetings like the one just described fall in a gray area of presentation. While she was starting the meeting, introducing herself and her style, most of the meeting was an open discussion. She had a negative viewpoint with "presentations" mainly with the idea of someone talking at a group of people for an extended amount of time. Because of her viewpoint on presentations, she was nervous about being hypocritical: if she hates to sit when people are talking at her, who is she to talk at a group of people, even if it's only for a few moments? The idea of starting with a traditional story was out—she thought it was going to be too much like a lecture for her innovative position.

Since she wasn't a big fan of comedy, we didn't think about starting with humor, and since she was a very cut-to-the-chase type of person, we decided she should balance her interactive style that she was developing with her direct nature. She started the meeting with, "Hello, everyone! Turn to the person next to you, and talk about one thing you want to accomplish in the department next year."

Her question was a smart one; she asked them to think about a goal for the entire department and share it with someone, creating a bit of teamwork as well as accountability. After letting them talk for a few moments, she got everyone back together with a tried-and-true statement of mine, "Take a moment to finish up your conversations, and I'm curious to hear your thoughts."

What she decided to do was grab focus. It's a clear way to assert the "Once upon a time" concept without playing to the "OK guys, let's get started" that usually takes a few minutes to get going. Getting focus is something we teach, and it's something, no matter how old our student is, we've learned is tough.

Imagine yourself in a crowded room—or even a room with five or six people—and everyone is talking. How do you get their attention? You might be thinking, she's done the opposite! When you have an objective like "talk to the person next to you and talk," you've given them permission to talk over you, and intentionally so.

How do you get focus without going "shh shh," or "OK, let's get started!" a half dozen times? One tactic is exactly what my client did: say something that can be missed to get attention. It's not pertinent that a group hears your "Hello everyone!" Some people will hear it, and they will stop talking. Some people will miss it, but they will hear the other people stop talking and slowly stop talking as well. Then by immediately going into an activity or direction, or comment, in this case, by turning to the person next to you and talk—you've given them a beat to ease into the moment.

I have to admit, this is pretty ballsy. There are a lot of opportunities for issues that are completely out of your control. The group might not want to share anything. The group might freeze up talking to one another. They might keep talking over you. They might not have any goals they can discuss.

Or it might work. This is the kind of risk that we should be taking to see what works for us and what doesn't. The possibility of success outweighs the possibility of failure. If it works, she has asserted herself by having the confidence to take focus, without worrying if everyone hears *and* listens to every word she says. And she would have gotten the group primed for the idea of talking to one another. Even if this turn and talk doesn't work the first time, it might work and succeed the second or third time.

Almost any phrase, if it's said with the same intention can evoke a "Once upon a time" sentiment. When you're planning your opening, make sure you've actually said the words out loud, not just in your head.

That line matters because you've got about seven seconds when you first meet someone to impress them. Assuming you know the people in the meeting you're leading or taking part in, that first line influences the rest. If you get it out in a confident manner, clearly establishing your role in the meeting, you've set the tone for the rest of the time with that single line.

I recommend writing your opening line down and memorizing it, but stopping there. Do not write out the rest or any of your presentation word for word. When you memorize things word for word, and one thing is off, you might lose where you are and only be able to move forward by starting over or backing up. It's because you're memorizing the *pattern* of words. You are not necessarily memorizing the intention behind those words. When you memorize the intention and the words, you've got some magic.

Memorizing intention is more effective than memorizing word for word. For example, if you're speaking about the creation of the perfect plate of nachos, you might talk first about the chips, then the cheese, then the layers, then the toppings, and finally the dips like salsa and guacamole.

Memorizing that—the flow of the story—is different than memorizing the specific word order in sentences about the kind and brand of chip. There is quite a bit more flexibility in memorizing intention.

TRY THIS

Here's an effective exercise to help you understand why we should not write everything out word for word. Try to say the ABCs. Don't sing them, just say them, and skip the letters *M, F, U,* and *L.* OK, go! How frustrating was that?

This helps you understand that when we memorize word order, it is simply that: word order. We tend to remember order over meaning. This activity is a reminder and awareness that this happens.

It is, however, pretty easy to memorize the first sentence. Say it out loud a few times, specifically before you start the meeting. Whether you are outside, in your office, or in a bathroom—or even in the meeting room, softly to yourself, know those words the best you can. These words are your "Once upon a time." They are the hook into your attention and the tone at which you start the meeting.

During the meeting, remember this improv mantra, whether you are leading it or participating in it: show, don't tell. Having a meeting that drags on and on without focus on crucial points and action items ends up being a meeting that is wasted time for everyone. If you're leading the meeting, be sure you are ready to tell them what's going to happen, make that happen, and move the meeting along. In improv moments, a lot of new students get caught up in talking about what they are going to do rather than just doing it. This ruins meetings too—if only we had just ordered the Post-Its instead of talking about ordering them.

Don't be the person who should have sent the email instead of calling the meeting. When you go into leading a meeting, be sure you've clearly defined your wants. What do you want to get out of this, and what do you want your audience (meeting participants) to get out of it as well? Are those defined with action items? When someone leaves the meeting, do they know exactly what they should do next? Even if the next step is open ended, do they have a goal they are working for? Keep your agenda on point and start on time. If people are taking over the meeting, remember the "Once upon a time" focus grab—start saying something that isn't imperative for everyone to hear like "to be sensitive to time"—everyone is already thinking it—and then go into "this is definitely something we need to discuss further, let's plan time to get together later this week and meet about *just this*." These pocket phrases will save you during meetings. Having a few go-to lines to move things along when you are guiding a conversation isn't a negative thing; rather, it lets you be prepared.

The end of a meeting is just as important—I can't tell you how many improv moments started strong and then quickly went in a different direction. If you keep your focus on those wants and what you'd like to accomplish, you'll be satisfied with the result at the end of the meeting. The reason those strong moments didn't finish strong? They didn't stay the course and focus on wants. Your "The end"—your button—needs to be just as strong as your "Once upon a time." I tell people consistently: the audience needs to know when to clap. In a meeting, they probably aren't applauding you. They might very well be excited it's over—but if you don't want them to clap, think about what you want them to do. Do you want them to leave? Follow up with you? Reach out to people, work on a project, check in during the week? If you're not clear and concise with what you want them to do after they leave you, chances are everyone is going to be disappointed—or it's going to be another one of *those* meetings.

TRY THIS

Spend some time brainstorming three "Once upon a times" and three "The ends" that contain action items: things that the attendees can do. If you're participating in a meeting, you can definitely use this skill as well. When people leave, what do *you* want them to do?

This helps you create options. If we have only one to choose from, we'll not only wonder "what if," we'll also have nowhere to go to improve. This activity helps you build the habit of editing choices, and you can pick the best beginning and end.

YOUR CHEAT SHEET

Always remember what we started with: reflect. The only way you're going to grow with your meeting style, whether you are leading or participating, is by taking a moment to think about how it went. Did you get what you wanted out of it? What were those glows and grows? Were there things you wanted to say and didn't? Next time, say it.

Not all of the charismatic leadership tactics will work for you—and that's OK! This chapter serves the greater purpose of the book: to arm you with a toolbox so you can pull out what you need in all of the different kinds of situations you might have around meetings.

- Know what you want out of the meeting.

- Keep your agenda on point.

- Pick a CLT and focus on it.

- Figure out the beginning and the end.

- Reflect.

Interviewing

Yes! You scored that interview for the bigger job or career change! *Finally*! So much is riding on this . . . .

Yes! You have that amazing candidate interviewing for a position that reports to you! *Finally*, help. So much is riding on this . . . .

Either of these statements sound like you in the past few months, or maybe you hope this will be you in the next few months or year? Before we jump into interviewing, it's important to note that according to LinkedIn, 70 percent of people in 2016 were hired at a company with a connection.[1] That whole chapter on networking? Tap into that first, then come on back here when you score that interview or are about to interview someone for *that* position.

This prep falls firmly in the improv space because of the planned flexibility you're preparing for. You're doing prework to eliminate some of the caught off-guard moments that happen when a question shocks you, as well as working to quell some of the feelings of, "I wish I would have said that." By planning and preparing for the obvious things that come up in interviews, you're allowing for a greater sense of flexibility in those moments. Again, this isn't about scripting answers. It's all about the prep work for possibilities and being open to those possibilities. This work also doesn't apply just to jobs. This can be anytime you're being interviewed—a little bit of flexibility with the activities and you've covered blogs, news, podcasts, you name it. Interviewing skills are often present outside of a traditional job interview.

Being interviewed isn't the only part you can plan and prep for. Diving in to that ever-present question of "Tell me about yourself," learning how to spin negative and be specific when answering questions, handling those questions without the #Humblebrag, and working your confidence are all make-or-break parts of the interview process, whether you're interviewing or being interviewed. Throw in the dynamics of group interviewing, while you balance the four main communication styles and learn to understand your own communication style, and you've got more than a simple question and answer. As always, prep what you can, and get ready to improv what you can. The preparation makes everything easier.

BEING INTERVIEWED

When you know you have an upcoming interview, you probably also know you should be researching the company, doing a bit of Google and social media recon and figuring out what they are specifically looking for. This is all about knowing your audience. When you're digging into the company and positions, specifically what they stand for and are looking for, you might miss one of the most important parts of your research: the person who's interviewing you.

According to Byrne and Nelson's similarity-attraction hypothesis, we like people who like what we like.[2] Figuring out who is interviewing you before the interview is often a good tactic. Don't stalk them on social media and see everything they have ever posted, but do take a look at their company bio, if they have one, and their LinkedIn. See if you can find any commonalities. If the interviewer is interested in social enterprise and you are too, find a way to get that into the conversation. A word of caution: you don't want to shove something into a conversation that doesn't belong, or worse, bring it up just because you really want to, no matter if it makes sense or not.

Tell Me About Yourself

A simple way to incorporate what you want to talk about into an interview is weaving it into your "Tell me about yourself" answer. You know, without a doubt, that will be one of the first questions that gets asked in every single interview. Tell me about yourself, what brings you here, why are you interested in this position—all variations of the same question, with the same result, your intro. While this can mirror much of your elevator pitch, it usually should be a little more than the quick sentence or two that talks about who you are and what you want to do.

Taking the prompt of "Tell me about yourself," think of *why* you care about your words, and *why* they might care about what you have to say. You're not necessarily selling yourself in this moment. At the same time, this might be one of the most important times to show your past, present, and future.

During performative improv, improvisers use something called a "wipe." It's a gesture and movement that indicates that one moment is over for the time being, and the person doing the wipe wants to move time or space in the moment. For example, two people might be talking about an upcoming vacation they are looking forward to taking for their honeymoon. They say how excited and nervous they are about the vacation, and another person notices they are talking more than doing, so they walk across the moment, swipe their hand through the air, and start the next conversation with whoever they might need to move the moment forward.

Essentially a wipe taps into the future. The present is generally what you're starting with in an improv moment, and that present is colored by the past you've come up with in your head (namely, who you are and what you might want). You need all three for an interesting moment that makes sense—if you don't have a backstory, your character will be flat and uninteresting. If you're not in the present, you'll spend all your time talking about what next, without worrying about what's happening now. Finally, if you don't have a want, you're not working toward anything and there is no future.

Using this past, present, future mentality in your answer to "Tell me about yourself," you want to craft your statement with where you were, where you are, and where you'd like to be. Thinking about these three, the most important to the person listening is often where you were (what experience are you bringing) and where you want to be (trust me, they don't want to be hiring again in two months, no one likes interviewing). Forming that answer in advance, and again, not memorizing it, but rather having talking points that you'd like to hit are key to nailing this question. Top it off with a (small) bit of personal information, and you have an answer that's going to kick off your interview.

Your steps are pretty simple:

Research company, position, and mission.

Look at the interviewer's LinkedIn or company bio/profile.

Think about where you were, where you are, and where you want to be.

TRY THIS

Even if you aren't interviewing, be sure to understand how to answer the "Tell me about yourself" question. Where were you, where are you, and where do you want to be? This is a variation of your elevator pitch, a bit more defined with a specific audience in mind.

This helps you practice the question we tend to overlook. Since the question is so easy, we think we have it in the bag. This activity helps you attend to it before you get stuck in the moment or get hit with the wouldas afterward.

Now think again about why they care. You're looking at all of this information piece by piece first, and then you start to link things together.

The Spin

A recent client was trying to leave a university tech job for another position at the university. She was staying at the same place, different department and coworkers, as well as a different set of people she would be reporting to, so while it seemed like it might be a big switch, she knew all of the people who would be part of her team. They were actually the people she gravitated toward on the regular—people she would try to collaborate with as well as people she admired and respected at work.

She had dropped a few hints to people in that department to try to get an "in" and realized that either no one was picking it up, or the less likely situation that she still worried about—that they didn't have a place for her in their department. She finally arranged a meeting with the person who would ultimately do the hiring. We had been working together this entire time because she was really nervous about letting her current (toxic) position find out about this new position.

Aside from working on a "quieter" way to make this transition and interview in a way she was proud of, we worked on her past, present, future statement. The struggle was making sure she didn't speak negatively about her current position, even if she felt that way—the move was all about growth.

One of the most important skills in interviewing you absolutely need to master is the spin. Remember Viewpoints, and how we used the emotional lenses we placed on our bodies and voices to see how emotion changed what we were thinking and feeling? When you're talking about things that have the possibility to be negative, spin to the positive, and a good rule of thumb is to focus on the growth.

For this particular situation with my client the need for a spin was crucial: the two departments knew one another and collaborated with one another. Yes, she was the catalyst behind much of the collaboration, but who knows if the two would continue to collaborate with one another? Furthermore, interviews aren't always about what a person has accomplished—that's what the résumé and cover letter screening process are for—interviews are often more about seeing if a person is a good fit for the culture. This means your personality is what's most important in an interview.

According to a 2014 study by Career Builder out of Chicago, three out of every four jobs care if you are a positive person.[3]

Again, I am *not* saying you should be someone you aren't. This isn't about being a unicorn that shoots rainbows out of their nose. This *is* about that spin!

Take my client as an example: she was in a toxic work environment. The only woman in a department of men, she was constantly treated as inferior. She had more skills and abilities than the newer hires, yet she was paid much less than the past four hires over the past few years. She wanted to leave not only because she had hit the ceiling in that department, but because it was also awful and wearing on her soul. She could tell the interviewer that she was tired of being treated with disrespect (past), she wanted to move to a position that was respectful (present), and this was part of her goal to speak at more events and lead a team (future). Sounds safe enough?

No way. Even if she knew these people in a collaborative sense, they could easily see her request for disrespect as a status issue. She might have been elevating herself in work situations, because the only time they saw her was with special projects and collaborations that she often initiated. They might worry that she would be demanding and looking for accolades or some other praise that wasn't a normal part of the department. Furthermore, maybe they had no clue how toxic her current job was. These might look like petty complaints.

She can say the same thing with a spin that lets her express growth and change. She wanted to leave because she was looking for a new opportunity and had grown as much as she thought she could with her old position (past). She was looking for new challenges (present), and this was part of her goal to speak at more events and lead a team (future).

Sure, she doesn't get to vent about her toxic environment. In her case, the other department probably knew that her current department was unhealthy. Regardless, what would the known quantity of toxicity do for her search for a new position? Nothing. It wasn't something that would help her cause, and as far-reaching as it might be, the chances of it hurting were higher.

Spoiler: she got the job and the new department knew 100 percent how toxic her old department was. Her new manager commended her for taking the "classy" route and not trash-talking her past position.

What if they asked her about the toxicity? Spin again, and add some "Yes, and": Yes, it was a challenging environment (affirming the situation, not lying). And I have been looking for a new opportunity, like this one. If someone asks you about something that is true and real, the same rule applies from small talk: do not lie. If they know, *they know*. If they bring it up, they might want to see how you acknowledge it. Do it, and move along to your future goals. Spin away.

Applying the positive spin to that statement in response to "Tell me about yourself" is easy. Remember you aren't trying to make it sound magical, you're simply looking at areas of growth. Showing it and a desire to is a highly sought-after trait. You want to grow in this new position. You've grown all you can with your last one. You have plans for more growth. For any business, human capital is the greatest asset and the key to achieving goals. According to the *Training Industry Report*, the average training budget for a small business is $234,850 a year.[4] Companies want their employees to grow, and by showing a desire, you're proving they won't be wasting their money on the opportunities they are providing you.

TRY THIS

Think of something you don't feel completely confident about. How are you working on this? Present the information as "in progress" versus "negative."

This helps you build spin skills. Because this skill takes time to build, practicing is critical to growth. This activity encourages that practice.

Stay Specific

When thinking of how to discuss your past, present, future, be specific. A specific answer is much better than a long drawn-out and overly detailed answer. People only have so much time to pay attention to you, and much like networking, you have to get to the core of the answer before you add the details. And as we discussed in active listening, it's a great sign when people ask questions that tap into their curiosity. In an interview, you don't have a lot of time to figure out your audience. Sure, you've done your research (hopefully) and might have some leads on the person you're talking to, but you can only find so much via internet searching. By having a clear and concise answer that is specific, the interviewer can ask you questions they are curious about instead of feeling like they know everything about you because you've just talked at them for a few minutes.

TRY THIS

There's an improv activity that is much like one we discussed earlier with trimming the fat, only a little more cutthroat. It's called X Word. Every one of your responses in a conversation has to be a certain number of words—no more and no less. This can be adapted by answering, "Tell me about yourself," with a past, present, and future statement(s) and recording it. After you have an answer, count the words in that statement—you might have to split it into several statements if it's long—and then assign an arbitrary number that is lower than the current word count. Try to convey the same meaning of your statement with that number of words. Continue to cut it down, more and more, until you get to the bare minimum needed for the statement to have the same meaning. That minimum isn't what you should be using in an interview. The purpose of this activity is to work on being concise so you can figure out the key points of your statement. When you have that limited statement, add a small amount of detail—not too much that you go back to that long answer! Focus on getting the point across with a small amount of flavor.

This helps remove words that are unnecessary. Words are currency, and this activity helps you understand where you are wasting money.

WHO. ARE. *YOU.*

If you're using generic statements that you can't back up in detail when asked about it, you aren't showing enough of yourself. It's also not a good idea to just throw a bunch of buzzwords together, because you'll look inauthentic. Buzzwords go out of style quickly; if you are made up of buzzwords, you'll not only be out of style, you'll also not understand who you actually *are.*

In 2018, I had my worst client ever. This isn't just an overly dramatic statement—she was 100 percent the worst client I have had in six years. She hired me to work on her brand statement for upcoming opportunities and interviews. When a client hires me, I'm very clear that I don't do all the work for them. I am not a ghostwriter, nor do I want to be. Continuing education requires work on both sides, not just by the person you hire. She was insistent that I do a lot of the work myself and then come back to her with results. I usually ask people to send me the information they have, anything that's floating out in the world that might be helpful in moving forward to really refine their brand for interviews. She told me that she would upload a lot of information, and in talking to her, she was bold, exciting, motivated, and ready for a fresh move forward.

This, in turn, made me so excited to work with her. She uploaded her CV, bio, short bio—I opened them, ready to come up with a fun, professional, and dynamic brand statement for the work she was getting ready to do . . . and all of her statements were made up of buzzwords. Buzzwords on top of buzzwords, qualified by buzzwords. It was almost as if someone took a stereotype of a Silicon Valley millennial founder and brain dumped all of their trendy words onto one document.

It's fine, just fine, I said to myself, looking through this. She said she needed help, so she's aware that it's fragmented.

Oh, but she didn't actually realize it. Not one bit. It was alarming, actually. I smoothed out her CV for a position she was applying for and cringed sending it back to her. When I suggested a word like *ethics,* she revolted. Not only did she have no idea that her CV was one giant buzzword, but she also wanted a brand statement that summed all of it up so she could have a great one-liner for these networking situations as well as phrases to use for interviews.

This has nothing to do with the psychology of an actual interview, and everything to do with identifying yourself and the version of you that needs to come out for each interview. That deeper understanding was lacking in a lot of her materials; when she was talking to me and we were discussing ideas, she was who she was—bold, aggressive, powerful, loud, and intense. Every single bold and powerful brand statement I wrote for her? Trash. She insisted she needs the quiet power of Michelle and Barack Obama. At first, I thought she was joking. She wasn't.

The problem with wanting to be someone and something you aren't? The inauthenticity of it all. If you aren't a quiet person, you're going to look awkward being the quiet person. Or worse, you're going to feel like you're constantly letting yourself down and not living up to your potential. The moment you try to be fine with being the quiet person and catch yourself for being too quiet, then you're going to end up being upset with yourself for being the loud person. See the issue?

When you're diving into the *who* you are bringing to the table for interviewing, look at all of your materials. If you walk in and you want to be seen as the quietly humble person, and you have a big voice, take up a lot of space, have a lot of accolades on your résumé, and have a considerable number of initiatives, maybe that's the wrong version of you! Embrace who you are when you're putting yourself up for a job: that best version of you. Look at your experience and examine what energy you put out as a person: Are you quiet or loud? Do you talk a lot, or are you shy? Do you feel comfortable talking about your accomplishments, or would you rather they simply show up on paper?

You're playing a character when you go into professional situations: the character of you. The interview-ready version of that character is the best version of you for that position. You're not making something up or creating what you think the other person wants to see. You're looking at who you are on paper and in person, and reorganizing it so the best parts come forward.

This client refused to see anything in any way but her own idea of what she wanted. She didn't want to be known as bold and outspoken, even though she was. She wasn't interested in working on making herself the best version of who she was. She wanted to be this person she created in her head, and it wasn't who she was. We finally parted ways (not in a good way) because I can't re-create someone. I prefer to bring out the person you already are, and you should too. That's the true authenticity.

Dig into *you* before an interview. Interviews are some of the best times in your career. Why? Because you have a chance at something *new*. A new opportunity, a new job, a new adventure. You essentially get to pick and choose moments from your past, refocus on the future you want, and apply it to the present. Whatever version of you that you bring to the interview, make sure it truly is who you are, who you represent, and where you want to go.

One more quick argument for being yourself. Interviews are stressful. Think about it: even as the interviewer, you're sitting listening to strangers talk about their job experience. Everyone wants something, or you both wouldn't be here. Sometimes desperation sneaks into those conversations. Desperation is pretty awkward to be around, so chances are the interviewer is at the very least mildly uncomfortable, especially if they have sat through a few interviews already. If the situation is already mildly charged with the awkwardness of desperation, and you're trying on a new personality for the first time, you will not only feel that discomfort from the person you're talking to, but also the discomfort of that new personality.

Dress for Success

This goes for clothing too. I still remember a project manager I was working with, and he desperately wanted to get a new, slim-cut suit for a job interview. He'd never worn a slim-cut suit. He wanted to look slick, like Bond.

Thankfully, he listened. He ended up wearing something that he liked a lot, he already owned, and made him feel confident. New clothes for interviews are a huge no—unless you've given them a dress rehearsal and wore them outside your house. Again, you're already nervous, you're looking to be the best version of yourself. Do you really want a wardrobe malfunction on such an important day?

Set yourself up for success, not for potential nerve-racking moments.

Think again about those things that make you, *you*. What professional qualities can you show, not tell?

This helps you take a personal inventory. We often identify ourselves as our jobs or careers, and we are more than our work. This activity helps you figure out how to talk about who you are, outside of your immediate position.

AFTER THE FIRST QUESTION

Once you've gotten yourself through the door, in the chair, and past that first loaded question of "Tell me about yourself," there are a few things you can do with improv and psychology that will help you along the way. Aside from the previously mentioned similarity-attraction hypothesis, mirroring the gestures of your interviewer contributes to the psychological idea of the "chameleon effect." The science behind it essentially states that people often like each other more when they are using the same or similar body language.

Mirroring is often part of improv—follow the follower. In improv, two people stand across from one another. One person "starts" and the other person follows them, making the same movements with their body. It goes pretty slow because accuracy is important in this activity. It's the idea of passing control back and forth, as well as sharing the lead.

Connecting this to the chameleon effect, by concentrating on mirroring, you focus your attention on details. Think about the last seated conversation you had. How was the person sitting? How did they move their hands? Did they have any place to put their hands, or were their hands in their lap the entire time?

You probably don't know the answer to most of those questions. We don't often remember nonverbal cues unless they are over the top or awkward—or if we are looking for them. When they are fine, they are practically hidden. They work for you, and you just look amazing. This is why practicing mirroring is a great idea, because you're working on focusing that attention to body language so you can easily match some-one in an interview.

One great gesture to mimic the day of the interview is leaning forward with your hands on the table. You can pull that off and your interviewer won't notice. On the other hand, if you start moving your hands in time with the interviewer, they might feel like you're having a dance off.

#Humblebrag

Aside from voguing with your interviewer, you also want to avoid the humblebrag. But wait, you're probably thinking, don't we want to work on sharing and celebrating our accomplishments? Being confident and humblebragging are very different things. Research from a 2017 study out of Harvard University defines humblebragging as boasting concealed by a complaint.[5] Statements along the lines of, "Oh, I'm such a perfectionist, it's just maddening," are often used for the answer to the question, "What are your weaknesses?" We all know that question is coming. Don't answer in a way that avoids the question and positions you in perfect light. We all have weaknesses—and that's OK.

The same Harvard study had students identify their weaknesses as if they were in an interview. Almost three-quarters of the group humble-bragged and answered the questions by saying they were too nice, too much of a perfectionist, too hardworking, and not surprisingly, they were less likely to get hired based off of that question. What you can do is spin to the positive. We discussed this earlier, and this question is a great place for the spin. You're being honest, showing you understand yourself. By considering this question and more, you're planning what you can.

Here's a concrete example of this: a client was interviewing for a position in customer service. She was really nervous about the interview because she had been unemployed for a while. We were working on her interview skills, specifically the typical questions that get asked in almost every job interview. She was preparing for the known quantities because she knew she often got caught off guard. This way she could bounce back in a slightly faster way, versus looking lost. When we got to this question, she immediately answered that her weakness was working too hard. That's not a weakness, so we dug a bit deeper. The more we talked about this, the more we realized that her weakness was that she got obsessed with what she was working on, and neglected everything else only to focus and fixate on this *one* thing. The real weakness was her tunnel vision and stubbornness to give space to a problem once she started working on it.

Instead of saying that she worked too hard, we got specific and added a preview statement that will help almost all of your answers to the question, "What's your weakness?" She started her answer with, "I'm currently working on [fill in the blank with your weakness]." This eliminated the humblebrag problem, and she didn't feel like she had to qualify her weakness with a strength or a joke. It also spun her weakness into a growth mind-set, which was appealing to her potential new company, since it heavily valued professional development and learning. Most companies, if not all, value professional development, learning, and continuing education.

Staying very specific to the actual weakness and not treating it as a vague statement will make this work. There is a stereotypical improv moment when one person hands someone a box, and tells them to open it and use what's inside without ever telling them what it is, passing all the choice and responsibility on to them. This is the same thing: if you leave a statement wildly vague, especially about your weaknesses, you're letting your interviewer make the choice on those specifics. For example, if you say, "I like control," that might be a dead stop for an interviewer, which is unfortunate because the reality might be that you enjoy control in taking initiative when no one else can decide what to do. See the difference?

How You Say It

Another psychological improv hack is to adapt those great presentation skills, specifically cadence. How you say what you say has always been a critical part of what we teach and do. One study by psychologists Amanda Feiler and Deborah Powell tapped into nervous behavior and how it's not the nervousness that hinders someone in a job interview, it's actually the speed and cadence of their voice.[6] The 2015 study showed that speech rate (words spoken per minute) and assertiveness greatly affected an interviewer's perception of an interviewee. Anxiety slows your voice down and makes you seem less warm. Solution? You've got to move it. Work on the cadence of your voice. If you're constantly speaking at the same speed and that speed is slow, you're hurting yourself. On the flip side, you don't want to be speaking as fast as possible; you'll exhaust the interviewer. Moving your voice around is effective: think fast and slow speeds. And remember what we said about smiling? Even if you have to imagine the best day of your life, pull out that smile once in a while.

Questions + Answers

The meat of an interview is usually a series of questions, and many of those questions are the same from employer to employer. Questions that you should be prepared for include:

Why should we hire you?

How did you hear about this job?

What are your strengths and weaknesses?

Why are you leaving your current job?

What is your salary expectation?

Why do you want this job?

How do you handle stress?

> Tell me about a difficult work situation and how you overcame it?

> What are your goals for the future?

Planning for these questions will give you the flexibility we discussed earlier, and answering these questions in a storytelling manner will definitely help you *not* memorize the answers but focus more on telling the story with Sit-Prob-Sol, which we discussed in Chapter 4.

The situation is the same. You're setting the stage. The task and action are the problems and the start of the solution, and the result is the solution. You're tapping into the bare bones of a story when you answer interview questions, and that's a nice way to make sure you're staying on track with your answer. Does what you're saying fall in the Situation, Problem, or Solution category? No? You can trim it out. Remember, it's always better to be specific and concise than long-winded.

One client went through the previous list of interview questions and worked out all of the Sit-Prob-Sols for every single question. She was very excited about the upcoming job interview and wanted to feel completely prepared. This wasn't something I assigned to her. It was a strategy she found really helpful in improv class, so she tried it on each of the questions. Once I heard that she did this for each one, I broke down all of the questions myself with Sit-Prob-Sol and came to several conclusions:

1. **Why should we hire you?** The situation is the specific company and job that were in consideration. The problem is not necessarily a company problem; it is the position itself. It's empty. The company needs this to be filled. And you as the candidate are the solution because you're amazing. The solution can be bolstered with a few details about why you're the specific ideal solution.

2. **How did you hear about this job?** This question is less effective with the Sit-Prob-Sol idea because it's such a simple question with a finite answer. Storytelling isn't really necessary for this one. Best to be clear, concise, and answer the question, because nothing about your answer could contribute to you getting hired—unless you know someone at the company or a mutual connection told you about the business. If it's as simple as "a Google search," it's best to keep it simple.

3. **What are your strengths and weaknesses?** This could benefit from some great Sit-Prob-Sol, as well as some editing. When you're talking about your strengths and weaknesses, examples are always more helpful than characteristics. Using the woman who gave me this idea in the first place, one of her strengths was problem-solving capabilities and her specific situation took place at her last job, where she worked as a marketing assistant. A problem came up with their social media engagement, and she not only quickly identified the core of the problem, but she also enacted a long-term sustainable solution. As for her weaknesses, she often found herself crippled by choices and options. A situation that showed this was deciding the aesthetic of the new brand for her new initiative. The problem came in when she got ultimate creative control over the look and she had to ask for parameters after being stalled on decision-making for a few weeks. Her spin: she was aware and mindful of situations where she might be overwhelmed. Through her awareness, she knew to give herself time to figure out the parameters she would need for success.

4. **Why are you leaving your job?** The situation is your soon to be ex-job. The problem is the reason—the spun reason—why you're leaving. If it's because you outgrew the position, that's the problem—you want to be challenged. If it's because of moving, salary, new interest, new focus—that's the problem. The solution is not necessarily a finite one: essentially you started a search as a solution and ended up here.

5. **What is your salary expectation?** This is one you should be straightforward about. If you have a specific number in mind, fantastic. If you don't, make sure you research what the position should get paid based on your experience and ask for that. If you aren't sure, your current salary is the situation and more than what you make now is the solution.

6. **Why do you want this job?** This is different than why they should hire you. Think back to why you're leaving your current job—that's your situation. The problem is you don't currently

have it, and the solution is all of the ways the job will help you achieve your next set of goals. You can also incorporate what you have to offer the company as part of the situation—you have skills that need a focus, and this position is perfect for those skills.

7. **How do you handle stress?** Again, a specific example works well here. Think about a stressful situation you handled well. Don't use one that ended in you giving up. Think of one where the actions you took could be adopted again to a similar situation. The problem is the stress that happened during that situation. How did it manifest? The solution is how you dealt with it. How did you *not* break down in tears and quit?

8. **Tell me about a difficult work situation and how you overcame it?** Ripe for Sit-Prob-Sol! Set the stage with the situation—whether it's at your last job or one a few jobs ago. The problem is the difficult part of the situation. Was it a coworker, a client, yourself? The solution is how you overcame it.

9. **What are your goals for the future?** This one used to scare me and often does still when it comes to next steps for me and my businesses. When I keep things intentionally vague, I don't end up disappointed with the result, so whenever I answer this question, I'm careful. The situation is where I currently am. The problem is actually where I want to go and the solution is the goal. Back to the client: she was a marketing assistant. She wanted to be a creative director, so she was looking for a job with mobility and possibility. Keep the goals attainable.

Sit-Prob-Sol does one of the things quite a few people miss in interview situations: it forces you to answer the entire question, instead of getting lost in details and information. If you're practicing answers in advance, keeping your Sit-Prob-Sol as short as possible is the key to a natural delivery. Some people find writing a few things down helpful, and others like talking it out. If you start by writing down a few key words related to your answer, be sure to write down words that will cue you, and use those words to extrapolate into a bit more detail. Sometimes, you're going to stick very close to those words you wrote down. You might only say a few more. Other times, you might feel that your audience wants to hear the longer version, or even better, they might ask for the longer version. You've got the main point down; now you can dig into the details.

In the moment, you can use the words *situation*, *problem*, and *solution* as long as they don't become so repetitive that your interviewer knows exactly how you practiced or wonders why you like those words so much. You can also use the Sit-Prob-Sol technique in answering questions you were not expecting. If you are asked a question like "How do you work with other people?" (a less common interview question, still one that comes up from time to time) or another equally unprepped question, you can pull out Sit-Prob-Sol for a clear, concise, and complete answer. Your situation is always for setting the stage; the problem is what breaks from the norm: it might be what went wrong, and it might be what is changing. The solution is how you "fixed" or changed the problem.

Keep in mind that although Sit-Prob-Sol is a great tool, it's not a catch-all for every question, as we learned from the earlier examples. Some questions require a simple answer. You can tell by spending some time doing what every interview needs to do more of—listening. As part of our work, we often sit in hiring rooms and listen in on the group and individual interviews. All too often the interviewee isn't answering the question directly. They aren't threading their answer into the needle that is the question. They get off on such a tangent that the answer might be there, but we all can't tell, because it seems so very far away from the question, and there was no summary, no recap, and no connection. If you actively listen to the interviewer, you can run a quick check in your head to see if you answered the question or not. This is where Sit-Prob-Sol comes in handy. Assess the question and see if you built out a situation, problem, and solution. If so, great! If not, you can quickly sum up your answer with Sit-Prob-Sol, and make it so very clear and concise that it's almost as if they are reading a slightly larger version of your very tight notes.

If you aren't paying attention to the interviewer, you'll miss nuances in questions. They are dropping gifts, and those gifts are great to use when your brain is quickly processing the answer to that question. Recall the work you did at home prepping for the interview as well as the work you've done in your life that you are drawing from. And run a quick check through Sit-Prob-Sol. Repeating parts or part of the question asked, even if you're simply using a few similar words in your answer, not only shows the interviewer that you're listening, it also gives you a natural stall tactic.

This prep that goes into an interview should feel a little exhausting, and the actual interview will probably tire you out as well, since you're required to be "on" the entire time with your focus and attention. That prep goes a long way, but take care not to overprep too much. Excessive overpreparation is where realness and authenticity go to die. If you've written out paragraphs for the possible answers to the potential questions, you've done too much. If you've written out bullets or words for the answers, and practiced saying the answers in a few different ways, you're on the right track.

TRY THIS

Break down a recent situation into a Sit-Prob-Sol. Does it work? Does it not?

This helps you look at a situation clinically. You can see consistencies that can be applied to situations moving forward by taking a step back and looking critically. This activity gives you the space to examine the technique.

CONFIDENTLY YOU

This next tip related to interviewing is one of the few times I'll tap into performative improv and theater. Think of the best live show you've seen. Maybe it was an improv show or a performance you saw at a local theater. Think of the best character you saw. It might have been someone off the wall. It might have been someone who was realistic and so close to someone you might have known in real life. Did everything they say completely connect so perfectly to who they were as a person? Was it simply so "them" and the character so rich they were believable?

When you're developing a new character for improv or working on one for a performance, you have to eat, breathe, and sleep that character.

You need to know what they love, what they hate, what they dream about, what they're afraid of, who their friends are, who they aspire to be—all of those questions need to have answers. If you are truly a character, you become that person. That's what you have to do in an interview.

You're not coming up with a character, but you are knowing yourself and your answers so well you are undeniably *you* in whatever you say and do. That's why you think about these answers in advance. All of this work gets done thinking about the audience and their wants, and how you can be the best version of you for that audience and their wants. And when you know yourself so incredibly well, you *can* answer those questions because you know how you feel about those subjects. Thinking about questions in advance isn't overpreparing, and neither is coming up with answers. You're focusing on presenting *you* to someone *who* doesn't know you and narrowing in on that best version. If you know yourself, you've got this interview in the bag on your end.

Sometimes, you know yourself and prep so incredibly well, and you still don't get the job you think you're perfect for. This is not on you. This might be seen as some of the most basic advice, but I truly think we need to hear this more. If you feel like you put your all into something and it doesn't happen, reflect on it to see what happened. If you can't find a reason why something didn't happen, then it probably isn't you. If you realize you brought stress into the room, sounded like someone else, slacked on your prep, were surprised by a question and froze, or any other of the laundry list items that could have happened, your response is easy: grow for next time. It's not a failure; it's a what next.

Even some of the most confident people I meet and coach have bad months or years. I was working with a woman who was a senior vice president of a well-known network, and her confidence in interviewing was in the trash. She was looking for a new position because her current one was incredibly toxic. She kept interviewing and having meetings about positions, and every single time, at the same time in the interview process, she couldn't "seal the deal," as she said. It would get to almost, often down to her and one or two other candidates, and then no luck.

After this happened five or six times (in a row), she and I started working together. She was, by all intents and purposes, a dream client. She went to improv classes, did her coaching homework (I am not the kind of coach expects you to work only when we're on the phone, in person, or on a Skype call—you gotta be working all the time) and followed up and reflected like a professional. Even while working with me, she had two additional interviews, got to the last stage, but no luck.

To this day, I'm not entirely sure what was happening. I have a pretty good guess that when she got to that final moment, she choked. She compared that moment to all of the other moments, and immediately started to think about how she was going to make a mistake here too and not get the job. Ironically enough, she might have been losing all of that confidence in one single, important moment.

What we worked on is the next segment of interviewing with improv: envision yourself in the job. It's something I don't necessarily recommend for all interviews because it's exhausting. When you are far enough along in the process—really past the first or second interview—consider yourself in that role. Imagine what it would be like going to work there every day. Think about what your typical day would look like. What would you accomplish if you couldn't fail and that job was yours?

We decided to do this activity late in the interview process on purpose because we couldn't figure out what was happening. One or two jobs, OK, that's someone else. We got up to eight total final interviews and no job, so desperate times called for desperate measures. She and I worked before her ninth and final interview and focused solely on getting her to envision herself in the role. We thought about the things she was planning on doing on a regular basis, what a typical day might look like, what she wanted to change, and what she looked to keep the same. All a very imaginary conversation, and we put her in that role. When the final interview happened, she went in with the belief that she had the position, and this was simply a conversation she was having with the people she would be working with. She got it.

There is something to be said for that energy you walk in with. She didn't proceed with a cocky arrogant attitude; she went in believing that she had the position because she had given them everything. There was no more convincing. She made her case as best as she could. Now it was this final moment, and one other person was between her and the position, so her best chance was to be the best version of her.

I'm not going to pretend I'm some kind of magic help, and it was 100 percent me and our work that made this happen. It could have simply been the right job and the right time for her. I can say with 100 percent certainty that her attitude was much more relaxed walking into that final interview because in her head she already had the job. She was going in for a conversation, and since we met right before this conversation and right after (literally, at the coffee shop on the next block), I got to witness her confidence. When we reflected on it afterward, she also had a much calmer disposition than she would have if she *didn't* get it. When we first met, even though she had been at her company for 15 years, was incredibly accomplished, and would be great for any position, she was starting to get in her head she wasn't good enough for another nontoxic position. Now, she said the conversation was fun, and if she didn't get the position, she was sure she would at the very least stay in touch and network with the group that interviewed her.

That confidence goes a long way.

Thank You

Have you ever gone up to someone after you watched them perform, and told them what a great job they did and meant it? That kind of gratitude, as a performer, feels amazing. I've had people come up to me after a presentation, and let me tell you, it's one of the nicest things you can do. After all the stress and commotion that goes into putting together something you care deeply about—the focus, energy, time, and preparation, it's wonderful to see someone appreciate all of that work.

Thank your interviewer, both in person and in an email or note afterward. Yes, I know you know this, but it's so important, it needs to be reiterated. That interview was a lot of work to prep and plan for them, too. You might think they are in the "easy" seat because they already have the job. Imagine how many people they need to talk to select one to take a risk on. Clearly, we all want a hire to work out and that person to be an asset to the team, but you have no idea what things were like leading up to this interview with you. They are also probably taking time out of their day to have this interview, so thank them, sincerely, for their time. This is also a great time to have that confident moment of envisioning yourself in that position.

I love the line, "I look forward to the potential of working together." That line shows you're interested, casts the imagination in the direction of working together, and exhibits that line between confident but not arrogant that we're often seeking in an interview follow-up. While many people worry about not being confident enough, when you first start displaying confidence, your first thought might be, "Oh no, I'm too confident and cocky!" The truth is, when people fear that line between confidence and arrogance, they probably aren't approaching arrogance, and when they are completely unaware of it, they usually cross over beyond the horizon line, dancing in the distance with their arrogance. It's a place where you might get stuck when you start showing confidence: just be aware of what arrogance looks like on you, and stay away from it.

When you're thanking them in person, you're thinking about that button again from storytelling—that "The end!" so the audience knows to clap. When it's wrapping up, a simple, "Thank you so much for your time, I'm looking forward to talking more," is usually effective.

Questions Please!

You've done it! You made to the end of the interview! This is so exciting, your hard work paid off, you can now take a deep breath and take some time knowing it's all out of your hands. You're getting ready to thank the interviewer for their time and then the inevitable, "So do you have any questions?"

Silence. You fumble, "Not right now," and mutter something about sending questions you have along in an email later, and you both know you don't have any questions. How should you answer this question?

Some people will tell you to always have questions. If you don't have any, they will think you don't care, they say. I do not think it matters if you ask 10 questions or no questions: what matters is doing it intentionally.

Three situations might come up around questions in the moment: you have none, you have some that you planned in advance, or you have some that came up along the way.

For the first, if you have no questions, answer clearly and concisely, "I have no questions, thank you." Don't pretend to think, don't make up a question that you don't care about, and definitely don't ask a question you already know the answer to. Just thank them for their time and move on.

For the second, if you truly have a question—maybe it's about the culture, salary, expectations, time off, family leave, sick leave, anything—

be sure to ask it in a clear and concise manner. This is your time. Don't worry about it being an "appropriate" question, because if it matters to you and might change your answer if you were offered the job, it is appropriate. Understand that your interviewer might be caught off guard if it's a tough question, and if you're asking something that is a hot topic within the organization, like parental leave, you might not get the response you want. For this situation, you've planned your questions in advance and you didn't get an answer during the interview, so go ahead and ask with confidence.

The final situation involves questions that come up based on information in the interview. Maybe you want to clarify something or ask for more information. You can do this one of two ways. You can use "Yes, and" by affirming what they said you have a question on and then adding the question. For example, if it was a question that came up because of a conversation about company culture, you might say, "You said the company culture is very involved, what does that mean for after-hour functions and events?" You've asserted that you heard what they said and then added your question.

The trouble with questions comes when you're waffling around your potential question. If you're throwing in disfluencies like *kinda* and *just*, or other fillers that do nothing more but take up space in a sentence, you're ending that interview on a low note. That waffle might undercut all of the confidence you've built up in the interview, all in one quick moment. If you're going to ask, ask—and if you're not, don't.

TRY THIS

Spend part of tomorrow being confident. No humblebrags, no self-deprecation—just good old-fashioned confidence. Move with intention through your day, and try not to second-guess yourself. Reflect on how it felt different than other days.

This helps you build confidence. Sometimes we need permission to be confident. This activity not only gives you that permission, it also encourages it.

INTERVIEWING OTHERS

And folks who *do* the interviewing? All of the previous information is important, and remember, nowadays, people are also interviewing *you*. The information for the interviewer matters because you can very easily see if they put time into preparing for this interview. You can also practice empathy skills and pay attention if they are simply nervous or unprepared. It's your place to make that space comfortable for an open conversation, as well as free of any sort of status and power dynamics you're looking to put into place.

The bit about people interviewing you: *they are.* A recent client who works with scalable businesses was interviewing people for a position with her, and this position essentially was her second in command. She was overworked and overextended. Like many new ventures, her company was greeted with *so much* excitement. With excitement comes *so much* work. She chatted with me about interviewing candidates and told me she found the perfect candidate but he turned it down. When she asked him why he turned it down, he said "Honestly, you were really disorganized." Mic. Drop.

Joking aside, she asked for real feedback and she got it. When she heard that, she knew she was projecting the feeling of overwhelm as desperation that was very real. She was overwhelmed and *needed* someone to work out, because she wasn't getting her work done in the way she was used to. She thanked the candidate and went back into her work life and looked at how she could manage a few things before interviewing another candidate.

When you are interviewing other people, it's important to establish a system. Too much creativity is just as crippling as not enough. The seat-of-your-pants manner of doing *anything* in a professional situation has the distinct possibility of massive failure. When you establish a system, you are thinking through what you *want* to know in the interview, all while assessing *how* you feel about the candidate and their answers, as well as the fit for the position. Well before the interviews, be sure you understand what the position looks like (you're defining the role!), what kind of person might succeed in this position, what success looks like in the position, and what you want the position to accomplish in the larger part of the company and its culture.

I often joke that some positions feel like warm-body positions, and it's because no attention was paid to the potential "best" candidate. Any breathing person will do! We all know that isn't generally true, but if you as the interviewer aren't attending to what you want in this position (and interview), you won't get what you want because it's undefined. When thinking about what kind of person might succeed in this position, think of characteristics: Do they need to be an independent worker? Detail orientated? Customer focused? IT skills? Open to rolling up their sleeves and doing anything expected of them? Hyperfocused on one task? Flesh this out, and stay away from things that are either unattainable or too close-minded. If you get too focused on what you're looking for, you'll be disappointed by every person who walks in, because they will never be it.

Disappointment often happens when people compare the new candidates to the last person in the position. If you had a stellar candidate in that position who left and you're sore about it, think about what qualities they had that made them great for that position. That's what you're looking for in the interview.

Once you have these ideas outlined, you are ready to interview candidates. This prep allows you time to pay attention in the moment to what they are saying. You've got the pieces; you're looking for someone to connect them. If you haven't interviewed people before (even if you have and you're not thrilled about it), be sure to plan a few questions in advance. Yes, you can let the interview be more conversational. You find out a lot about a person in a conversation if you know what you're looking for. If you have specific things you would like to know answers to, don't be afraid to preselect questions you feel could accomplish your goal. You have a few kinds of questions to select from and a few that put your improv skills to the test.

Icebreakers. For the love of all things, please don't make this question awkward. Calling it an icebreaker, and using something like, "if your life could be a movie, what kind of movie would it be?", or another question that might be more appropriate for a first or second date, usually is not the best question to lead with, especially if this is the first time you are meeting. Keep it simple, and always remember the point of interview questions: you're not trying to trick or trap someone. You want to find more information. You're seeking to get to know them in a professional manner, and with an icebreaker, you're trying to make them feel comfortable. This isn't time for you to share your creativity.

You might be chuckling right now, thinking, "No one would ever ask what kind of movie represents their life." And you would be wrong. I was working with a new graphic designer, and he really wanted to get an idea of an assistant's personality. He had this question as part of his survey. After my initial shock, I asked him how his results were, and not surprisingly, they were not what he expected. Interviewees seemed to struggle with the question and their answers didn't really help him figure out who to choose. They ended up talking more about movies than anything else, and while it was nice to get to know the person, that wasn't the point of the question.

Do not make the icebreaker question difficult for the responder. If they can't figure out how to answer the question, or they can't make the creative jumps to express themselves correctly, or worse, they get so caught up in it they can't focus the rest of the time, you've done yourself a disservice when all you wanted to do was make the other person comfortable. Ask a simple icebreaker: Tell me about yourself.

Traditional questions. Have a few of these in your back pocket. These are the questions that are expected in interviews. Pick out a few and really practice active listening with the candidate's answers. Look for those gifts—the little bits of information you can easily grab on to and ask more questions about, or information that leads to a larger conversation. If you have these picked out in advance, you can spend time being present. Some of these are mentioned earlier in this chapter, a quick reminder of a few:

Why do you want to work here?

What are your strengths and weaknesses?

Why should we want to work with you?

Situational questions. These ask the interviewer to put themselves in a specific situation, and you get to see how they would react (in their own words) during these moments. The best way to use these kinds of questions are pulling from actual situations the candidate might be in. If they will not be customer facing, you're wasting time asking them how they would deal with an angry customer. Again, prepping these in advance not only gives you time to think about real situations that might happen, but it also gives you the space to attend to their answer: Do they look uncomfortable? Does it seem like they've dealt with something like this before? Do you care if they have been in this situation many other times, or do you not mind if they've never dealt with something like this? In the end, you're looking to see their thought process.

Behavior-based questions. The difference between these and situational questions is simple. Behavior-based questions refer specifically to situations that have already happened, while situational questions tap into a possibility. These are the "tell me about a time . . ." questions that ask the interviewee to tap into past experiences. These are very important for observation: when you're asking these questions, you're asking the interviewee to recall situations that might mirror a situation in this new position. In the end, you're making a judgment based on their re-telling of a past situation. For what it's worth to the position they are interviewing for, this is a good time to see how the candidate connects with information, gets it out in a clear and concise manner, and actually answers your question. Candidates may spin the information in a way that is beneficial to them (see humblebragging and pivoting) or answer around the question you've asked. Again, active listening comes into play. If something sounds a little off, ask a follow-up question for more information.

Culture-fit questions. This segment of questions is one that you have to prepare for more than the candidate. Do you understand your culture? Is praise given regularly? Are you open communicators? Do you expect people to immediately reply to emails? Do you send texts in or out of the office to coworkers about work issues?

This is an opportunity to see if the candidate is a good fit with the culture that you either already have or want to build. The critical factor is you. If you don't understand the culture you *have*, then how can you judge someone based on their answer to a question that essentially doesn't matter? Think of building a world in improv. Every little bit contributes to the whole, so think about what you want that whole to be. If you have a considerable amount of extroverts on the team and you'd like some quiet thinkers, consider that, and vice versa. Again though, you need to clearly define these aspects to either achieve or discard them. If they aren't defined, you'll be disappointed 100 percent of the time.

Whether you are interviewing someone or being interviewed, your biggest advantage will come by preparing ahead of time and making a choice to actively listen to the person in front of you. If you start spacing out, work to snap back to focus.

Soft Skills

Remember your soft skills. While I hate the term *soft skills*, I love what they are and how important they are to an effective work environment. Soft skills, at their core definition, are "personal attributes that enable someone to interact effectively and harmoniously with other people." Essentially they are people skills, specifically things like communication skills, critical thinking, leadership, positive attitude, teamwork and work ethic. So . . . skills that work improv techniques.

While this might not necessarily sound like something every person will immediately say "oh, but of course!" to, the latest findings from the World Economic Forum predict that by 2020, soft skills that are crucial for the job will rise by a third.[7] What does this mean for interviewers and interviewees? Well, aside from a clear need to develop these skills for interviewees, interviewers need to start to think clearly about what skills are necessary for a candidate to succeed, and what skills might be grown through learning and development initiatives on the job. Many of these skills aren't immediately apparent when interviewing, which makes another argument for preparation. How can you show things like social skills, complex problem solving, processing skills, or cognitive abilities if you are worried about relaying your strengths and weaknesses in a clear and concise manner? For interviewers, how can you measure and attend to these not wholly apparent skills if you haven't thought about your next question or the critical parts of your office culture? Prep for what you can; let yourself follow along for the ride once it starts.

GROUP INTERVIEWS

Group interviews deserve their own place in this chapter. A group interview can mean multiple interviewers, multiple candidates, or a combination of both. Many of the same essential ideas apply, with a few adjustments to help a candidate stand out, and help an interviewer manage the potential of a person who is monopolizing or being monopolized.

Before diving in, it's important to note that group interviews are uncomfortable and awkward, and people often can get lost in the room. It's up to you, the candidate, and you, the interviewer, to attend to this. The majority of this responsibility does fall on the candidate. However, the interviewer has some responsibility to manage the room.

First, as the candidate, treat this situation like a mini-networking moment. Say hello, shake hands, and introduce yourself. There is no need to dive into your elevator pitch. If this is a first interview (which is often the case with group interviews), chances are the first question will be an icebreaker of "Tell me about yourself," and you'll get to dive into that (abridged) version. Remember: you get the energy you put out. If you're there sizing up the other people in the room and doing that awful once over that is both insecure for you and incredibly intimidating for the person who is receiving it, you're definitely not showing any sort of people skills or teamwork. Sure, these folks are "competition," but you are mostly competing against yourself in this moment. Don't get in your own way, and include the other candidates in your conversation by (1) making eye contact and (2) using "Yes, and" to their comments if you can truly add something. Here's an example of this working . . . and not.

For quite a few years I was part of a luxury department store's learning and development team and human resources. We trained new hires, led growth opportunities, and participated in the hiring process. The initial interview for their brand ambassador positions was in a group setting. In every interview we would have several types of people, including the person who nailed the group interview and the person who ruined all chances of working there through the group interview.

The candidate who would nail the interview was one who came in confidently, greeted everyone, and made eye contact with the entire room while they were talking. They looked everyone in the eye for a comfortable amount of time while they were answering questions, even looking at the other candidates. You see, it's very weird being in a room with someone in the same conversation and having them never make eye contact with you. It's even stranger when you're watching the conversation happen and you see them purposely avoiding that eye contact with others for whatever reason, and making very intense eye contact with people "who matter." The person who would clearly get to move on to the one-on-one interview would talk to everyone and include everyone in the room. They also listened to other people, and if they had a similar answer, they would build off of the previous answer.

I met one candidate in particular who strikes me a few years ago during one of the biggest group interviews I've been present for. About 12 people were in the room as candidates and 5, including myself, as interviewers. While I didn't ask a single question, I was there for observation purposes only. I watched one candidate walk in, greet everyone, including the other candidates, and ask their name. He then proceeded to weave the other candidates' answers into his, appropriately crediting them and building off of what they said. One question, a behavior-based question, asked the candidates how they have handled an unhappy and loud customer in public situations. He answered later, and said, "Much like Steve, the customer is my priority. And like Tara, I also have a responsibility to the store and other customers," then added his own personal addition: "My go-to response with an upset customer is to make sure they are heard."

Mic drop moment. Do you see what he did there? He not only said his goal is to make sure a customer is heard, but he also showed how he does indeed listen to other people. He included the answers that resonated with him and his answer, and instead of wasting time repeating what every person before him said, he confidently affirmed that *yes*, these folks said a great answer and I agree with them, *and* I have this additional information to add to this situation. "Yes, and" is magic.

I asked him afterward, much, much later down the line at a work summit (he got hired) if he knew what he was doing. He said that he took an improv class a few years ago, and his biggest takeaway was to affirm and elevate with "Yes, and." It changed his perspective on work conversations. See? Magic!

The candidate who ruins their chances of moving forward to a one-on-one interview might look like everyone else. They might come in and be a little nervous with the number of people there. They might start to size up the other people, not interested in introducing themselves to anyone and keeping to themselves. This is more than being introverted. Some people are simply shy. They keep to themselves in situations like this. This looks very different than the person who ruins their chances at the one-on-one. Introverts still listen and answer questions when they are asked. Being introverted doesn't mean you're going to lose the opportunity.

Being a jerk means you're going to lose the opportunity. The jerk behavior is simply defined as someone who lacks the people skills and empathy part of soft skills. Yes, this is absolutely between you and the other people in the room. Do you think the interviewer wants you to be cutthroat? Or insulting to the others? Interrupt them? Say they are wrong? Not address anyone else in the room, and talk as if you and the interviewer are the only people in the room?

It might be better described as agenda-oriented and "selfish" behavior. This is the person who walks into an interview and is so focused on making themselves known, they don't think about potential reasons for the group interview, or more often, the impression that selfish and agenda-oriented behavior gives off.

A few years ago, with another company, I got to see the worst of this. It was a financial firm in New York City, and they hired between 10 and 20 people a month. Because they were hiring so aggressively, they clearly had group interviews to simply "weed people out." It was an afternoon interview in the fall, and about six people were being interviewed at once. For this particular client, I would sit in the interview "holding" room and often pretend to be an interviewee. They would eliminate people who couldn't work well as a team, which was a big part of company culture. My job was to speak when spoken to by the interviewer and answer questions in a benign manner. I would never be the best person there, and I would never be the worst. Before you start looking for a plant at your next interview, this isn't something I did often and it's usually not something a company can spend time on.

This particular day, I got there first, got briefed on the candidates and sat down, typing away on my phone as people came in. Just about everyone was there and we were about to go into the other room for the actual interview, when the last candidate walked in. Since my job was to watch people for personality and soft skills, I can safely say I have never seen anyone walk in with so much arrogance. He came in, looked around, and said, "Oh, this should be easy." We went into the room where he "pushed" his way to the front and selected the chair in the center. I tentatively say "push" because as the last person in, he probably should have been the last person down the hall. He managed to get to the front of the entire group to pick the chair he thought exuded the most power.

When it came time for the actual interview, he interrupted people on four separate occasions, when he absolutely did not need to. When he spoke, he looked only at who he presumed to be the lead interviewer (there were three) and didn't make eye contact with anyone else. I'll give him credit, he was semi-listening to some of the people talking, but more to say things like, "I disagree with what they just said."

When the interview was over, he immediately got up, walked to the interviewers and proceeded to talk to that lead for about 10 minutes, oblivious to or because of the other interviewees in the room. When I came up to possibly save the people who were paying me, I was promptly dismissed with an, "Oh, we're having a pretty serious conversation here, I don't know if you'll get it."

He did not get the position or a one-on-one interview. Worse, no one in the room did either.

First, his behavior—he knew what he wanted. Great, A+ for task one. The problem he showed everyone was his lack of respect for anyone he deemed "unimportant." This wasn't an interview for a senior vice president position. And even if it were, it wouldn't matter; the behavior was awful. This was an interview for an entry-level position at a huge financial firm. How would he treat his coworkers? People in other departments? He made his status *very* clear from the moment he walked into the room and confirmed it by the end. His interrupting during the interview, combined with his lack of eye contact—which, on top of being awkward, is extremely rude to the other interviewers in the room—confirmed his perceived status. At the end, I'm sure he thought he was showing "strength" and "leadership" by talking to the people he felt would influence the decision. The behavior he showed toward me aside, his awareness was severely lacking, and all graciousness was lost long before that moment.

While some companies may value skills like this—we do hear, "Oh, they are a great performer! Not really a good team player though," all too often—many companies don't. Companies are evolving to invest in candidates that increase company culture. On top of that, when a person is that self-centered in their own importance, you have to wonder: is this just a step to another position, or is this person going to be around long enough for this all to be worth it? We know that people want to grow, and movement is crucial for growth. But few people *like* the interview process, so the last thing you want to project in an interview is the idea that you'll be gone by the time you've gotten to know everyone's name.

I mentioned that none of the people in the room got a one-on-one interview. The dynamic that happened was uncomfortable, to say the least. I quietly watched as the other candidates shrunk because of his behavior. The first interruption took out a few people, who then started to answer questions in a tentative manner, looking around at other people for approval. By the time the interview was over, half the room left immediately. The other half awkwardly waited for their turn to thank the interviewers, but gave up after a short amount of time when they saw how long he was talking to the interviewers.

While the interviewers saw the arrogance and rudeness of that particular candidate, they also saw what happened with the others. They let that behavior destroy their own answers and confidence, and in turn, all of their answers were short and not nearly as good as they would have been if they felt good about their own worth.

What do you do in a situation like this? First, I can say this was an extreme example, as many of my examples are. I pick out the one in the dozens that make a point, so while he wasn't the only arrogant interviewee I've seen, he was definitely the worst. You very well might see people who exhibit some of those qualities, and the best advice I have is what I've been saying all along: know yourself. Know yourself and your answers so well that nothing can throw you off, including some person who thinks they already have the job and this is just a fun HR routine. Keep your eyes on the prize, and the more you focus on that, the less some noise will throw you off.

Let the energy happen around you and keep yours intact. If you give off the impression you no longer want to be there, the interviewers will feel that and apply it to you as a candidate, not to how you deal with difficult people. If you are constantly getting interrupted by another candidate, you have a few options. Patiently wait until they are done (or until they take a breath, or hit a punctuation mark) and then say something to the effect of, "Thank you for that. As I was saying . . . ." and pick up where you left off if you didn't finish your point. Be gracious, and take the focus back. You also can politely say, "I wasn't finished talking, can you hold your thought for one moment?" That one is a bit harder to pull off without getting into an interrupting war. You don't want to start going back and forth and struggling for power. If you make it known, politely, that you're not finished talking (and hopefully when you are answering the questions you're putting a button on the end of that story so people actually know you are done), a good interviewer should take the control back from the interrupter and return focus to you.

As an interviewer, group interviews are a great time saver if you know what you're looking for. Like every interview, preparation is incredibly important. Be sure you know what you're looking for in a candidate before the interview. It's almost even more important to prepare for a group interview, because of the number of personalities in the room.

A big part of preparing for a group interview for the interviewer is understanding the different types of people who might be in the room. This isn't to say you need to prepare for every single personality, but it is critical to be ready for several types. You have your personality all set, but how is that version going to interact with everyone else?

The Communication Styles

There are four main communication styles: passive, aggressive, passive-aggressive, and assertive. We spend a lot of time with these four communication styles in our improv class. Each one of the styles is very distinctive and is shown both verbally and nonverbally. This is another added consideration for *who* you are in the room. When you're planning your *who*, be sure to take note of these styles as well as your own.

The **passive** style is often encompassed with indifference toward decisions and consistently taking the passenger seat in conversations. In improv moments, passive persons often "Yes" instead of "Yes, and"—they go along with decisions that are made and won't make additional decisions. Their indifference can lead to resentment: if you're never making a decision and constantly going along with everyone else, sooner or later you're going to do something that frustrates you or makes you uncomfortable. In conflict, they most likely defer to others or make accommodations to make the other person feel "better" to avoid a conflict. Finally, they often avoid eye contact and don't stand in that "open" stance with their feet under their knees under their hips under their shoulders. They often make themselves small and take up less space.

Passive communicators use phrases like "It doesn't matter," or "Whatever you think." They might also use qualifiers to not offend the people they're talking to. In improv conversations, black-and-white decisions make them very uncomfortable and they often have a hard time determining what they want. When they *do* determine what they want, or lead with it, they often end up deferring to the other person and their wants. The idea of taking focus and running with an idea can cripple a passive communicator. People usually like passive communicators because they are easy to get along with. The passive communicator can feel like a doormat.

The **aggressive** style of communication is also very apparent. Aggressive communicators are clear with their style. They rarely care about the needs and wants of others and are very driven with their own needs and wants. It's a style of communication you can hear, see, and often feel. Aggressive communicators often speak in a loud voice and use influencers like intimidation, criticism, threats, and blame to get what they want. They usually lack active listening skills (listening skills as a whole), interrupt, and speak with a demanding voice.

Aggressive communicators also tend to be seen as leaders, which is what often makes them so dangerous. In EE's experience, these tend to be the people for whom we go in for empathy training. They are very, very good at taking action and making things happen—sometimes at the expense of other people. When something doesn't work out in their favor, blame is always on another person.

In improv moments, these folks make the decisions and *push* the decisions. They won't often "Yes, and" a situation. They are usually waiting for someone to "Yes, and" them. Often the driver in a conversation, they fight for what they want and make those black-and-white choices. The examples earlier in the book of people not listening, specifically those who miss the gifts dropped by other people and often to the determent of the conversation, illustrate this type of communication. Eye contact is often intense and used more as an intimidation technique rather than a communication technique.

Passive-aggressive communicators are an interesting combination of both. They seem very outwardly passive yet internally aggressive. The resentment that builds up with passive-aggressive communicators usually leads to those little comments that can be interpreted as "acting out" or veiled in kindness, with anger underneath. Passive-aggressive communicators avoid conflict, but then talk behind someone's back or spread rumors because they can't deal with the aggression building up beneath the surface.

Oftentimes, passive-aggressive communicators are aware of what they want; they have a hard time getting it because they can't effectively voice it. That person that mutters comments to themselves or is constantly talking about other people, definitely not dealing with things in a way that is healthy. Most likely they are harboring a lot of unresolved conflict.

In improv moments, and real life, passive-aggressive communicators are usually saying "but" to *themselves*. They worry about presenting their full opinion on something, so they often temper it with an agreeable solution, adding what they actually think afterward—the structure of "Yeah that's fine, but this might happen." They make a statement and then walk it back because the passive part of their communication style kicks in. It might also be the opposite. They go with the flow and then mutter something under their breath that some people might giggle about but is actually really harmful and aggressive.

Their body language is all over the place—if someone is upset, they'll shut off, cross their arms and legs, and give the silent treatment to people they are upset with and if they are feeling OK with someone, they might open up, only to close off when they are bottling up emotions. Think of passive-aggressive communication like a shaken-up soda before it's carefully opened. The pressure builds and builds, and when you open it a little bit, some soda sprays out. Now think of that soda that sprays out as words—unless the can is opened quickly, it comes in short bursts.

The final communication style is **assertive**—many people consider this to be the most effective communication style. It's often categorized by being aware of your own needs and balancing them with the needs of others. You can also express those needs in a clear manner, and when you are expressing those needs, you are minding others' needs as well.

"I" statements are big in assertive communication. By owning the statement, opinion, and comment, you aren't blaming another person or making things vague. You're very clearly owning the words coming out of your mouth.

"Yes, and" is a very assertive manner of communication. You are acknowledging the information, opinion, and thoughts of another person, and you're adding how you feel, equalizing both. Say you're having a conversation about politics, and you don't agree with the person you're talking to. You can easily get aggressive with your opinion, insisting you are correct and the other person is wrong. You can say, "But what about [insert opinion here]?" and then you elevate your opinion in an aggressive or passive-aggressive manner.

Again, this is not to say we're looking at always agreeing or not having heated conversations. You can be aggressive in your opinion, or you can be assertive. By elevating one opinion above another, you've introduced status and emotion into a conversation that usually is better served by facts. Sometimes, those facts are things that can be proven, and sometimes, those facts are simply the fact that someone feels a certain way. Here's an example: I love dogs—way more than people, most of the time. It is a fact that I love dogs. The statement, "I love dogs," is an opinion. Not everyone has to love dogs. You're not better or worse than me if you like dogs. You don't have to pretend you love dogs to be part of my team. It is a fact that I love dogs; the belief that I think dogs are awesome is an opinion. Make sense?

Back on the assertive style with "Yes, and." Your opinion is still an opinion if it has to do with an office matter, a political movement, or dogs. You might be able to back it up with your set of facts, but it's still your opinion. Which is why the "Yes, and" is so powerful in these moments. That other person over there? Their opinion is also simply their opinion, backed up by their set of facts. Neither one of you is better than the other, and that's important to remember. The key factor in assertive communication is the "I" statement. In conversation workshops, "I" statements make some people nervous. Shouldn't we be opening it up to everyone? The difference is that an "I" statement is assertive and effective when it comes to owning feelings and behaviors. Saying, "I am frustrated explaining things to you every morning," is assertive. It might seem rude to some of you, and that's OK. Let's dissect it.

In "I am frustrated explaining things to you every morning," the emotion and frustration lie with the person making the statement. They are stating a fact—they are frustrated. They are saying why—they are explaining things every morning. There isn't blame on the other person. Imagine having a discussion on the frustration. The other person might respond with, "Well, it's your job to explain everything to me!" You can respond with, "Yes, it is my job to explain everything to you, and I am getting frustrated with it." You own the emotion, and ownership is a huge part of assertive communication.

Other ways to show assertive communication aside from "I" statements include constant eye contact, learning to say no, and a consistent, confident manner of voicing needs and desires.

Managing Communication Styles in a Group Interview

When you're working with a group of people, pay attention to what communication style goes with each person, because as you can see, it's indicative of personalities as well. The relation between the styles is also something to watch. If you have a few aggressive styles in the room, they might be talking over or interrupting the passive or even assertive communication styles. Passive-aggressive communicators are not necessarily the best to have on a team, and they possibly are that way because of working with aggressive communicators. So they are also one to manage—not in the sense of helping them speak up, but specifically addressing the aggressive part of their communication.

Assertive communicators can effectively "stand up for themselves" and "hold their own" in group situations. Passive communicators, like the ones in the earlier example of the terrible group interview I sat in on, often try to blend into the group and defer to the more aggressive communicators. Backing up further, if you are looking at a specific candidate, and they are being extremely quiet despite being very vocal in email and written communication, look at the situation as a whole and see if perhaps they are being shut down by more aggressive communicators.

Tactics for running an interview in the moment with aggressive communicators can be a little stressful for people who are not always comfortable with assertive communication. This is why it's important to assert confidence at the beginning of the interview. Sure, you're interviewing them, so you're automatically "in charge," but aggressive communicators often see other types of communicators as weaker and try to run over them. In that earlier example, the aggressive communicator identified the person he thought was "equal" in communication and addressed only them. Sometimes the strategy is less about finding the equal and more about shutting down the possible opposition or competition. It might look like talking over people, interrupting, or using aggressive language.

Having a few prepared statements like, "I'd like to hear the rest of your thoughts," when an aggressive communicator interrupts a more passive communicator, or "Thank you for that and I want to hear more in a moment. I would like Steve to finish his answer first," are simple ways to not only assert your own authority in an interview, but also redirect the focus to the more passive communicator. You can also specifically ask people the question versus posing it to the entire group. By naming a candidate and then asking the question, you can direct the conversation toward people who you're looking to get information from. While you will need to ask questions to the aggressive communicators too, you're holding the power in the conversation.

There's also the school of thought that the candidates should fend for themselves and figure out how to be heard—not my favorite. Aggressive communicators can be high-performing and incredible workers. They also can shut down other communication styles very easily. Because they are so forward and focused on their own needs and wants, they often can push their own agenda and desires *so hard* they shut down everyone else in the conversation. While they might be great on paper, they are usually very difficult to work with if any part of the job involves a team mentality. Furthermore, if you are looking for someone who works and plays well with others, an aggressive communicator isn't the best team player, because they are so often fixated on *their* needs and wants.

If you're looking for the group to "fend for themselves," then you need to truly consider what kind of work culture you're looking to build. If you have an opportunity to create a culture through an interview situation, or effectively elevate (or dissipate) a culture that's currently in place, you should be taking the opportunity to do so. This is important for those smaller businesses without an HR department to manage the culture, as well as those larger businesses. Changing work culture is not impossible. It's also not easy, so any time you can put in to effectively making it "better," including who you bring into the culture, you're doing yourself a favor.

TRY THIS

Identify your communication style at work. Remember, this might change person to person, situation to situation. Look at your last conversation as an example, and look at it like an improv moment. Who was assertive? Who was passive? Maybe both of you were aggressive? Build this into your reflection after conversations.

This helps you understand your personal communication style. Prior to reading this, you might not know your go-to style. This activity forces you to examine how you communicate at work. You can't change how anyone else communicates, just how you respond to them.

When you're managing a group interview as a facilitator, you'll need to remember *your* assertive communication style. Using "I" statements and remembering you control that narrative are critical. If you have a candidate who is attempting to run the show, it's up to you to get it back, because you truly can blame only yourself for not holding the control. When you're managing it as an interviewee, balance personalities and remember it's often between you and yourself for a job.

YOUR CHEAT SHEET

Interviewing is a nervous, awkward situation for everyone involved. *No one* likes to be interviewed, and likewise, interviewing people is an exhausting process. Like many verbal communication situations in professional environments, by preparing your tool kit you can remain present in the moment.

In the beginning I mentioned that many of these tactics work for non-job-interviews. A great place to start is with Sit-Prob-Sol—if you're being interviewed for anything, it's a surefire way for clear and specific answers. Good luck, and remember to:

- Do research.

- Know your questions and answers.

- Mind your communication style.

- Pivot and spin, but don't lie.

- Stock your toolbox.

- When in doubt, remember to Sit-Prob-Sol your answer.

CHAPTER 6

Get Out of Your Own Way

S elf-advocacy is difficult for many of us, especially in professional situ-ations. Whether it is "selling" yourself or your business, asking for a raise or a new position, negotiating or resolving conflict, or standing up for yourself and speaking up, when it comes to professional advocacy, many people stall and struggle. It's difficult to sell without seeming like you're selling, asking for a raise without demanding or backing down. When it comes to negotiating your worth, professional situations often make it harder because of the degree of professionalism that needs to be maintained. When you're advocating yourself in personal situations, often you can go hard and not worry as much about the reactions and effects. In professional situations, you worry about the audience and the people the audience know, and the people they know . . . .

Many times it all comes down to you and how much you get in your own way. At all stages of improv education, people get in their own way. This might look like a lack of confidence, a nervous energy, self-depreca-tion, or not standing up for yourself. It might come from a lack of prepa-ration, lack of listening, missing focus, or missing presence. It's "easier" to play things safe a lot of the time. If you're constantly trying not to fail, you'll never succeed.

Let's get out of our own way.

PITCHING A BUSINESS

Personal elevator pitches have been covered, but what about business pitches? Generally speaking, when you're pitching your business, no matter what size, you have to think about your audience first. I've seen some horrific business pitches before (and if you've watched *Shark Tank*, so have you), and I've seen some that knocked it out of the park. The winning pitches have something in common I bet you can guess by now: they attend to the audience.

Think about who you're talking to and what you want your audience to do. Talking to customers is different than talking to investors, which is different than talking to a potential board. Every audience needs to be handled very differently. Let's compare pitching to customers versus pitching to investors. A customer needs to know what the product or service does for them, while an investor needs to know the business's capability. The investor cares about the customer, but they also care about the bottom line, customer acquisition cost, marketing cost, distribution, and potential, among others. In efforts to not dive too far into the rabbit hole, it suffices to say that the customer and investor want two very different things to buy in to the product or service and will spend two very different amounts of money.

Aside from thinking about the general audience, since you're pitching to a specific audience, you need to think about what's in it for them. Since the purpose of most pitches is to get buy-in, you want to think about what the person you're talking to can gain. Once an investor told me that businesses are either painkillers or vitamins. That makes so much sense to me. Is my business solving a problem as a painkiller, or is it making life better for someone as a vitamin? The key to this? You're thinking about the result with *them*, whoever they are. You're not thinking about anything else. You often want to start using those influence techniques when you are showing worth to whoever your specific audience is, *and* they most likely want very different things!

Pitching your company is much like going on a job interview for your business. Before you even walk in the door, you should think about potential questions and answers and how could you adjust if necessary. You've got to get straight to the point in job interviews; you have to actually be at the point before it even begins with pitches. We shouldn't be left wondering why you're here.

Employ a strong sense of excitement. If you have to use Viewpoints and see what your body and voice look like when you're excited talking about your business idea, go for it. If you can't excite your listeners in a pitch, you've lost before it even started. Again, control the room by walking in with the right energy for the audience. Once you've got the ideas of the pitch out, do that 90-second, 60-second, and 30-second version. Get it sharp, tight, and clear. In an interview, the interviewer is usually looking to meet a need and wants to hire someone. In a pitch session, investors don't necessarily *need* to spend their money on someone. They want to or are interested in the possibility of it. Your product or service is the candidate they want to hire, whether it's a room full of investors or a room full of customers.

You need to start your presentation with a bang. If you're going in front of customers or investors, they need to be impressed in the beginning. Having a tight first line or two is critical in getting your audience's immediate buy-in on your concept. Storytelling is critical: bring back Sit-Prob-Sol—the situation is the market, the problem is the problem, and the solution is your product or service. Finally, end with what makes you special. Why are you the best person and company for this particular group's problem? "Show, don't tell" is another improv strategy critical to pitching. By showing the effectiveness of your idea, product, service, and how your customers or investors can benefit from *you specifically* versus telling them, you're connecting back with the storytelling component of how we learn and process information. Finally, make sure they know what you want, and be clear with it yourself. If you can't describe what you want in one or very few sentences, you'll never be able to connect your audience with what you want them to do. Easy, right?

Now is a great time to take a moment and step back—this sounds remarkably like a job interview, doesn't it? That's the trick—they are so very similar. Conversations, too. If you understand who you are talking to, what they want, what you want, and how you can provide it, you've got so much in the bag. Listening and responding make up everything in verbal and nonverbal communication, no matter if it's a conversation in the office in front of the bathroom or a meeting with a potential multimillion-dollar investor. At the core, it's all listening and responding; which means it is all improv.

Tying pitching back to interviewing, when you are practicing your pitch, make sure you know it forward, backward, left, and right, because most of the time, unless you are giving a pitch for a competition, you'll be stopped and interrupted. Remember, if you are memorizing something word for word, you'll memorize the word order. If you memorize the word order and get interrupted by a question or five, you won't be able to restart that confidence that got you in the room in the first place.

TRY THIS

Even if you aren't an entrepreneur, you might be "selling" something that you care very much about. Persuasion is an important skill. Look around you. Grab a random object from your desk or home. Go ahead, do that, and come back.

Now that you have your object, your mission is to sell this object. Don't worry about who you're selling it to. How can you convince *anyone* to purchase this (probably benign) object? Use skills you developed earlier in the book, and remember: it's all about believing in this object and proving its worth.

Now reflect:

If you're an entrepreneur, was that easier or harder than selling your own business? Did you struggle to find the worth or was it easier?

If you're not, how did that feel?

This helps you build your persuasion tactics. When we understand why something is important to us, we then have to work on conveying that importance to others. This activity allows for playful practice of this skill. If you can sell ChapStick, you can sell anything.

THE UGLY: IMPOSTER SYNDROME

Ah, that confidence. Quick, check in: Have you ever felt like a fraud? Thought you don't belong in the room? It's all luck and will come crashing down when someone discovers you? I feel you. Both of my businesses are successful. I don't work another job, I don't worry about finances . . . and even writing that sentence, I almost wrote "knock on wood" because of that little nagging voice inside my head.

For most of this book, I've used student examples and have saved my own personal examples for very key moments. This is one of them.

I had left New York City after a long tenure, ready to move along to a life that was cheaper and calmer in Winston Salem. I still had that New York City hustle, so one of my big goals in the first few months of my new city was to meet as many people as possible and try to get EE off the ground. Getting the meetings were easy. Showing up with confidence wasn't. There was one meeting in particular that I will never forget. It was the meeting that changed everything about how I introduced myself and my business.

In my move, I sent out dozens of emails for meetings and set one up with the woman who was in charge of one of the artistic entrepreneur organizations in town. Being the City of Arts and Innovation, Winston had a few organizations that helped art-based businesses succeed. This particular organization was one I had heard so much about; it was one everyone told me to talk to because what we did with EE was such a fit. Seriously, we used a dramatic art—improv—and focused on professional development for businesses. I still remember how excited I was to meet with the executive director.

As for the *who, where, what,* and *how*—you've got me (who), this executive director (who), me sweating from a non-air-conditioned Jeep in the South and into the historic house turned office (where). I wanted to be welcomed into the arts scene here (what), and I felt excited, nervous, and uncertain (how). I had notoriously bad imposter syndrome. Whenever it would come time to introduce myself or my business, I would downplay, say I wasn't sure how it happened, act as if I didn't know what I was doing, or just wave off any successful things people may have heard about me. Internally, I felt like a fraud: all of this was luck, and I got here because . . . who really knows? This meeting was no exception: it could not have gone worse.

Well, it could have. She asked me to introduce my company and I could have frozen, broke into tears, walked out, or threw up. I totally could have done one of those things. Didn't do any of those things . . . the things I could forgive myself for or give myself grace about.

She asked me to introduce myself and my company, and I did what I always did: I downplayed. I'm pretty sure I said I was just along for the ride to see where it went.

And she tore me apart. Aside from telling me that what I was doing didn't sound very innovative, she pointed out a few different organizations that were doing similar things (they weren't, but I did a terrible job of explaining what I did). She suggested I could work for these companies because what I was doing and trying to do in Winston wasn't something that would "make it." On top of that, she said no one cared where I was, that people care where I'm going and what I'm changing now, so the fact I was an actor wasn't a big deal—and didn't matter in the end.

I slunk out of that meeting, sat in the hot car, and cried. I got home and kept crying. I texted my New York friends and cried more. I started looking for jobs, applying to schools for teaching positions, used my time to look for a job, and went along with being something that wasn't very special, angry that whatever luck happened to me in New York City wasn't worth anything in Winston Salem. A few weeks passed by, and I realized this woman wasn't a horrible human being who was just trying to smash my soul in a million pieces and get me to conform. She based her understanding of me on my awful, self-deprecating, and insecure introductions. The qualifiers! The awkward apathy! The "oh I don't know how I got here!" I knew how my business became successful: I worked so damn hard, slept very little, and pushed myself and my limits. We had been working with major clients, and we were successful because of the work I put in.

Yet I showed none of it. I didn't own the success of my business, didn't show how much I cared about it, and didn't speak up about what it really was: I spent so much time trying to be friendly and cool in that moment, hoping for her to "just see" how successful I was, and maybe my luck or whatever everyone else saw in me would work out again. Ironic, right? I help people speak up about their own professional accomplishments and worth. It's not always easy to see the forest when you're stuck in the trees, no matter who you are.

I did a hard stop on all introductions and job applications. I took a moment and wrote out my introduction for both myself and my business. I knew how to introduce myself, but clearly not in a professional way that incorporated my business in a confident manner. Then I started to introduce myself again and kept working. I would be lying if I said it was the only time someone had doubted my worth or I introduced myself in a terrible manner. It was far from it—but this time, I knew how to quiet my imposter syndrome in the moment.

A few years after that moment that changed everything, I ran into the same woman at an arts event. As small as Winston is, it was definitely the first time I had seen her since we had our meeting. I walked up to her, and while I'm not entirely sure she remembered our meeting, I thanked her for it. Specifically, I thanked her for making me feel so awful that I realized my introductions completely did not represent who I really was and how great my business actually was. She looked a little caught off guard (I mean, I came up to her at an event and basically said thanks for making me feel terrible), but I felt I really needed her to know how much she changed how I viewed myself. It was *that moment* when I knew my imposter syndrome was holding me back.

Imposter syndrome is no joke. It's a psychological phenomenon that is categorized by the belief that you are inadequate despite evidence that you are actually quite successful. According to Dr. Valerie Young, an expert on imposter syndrome, there are five types of imposter syndrome.[1] Certain activities can help combat each of those types.

The first is the **perfectionist**. Control freak, anyone? This type always feels like they can do better and success is never achieved, especially not in a situation where people are assisting with the final project. It could always be better if you did it, and you could have always done it better, so the vicious cycle continues. The second is the **superwoman/man**. This type is the one constantly trying to prove their worth despite their success. They work longer than everyone else, pushing their own physical limits to prove to themselves and the world that they are worth it, even when no one questions their worth. The third is the **natural genius**. Irritated when you don't get something immediately? Feel like you should have understood something by now and beat yourself up if you don't? This is you. The fourth is the **soloist**. Need to do it yourself? Does asking for help sound like a failure? You might be a soloist. The final is the **expert**. You fall into this type if you're measuring yourself on what or how much you know, feel like you'll never know enough to be competent, and fear you'll be uncovered as a fraud because you don't know enough.

The cure for all of these? Know the phrase "eat, sleep, breathe x"? Well, do, think, and live improv and go back to the basics. Remember Zip, Zap,

Zop from Chapter 4? You stand in a circle, one person points to another and says Zip, that person looks at another and says Zap, that person looks at another and says Zop, and the game begins again. When one person makes a mistake, *everyone* makes that mistake, puts their hands on their hips and says, "AaahhhOOOgah" while doing a hip thrust. Failure becomes funny. You're practicing failure and training yourself to accept that *yes*, you fail, *and* not only is it not as bad as you think, it's always OK. This is true in all of improv as well as in taking initiative. You might not have something ready but you have enough to move forward and figure it out while you are listening and responding. While you're listening and responding, think: Did anyone question your worth? No? Then you probably are proving it. Yes, someone is asking? Like, literally asking for your receipts? What does it look like? Why are they asking you to prove your worth? Is it real, or something you are imagining? What is true and provable in this moment?

This takes time and effort. Remaining present with yourself isn't easy. Ask what is real. What do you know to be true about your abilities and worth? Are you questioning or is someone else? If this is hard, don't worry, you aren't alone. Think of all the people who suffer from imposter syndrome. According to a 2011 article from the *International Journal of Behavioral Science*, some 70 percent of people suffer from imposter syndrome.[2] Ask three people in the next day if they have ever felt like a fraud, or if their successes are simply luck. The unfortunate truth is that many of us feel this way, and often that's what makes advocating for ourselves professionally difficult at the very least. Sure, talking about your business, idea, or personal accomplishments might be easy if you stick to the facts and present them in an unbiased manner, but you are much, much more than that. Furthermore, when you are pitching a business idea or yourself, you need to have the confidence that you're the best person for whatever you're pitching. If you don't believe that, why should anyone else?

Confidence is one of those funny side effects of improv, mainly because you can't necessarily pinpoint specific activities that help with confidence. Yet at the same time, I can say without hesitation that they all help. The secret sauce once again? "Yes, and." When I'm talking about improv, there are so many times I bring everything back to "Yes, and." It's one of those lessons that I really believe is a game changer. Since you already know "Yes, and" is great for conversation (affirm and equalize) and ideation (affirm and elevate), as well as listening (recap and confirmation), you already know how it can easily be brought into all areas of your life—not limited to professional.

Confidence in professional life often comes from understanding that you can indeed handle whatever comes along. You are prepared for anything and you can roll with whatever the world and work throw at you. Those blips? Simply that—a blip that you deal with.

Building Confidence with the Power of "Yes, And"

When you have confidence in your own abilities to handle anything that happens or could happen, no matter how unexpected it might be, you start simply absorbing and reacting to all of the other stuff around you as part of life. Remember the *yes* in "Yes, and" isn't agreeing. It's affirming a reality. If you start to *yes* to the reality around you and affirm that "Yes, this is all happening and I have to deal with it," things simply become a small part of the larger picture of your life. Also, when you are attending to things happening around you, you can incorporate them into your life instead of fighting it, pretending it's not happening, or worse, resenting that this is "always happening" to you.

We have quite a few clients who are small business owners. It's interesting to see the ones who take things in stride and incorporate bumps into their every day, and those who build resentment when things aren't happening in the specific way they planned. It shows up in improv conversations, and those conversations are indicative of how they are in life. One workshop for start-up founders brought a group of people together that were all starting new businesses with grant monies. Each business idea was their own, and each of them was part of the cohort that was supposed to launch at the same time. We taught a few improv for confidence classes and got to know quite a few of the founders through our partnership with the organization. Some of them really wanted the polish for their public speaking: they believed that if they presented well enough, they would be completely fine in securing more funds for their business. Others wanted to develop presence and confidence—they felt like they were fine presenters, and knew they wanted to really do well with how they walked into a room and worked the people in the room.

Both are correct, really. To be a confident speaker—and not an arrogant speaker—you need to constantly have your finger on the pulse of your audience. Yes, the polish is incredibly important. It's also the secret sauce that some people think can't be taught.

We discussed really digging into what made someone confident when they were pitching their ideas and business, and how was it different from someone who thought their business was unshakable. No one wanted to seem cocky, but at the same time, the balance between the two is difficult for many people to understand. One of the things that came up consistently was the acceptance that it could fail—someone could make a bigger and faster version of it. The reason why it wouldn't? Because of the person behind it and the work they themselves were putting into it. They discussed that attending to reality and everything that goes with it, like competition, market, cost, and more, made their business stronger. They were planning on hitting reality head-on, taking it in, digesting it, and using it. That awareness is developed by the "Yes," and dealing with it is the "and."

The sneaky side effect of applying "Yes, and" to the world around you? You start to "Yes, and" your own ideas, thoughts, concerns, and dreams. When is the last time you were around a table discussing something you had a stake in, and you got a glimmer of an idea of what to say that was very much yours? And instead of saying it and owning it, you shut it down and let the moment pass only to have the reaction of, "I wish I would have said that!" Or worse, someone else says the exact same thing and at this point, you have nothing to add. By using "Yes, and" to your own thoughts, even if you start in your head, you will notice you've probably put limits on ideas and inspiration.

TRY THIS

Come up with an idea for a new thing. Take your object from the last activity, and your job is to "Yes, and" yourself for this new idea, becoming more and more creative with each thought. For example, if your object was a tube of ChapStick, you might say:

I'm going to come up with a new ChapStick.

Yes, and this ChapStick won't dry out your lips.

Yes, and it won't be waxy.

Yes, and it won't melt in your pocket.

Yes, and it will be available in all sorts of flavors.

Yes, and you can get your daily dose of coffee in the
ChapStick.

Remember: with "Yes, and" you aren't worrying about being right
or coming up with something that won't fail. You're working on
creativity!

This helps explore the creative possibilities using "Yes, and."
Brainstorming becomes harder and harder as we settle into
"adult." This activity gives you a tool to ideate.

"Yes, and" makes you think about what the possibilities beyond your
original idea could be—you are yes-ing the possibility. You are saying
there is a possibility and chance it could happen, and it's a path. One
of the guys in my start-up group I mentioned earlier had the idea of a
brunch food truck. So we discussed late-night food, specifically bar food,
as well as straight breakfast. Then we selected one alternative possibility: brunch and late-night food on the weekends at bar time. After that
decision, we thought about being at the same location in the morning
for brunch and pairing with the bar for a brunch drink special, as well
as in the evening for patrons who needed to grab some late-night food.
Then what if he also had a deal with the bar where if they brought a
receipt from the bar, they could get a brunch upgrade from the truck for
free—which would make the bar more than happy to promote the truck
because it was a win-win.

Nowhere in this scenario did we start to think, "Well, what if the bar
doesn't want the truck outside?" or "What if the bar already serves food,
wouldn't they think that's competition?" or "Am I even good enough to
make this crazy idea happen?" None of those issues, or really any of the
issues that come up with a lack of confidence in your own abilities or the
ugly imposter syndrome voice, have any place in "Yes, and." That's not to
say you won't deal with problems or that nasty self-doubt if you start to
"Yes, and" things—you'll still have issues, no matter what! If you use those
issues when you're using "Yes, and" to some creativity within yourself, you

stop the idea much like you stop a conversation with the word *but*. You don't need it right now, so don't use it or bring it out.

Often, I have to tell small business owners to rein it in. When we say this, it is *not* to limit the "Yes, and"—it's to focus it, like a beam of light. If you have some highly dispersed light, sure you'll light everything just a little bit. If you have a focused beam, you shine all the light on a specific point. Same for business: if you have 10 ideas and are trying to "Yes, and" all of them, you'll have 10 wildly creative paths you could follow. Take one idea and "Yes, and" that idea first—then finesse it, go back, recalibrate it, and "Yes, and" it again. If that idea doesn't work, then your job is to "Yes, and" another one of your points. By focusing your light on one thing when you're opening up a possibility, you build a sustainable structure for your business. And there's less possibility for you to get overwhelmed—if you're not overwhelmed by options, you can monitor the imposter syndrome and handle it with that focus.

On the same token, if you start to "Yes, and" yourself often, both in professional ideas and in settings where you are offering ideas, you make speaking up a regular thing. The more you speak up, the more you're either going to get told "Brilliant!" or get ignored because someone won't like your idea—or almost always the more likely response, something in between the two. The more you experience all of those things, the easier speaking up will be. You're lowering your bar for speaking up. It quickly becomes a very normal thing; so you do it, embracing each outcome as the norm. If the outcome is good, you digest it instead of basking in it, and simply deal with it. If it's negative, you digest it instead of basking in it, and simply deal with it. It no longer becomes a big deal. It's simply part of a normal day. Now when your imposter syndrome acts up, you can shut it down with a simple, "Well, sometimes people don't like ideas, but yesterday they did, so maybe tomorrow, someone else will again." There's more empirical data to draw from to shut that negative voice down.

Yet another win with "Yes, and" comes with being in the moment. You absolutely cannot be thinking 10 steps ahead when you are actively using "Yes, and." If you are constantly overthinking everything you say, you cannot "Yes, and." "Yes, and" keeps you connected to your thoughts— and you own each and every one of them. Sounds a lot like assertive communication as well, doesn't it? You're taking little steps to become assertive, and you're following and owning your own thoughts along the way. On top of that, you have to pay attention, so you've checked in to your own moment and the people around you, to correctly "Yes, and." If you're in the moment, you also can't catastrophize situations, a common side effect of imposter syndrome. You're too busy attending to the present to dive into the "What if?".

TRY THIS

If you need some help on speaking confidently, there's an activity for that. The History of the World is one of my favorite activities to get people working on confidence and start to work against imposter syndrome. This is also one you can play with yourself or with a friend (or two). If you're doing this by yourself, take a moment to write down a few things or events; they can be anything from a horse, cat, or bug to a holiday, a taco, or a church. Pick one at random.

Now rehash the history of it. No, really, start talking about the history of that horse or how the bug got his wings. It doesn't need to be factual history. Your job is simply to talk about the one- to two-minute history of that horse (or bug wings, or taco, or whatever you chose). The key here? Sustained credibility. You need to project confidence and knowledge about a topic you know nothing about. When you start, you'll probably feel a little weird and awkward. After a bit, you might pick up some steam, and when you get to the point of bringing it home, you'll get a little awkward again. Try it and reflect on how you felt when you were on a roll with your story. Did you get to a point where you were very excited and really believed the crazy story you were concocting? That's the excitement you should channel—because that excitement looks a lot like passion, and passion lends itself to confidence.

This helps you build confidence. When you're practicing with something benign, there's no risk! This activity uses play-based learning to explore confidence.

ASKING FOR A RAISE, PROMOTION, AND NEGOTIATING

Before starting this section, I'd like to take a moment to tell you that you absolutely deserve a raise or promotion. Maybe this moment isn't the best moment or the "right" moment, but you deserve one because you've worked really hard, you've gone above and beyond, and you deserve to be paid your worth.

If you thought about applying improv's core structure of *who*, *where*, *what*, and *how* here, you're absolutely correct on the place to start. We'll dive a little deeper into each of those when it comes to asking for a raise or promotion, and then take a bit of a turn when discussing negotiation.

The *who* is you, and the you that is the best version of yourself at work. When you're thinking about asking for a raise, take a moment to review recent accomplishments or guideposts. For example, I've been working with a social media manager who was looking for a raise and didn't know where to start. She came in telling me that everyone who had coached her prior said she needed to ask for a raise after a big accomplishment. But as many of you might know about social media, there isn't an outpouring of viral content in the everyday life of one person. So if you aren't causing a terrible social media issue, you're probably doing it right, but there won't be a big shining moment that can be referred to as an accomplishment. So she didn't know what she could pinpoint as her reason for a raise and was looking for something that didn't exist. Because of this, she had probably gone a little too far between raises, and thus that vicious cycle of feeling like you're not being valued, to looking for value, to not finding it and knowing you're working hard.

This *who* is not just the who you are right now—it's who you've become at work. What changes have happened? In the case of the social media manager, we looked at the additional followers, average engagement, and analytics for all of the accounts when she first started to present. The increase? That's an accomplishment. Seems easy for something that already measures analytics. Understanding the changes you directly influenced at your job is an excellent place to start when you don't have multiple points of accomplishments. Essentially what you're doing is making a résumé of your work for your work. This is something you should prepare for. Have it ready, even if you don't have an annual review. It's crucial to have this information at the ready *before* you ask, before you make an appointment to talk, before you even think of making that appointment. Take a step back and understand that *who*.

When you're making this résumé of milestones for your work, keep it as quantitative as possible. Stick with measurable outcomes versus feelings or qualitative issues. If you can measure it, whether it's in people, money, or time, it should go on the list. Right now, *do not worry* about making it too long. Start it with the ones that immediately come to mind, and then keep going. You're looking to get it out there, not to debate it in your head. This brain dump of information is important: you don't want to edit yourself. If you get stuck, there's a pretty great stream-of-consciousness activity that we do for creativity.

TRY THIS

Think of a word, any word at all. If you're stuck, then think of your favorite holiday. Now, what's the first thing you think of when you think of that holiday? What's the first thing you think of when you think of that thing from that holiday? For example:

Holiday: Halloween

First thing: Candy

First thing: Dentist

First thing: Pain

First thing: Hurt

First thing: Cut

First thing: Blood

And so on and so forth. Let yourself give in to that stream of consciousness: don't worry about making "sense," because you're not showing anyone this activity and you don't have to defend your thought process. Try it with a holiday, or food, or a hobby: something very benign to start with so you can get used to giving yourself that break. You're trying to free up those creative and mental blocks that happen when you start overthinking things. That overthinking? That ends up getting you trapped in a circle, especially when it comes to talking about accomplishments.

This helps you work on creative jumps. Too much creativity is just as bad as not enough, and saying, "be more creative" isn't helpful. This activity builds creativity.

After you feel comfortable with the process, look at your accomplishments again, and try it with an accomplishment. This is going to be infinitely harder. Start with one accomplishment and move from there. I'm going to use another client example, a woman in human resources (HR) who was looking for a raise:

> Accomplishment: Less turnover
>
> First thing: Happy
>
> First thing: Relaxed
>
> First thing: Easy
>
> First thing: Calm
>
> First thing: Yoga
>
> First thing: Stretching

In this example, you've got a few pathways to take. One, think about employee satisfaction: were there any surveys or internal reviews that talk about the happiness of employees? Another: how are the management teams? If you think about work in HR, you might be working with professional development or leadership training, which might be making work easier. On the same note: Do you have any health initiatives? Have you added any or enhanced something that was already there? This exercise helps you examine the work you've done, as well as the work you might want to do with this raise or promotion.

This activity leads to the *you* that you could be with this raise. What are your plans for your position? What do you want to accomplish? You can use this stream of consciousness or "Yes, and" to brainstorm the possibility. Sure, you don't necessarily want to admit you'll work harder, stronger, or faster with a raise or promotion. Real talk though: we work harder when we are appreciated. Money, specifically a raise, is a way employers often show appreciation.

When you have the *you* part of *who* worked out, think about that person you're asking. How do they work? Do they need a dossier of why you should get this raise or promotion? Are they the decision maker? What style of communicator are they? Have you asked for a raise in the past, or has there been any conversation about a raise? What is your relationship with this person like?

One client was an associate dean for a college in New York City. She was overworked, underpaid, and exhausted. So much to the point that if she didn't get a raise, she was looking for another job. This had gone so very far that before even thinking about asking for a raise, she had started looking for another job and came to us more for interview skills than anything else. After a few conversations, she admitted she used to love her job and wanted to stay, but she didn't think her health, both mental and physical, could handle it. We started to help her asking, and it came out that she never once told her supervisor she was feeling this way, and never once (in *five years*) asked for a raise. They had minor pay increases but no annual review or official increase based on merit.

Since I didn't know what we were dealing with, we halted some prep, and her new homework was to go into his office and set up an appointment to talk about the possibility of a raise. Since it never came up, we didn't know if he was even open to an increase that was outside of the yearly (minor) increase. She made the appointment, and he accepted it. Her ask was simple: she was looking to have a conversation with the person who would be responsible for a possible raise or promotion in the department.

He gave her a raise that day. Now this is a magical situation: also a terrible one. He said, and I quote (from her): "You never asked for more money, so I thought you were fine." This is one of the most frustrating things I can think of but also incredibly telling. They never once had a conversation about *who* would be the person in charge of granting a pay raise. Our client didn't actually know who she needed to ask, and a lot of the appointment was based on the idea of figuring out who she needed to talk to and what the process was for asking for a raise. Her situation was really one of the best- or worst-case scenarios. Because she didn't ask, she didn't know he was in charge of raises. Because she chose that moment to ask, he either realized they had never talked about it, or it simply took that ask to make the raise happen. This is why both *whos* are important in this situation. You and the person responsible for that raise. Do a bit of digging and figure out what you need to make your case.

Once you understand both your accomplishments as well as the person you'll be talking to, it's time to think about *where*. The *where* this time around encompasses a when. There may never be a perfect time to ask for a raise. Some times are better than others. For example, if you did just accomplish something major, you can "Yes, and" to ask for a raise or promotion. If you have a review policy at your work, figure out how that fits your plan. Did it just happen? Is it coming up? When you think about timeliness, you don't want to go too far from said accomplishment; otherwise, that momentum is hard to replicate.

If you don't know, ask around. Talk to people who have been there longer or people who have gotten raises or promotions. The *where* is also on your terms. Don't surprise someone with a raise conversation if they think they are just having a status meeting, because you're going to end up with a potentially annoyed raise-giver. On the same note, do your planning before you ask.

We were working with a museum professional who had been at his job for about three years with no raise aside from the yearly inflation increase, and we decided to do a lot of the planning before any whispers of an ask happened. He figured out who he was now compared to who he was before he started the position, and from there, what he had accomplished. Once he had that information together, he decided to ask for a meeting with the person who was responsible for any raise requests: the executive director. That executive director took the request, scheduled a meeting, and then a week before the actual meeting, requested they meet in the building—not in his office, but in the auditorium down the hall from all of the offices.

Shake your head, it's fine. I did too. This was an interesting situation. On one hand, I have to give the director credit. He was trying to throw the museum professional off his game, potentially getting him in a place where it could be refuted, or in a place where the museum professional didn't do enough research or prep for the raise. This is a strategy by people who are interested in power plays, as well as status plays. Set a meeting to discuss something, then throw them for a loop by asking them to meet early and in a place that was less formal. Lucky for the professional but not lucky for the director, we prepped prior to the ask, with notes and everything, so the change was not something that tossed him off guard. On the contrary, it threw the director off that the professional came in with so much information and ready to ask for the raise.

This is why I recommend preparing in advance, even if you are interested in setting up a meeting. On top of the advance meeting, the director in this particular example decided to select a location that was a little more casual and less private than an office, which hosts an entirely new set of things that might throw a person off their plan. By preparing in advance, all of the changes and alterations are simply noise, because your focus remains the same.

When it comes to the *where*, be ready to have this conversation anywhere and at any time. Sure, it's highly unlikely you're going to ask for a meeting and then on the spot, someone says, "Oh, I have time now!" but it *could happen*. So hold off on your asking until you have an understanding of *who* you are.

Patience is also important here. Please don't wait years to ask for a raise, but don't ask for it a few months into the job. A good rule of thumb is a year, if you haven't gotten an increase—and I'm talking about an increase that only you get, not an increase that everyone gets because life is expensive—then it's time to start thinking about it. If you took a job at too low of a salary and realize it a week into the job, then you might be stuck a bit until the timing is right to ask again. You also can't get a raise every time you hit a new goal. As amazing as that would be, patience pays off in this situation.

In the same area as *where*, please do the asking in person. You can definitely set the appointment in an email, but when it comes to the actual *asking for a raise*, be sure to sit in front of that person. If you work remotely, ask for a video chat. At the very least, be on the phone with that person. Too much gets lost in written communication, and you want to be sure to keep that connection in person as much as possible.

Another thing to consider in the *where* is what else is happening in the company culture. Did something stressful just happen? Has there been a lot of turnover, or did a key position just leave? Read the room, and see if it's an appropriate time to ask. Your chances are not going to be the best if you ask when everyone and everything are stressed. Look into what the other person's schedule looks like as well. If they have *their* yearly review coming up, you definitely don't want to dive into that moment, because how they currently feel is going to affect you and your chances. Stack the deck whenever possible.

Into the *what* you want: you might have to use some persuasive tactics to get what you want. Sure, you want a raise! Have you thought about how to get that raise? Your first step with this should have already happened—that list of quantitative things you've accomplished. That's a big part of persuasion—you have facts. The more specifics you can provide, the better. Often, you're going to be talking to a person who doesn't have the final say in your raise or promotion. This is why you have to show and not just tell. If you aren't making a clear case for yourself, you can't expect someone to make a case for you. You need to relay that information in the best way possible so they can take it up with the actual decision-maker if they aren't. That list? Make it look clear and clean, and print an extra one out or email it after the meeting. By giving them those resources before or after the conversation, you're giving them the prep for what they have to do next.

The Don'ts in Asking for a Raise

Something to avoid in conversations about raises: don't make it personal. By keeping it business focused, as well as merit focused, you up your chances. Yes, more money would make many lives easier, but you deserve a raise for your hard work and the things you've accomplished, not because your rent is going up. Keep your *who* as that best version of you at work—not the real-life person who pays bills. Also, when you're digging into conversations about money, keep the reason for your want focused on yourself. There is no reason to bring up colleagues' salaries, because this is between you and your raise and should have nothing to do with the other people in the office. Remember the idea of talking to the person in front of you and not about people who aren't in the room or conversation? You want to focus on your own experience and keep communication assertive. You're owning your ask as well as your accomplishments. Bringing in other people and what they make doesn't help.

When you're thinking about your influencers, you want to be very careful. If you aren't ready to lose your job, stay very far away from ultimatums or threats. *Even if* you are planning to leave if you don't get a raise, it's often not a good idea to use that to get what you want, because in the case that your bluff is called, you might end up looking for a job faster than you're ready to. Emotional influencers aren't a good idea either. Guilt trips and the like aren't professional and are not suited for a professional environment. Keeping it fact-based is best. If you've done the work in outlining your accomplishments and the changes you've contributed or caused, then you'll be able to make your case without needing to pull out threats or emotions. If you are prepared to lose your job, then go right ahead and do it.

The next two examples are of people who did it, and one worked, and the other didn't. Both were improv students of ours; both were looking to negotiate a raise. The first was an arts-based professional in New York City. He was frustrated being the lowest-paid employee who seemed to do the most work. While everyone feels like this at some point or another, he seemed to make a pretty decent case for it. Since it was an arts-based organization (read: nonprofit,) he was getting a yearly increase, but no *actual* raises, even though he had a new title that was essentially a promotion and more work.

We started with all of the homework, picked the right time, looked at the organization as a whole, and then he met with the executive director—and nothing. The director agreed he was a great employee and highly valued, but each time after they met, he would give another excuse as to why he couldn't make the raise happen yet. This went on for over a year—which in my opinion, is way too long for someone to wait on something like this. Some kind of answer was necessary, even if it was an answer that led to a "no." At this point, he had tried several influencers and was clearly expressing his wants. More than anything, he wanted to know if a raise was even a possibility because otherwise, he was planning on leaving the position and starting the very long process to find another comparable position. He started to apply for other jobs and got a few calls and interviews, and then asked me if he should pull that card in the next meeting.

We discussed it, and he understood that by doing that, he was playing a very dangerous game. If the director valued him, he would work harder to figure out this raise situation. We were both under the impression that the director was more passive than he needed to be because he didn't seem to think my client would leave. If the director didn't value him, the response could be anything from inaction all the way to letting him go. The problem in this situation was that the odds of either situation happening were equal. The client was valued: he brought a lot to the table and he had done a lot of good at the institution. At the same time, these negotiations had been going on for a year, which is incredibly frustrating, to say the least. He decided to go for it.

The other client worked for a sales organization. She had been there for four years, with no real raise aside from her commission. She had a meeting with HR and got a very small raise, only to find out that a new employee was making more than she was and another person with similar experience was making more as well and had recently gotten a larger raise than she did. It had been about a year since that raise, so she was ready to ask for a larger one, and if not, find another job. She was pretty set on that decision to get more money or go somewhere else and felt as though she could find a job if necessary. Since she had been looking, she knew the market was fine for her kind of position, and she wasn't hurting financially to take a few lean months if something were to happen. We prepared in the same way. She asked if she should give the semi-ultimatum that she would be leaving and looking for another position if she didn't get an appropriate raise. She wasn't planning on mentioning her knowledge of colleagues' pay (bad idea, remember) but was planning on leveraging her experience and the general pay in the market for her position.

We discussed it, and it was going to be less of a threat ("I'm going to leave if I don't get this raise!") and more of an ultimatum ("I'm sorry to hear that, I will have to start looking for another job") and she was going to pull it out *only* if she needed to. Again, she was valued, got affirmation from her boss and coworkers, had performance reviews, and knew this information about her counterparts. She knew they were similar in experience if not less experienced than her and making a considerable amount more than she was. One even got that raise the same time she did. She decided to go for it.

What do you think happened? Before I get to that, as the coach, I can safely say both had the same chance of getting a raise as they did getting let go. That's the improv part. You can put anything you want into the world in an interview, negotiation, conversation, and you have no idea what someone is going to do back to you. Things might go in the expected direction, and they might not. All of that is up to chance. You can only change how you respond to the situation. You can't change how someone communicates.

Because you're surely waiting with bated breath to hear what happened, I'll tell you. The art professional got his raise and the woman in sales was told to find another job. The art professional asked for the raise and was told, "I'm working on it," for the seventh time. He told the director he was at the end of his waiting time, because it had been too long and he was going to start looking for other positions. He said that he would keep the director informed if any interviews came up and would put in a notice if necessary. Simple, transparent, and direct. The director quietly took the information, told my client that he would "do what he could," which is what he said every single time, and the meeting ended. The client did exactly what he said he would do, but two weeks after the last meeting, the director called him into his office, letting him know that he got a smaller raise than what he was asking for, but it was enough for the arts professional to stay in the position. He's still there.

The woman in sales had another experience. She went in, asked for the raise, and made her case. Her supervisor took in the information and told her that he would see what he could do. She followed up in two weeks (a nice amount of follow-up time) to see where things were at, and he said he didn't think it was possible this year but he would try. She told her supervisor she was disappointed and was planning to start looking for other options. This was buttoned with, "I really don't want to and appreciate working here, but I believe that my work is worth more." He took that information quietly and spoke with her the next day, telling her he didn't think she was in a position for a raise anytime soon and she should look for other options. Not a firing, per se—just a definitive no. She found another job that paid her what she was looking for and life went on.

Why did each of these situations turn out so very differently? Who knows! Both were set up in the same way—two people who each deserved a raise. They were overdue, and while I only know what the clients tell me, I didn't get any ideas that either of them were making up any of the experiences we discussed, which ultimately meant that they were in a fine place asking for the raise. By using a threat or ultimatum, they made a choice to force a hand, which in both situations resulted in an answer. The key here is knowing the potential outcomes and being comfortable if you get a "negative" one. Both people were ready to leave their job, regardless of the answer.

This wouldn't be a good choice if you really needed your position and weren't ready to lose it. Most people need their jobs (otherwise, why would we be working?), but some people are ready to take on another no matter what it is, have some savings, or have a plan B in case of emergencies. I personally would never advise someone to do this unless they were ready to be unemployed—even though sometimes it works out.

Improv-ing Your Negotiation Skills

Very few people like to negotiate. Like public speaking, it's why people fear it: they try to avoid it, and then they never get better at it. It becomes this big scary thing that is often necessary for success in business—whether you own a business or work for one. The issue with negotiation for many people? They think it's a competition of "winning" versus communication. Before diving into improv-based negotiation (because so much of getting what you want in improv *is* negotiation), let's think about negotiation and what it actually is.

Negotiation is simply a discussion that seeks to reach a common goal. It's a way to come together when there are differences and reach a compromise, all while avoiding an argument or dispute. When people disagree, so often they look for the outcome that is best for *them*, versus thinking of the greater good of both parties. Negotiation can't be scripted, and using improv to help negotiation skills isn't a new concept. Negotiation is very much listening and responding to finesse a solution that works for everyone. But you can only control your own responses, not the responses of anyone else. This is the very definition of improv.

Improv isn't as simple as go with the flow. The best negotiators have plans A, B, C, and D in their heads. This means that following an improv mind-set lends itself to being a great negotiator. Specifically, one of the things that improv lends itself so well to in negotiation is taking the first step. Taking initiative is a nerve-racking experience for a lot of people. In classes and workshops, watching people take the first step in those three-line conversations previously mentioned in Chapter 2, an activity where success is possible 100 percent of the time, makes it incredibly clear that people don't like to go first. During that activity, I usually have the group split in half. Half of the group is on one side of the room, and the other half of the group is on the other side. They often face one another, and I *never* pick a side to go first. I simply let them know they have to decide who is going first by someone simply starting, and if they say, "you go first," that counts as a line.

It doesn't matter how clear or how vague I am with my description, people will always get nervous and try to "indicate" who is going first. And no matter what, a lot of people will want another person to go first. When I ask why, the answers range from, "I don't want to make the wrong choice," to "I'm not a leader," to "I can't think of anything."

In negotiation, making the first move shows confidence. Since this isn't a competition, you're helping the negotiation along to come from *some* place and give the person you're talking to a place to jump off from. This is also why doing your homework in advance of the moment is incredibly important. You want to know what you're looking to accomplish, what the other person wants as well, and what the "middle" looks like. It's a win-win situation you're working for. If you don't understand what you want, or you don't understand what the other person wants, you won't understand what the win-win actually looks like.

Make the first offer, and make it the best case, win-win, in the middle situation. If you don't know what the other person wants, transparency is confidence. Simply ask the person you're negotiating with what they want, and figure out the middle. This is assertive, not aggressive. Understanding what *you* want and what *they* want is assertive. You're owning what you want and understanding you're going to have to work together to get as close as possible to what you both want. Aggressive would be demanding what you want without considering what the other person wants.

After you've made the first offer, *be quiet*. Remember those active listening skills? Put those in action and listen more than you speak. By listening, you can pivot and work through your original offer to get as close to win-win for both of you. If you have a question, ask it. Another element of keeping quiet and not filling space with chatter? You might find out more about what that other person wants by waiting. People chatter nervously. Silence is *scary* for many of us. We tend to fill the silence with information, so if you take a moment to stay silent, or ask a question and simply wait in silence versus following up with another question or an answer, you're not only exhibiting calm, you're letting the other person potentially fill that silence.

There was a period of time during workshops for sales teams when we would practice a silence activity. We'd partner up, and then I would instruct everyone to look into their partner's eyes, take a deep breath, not to stare, and silently stand there while making eye contact for 60 to 90 seconds.

The room was so uncomfortable. Many people wanted to fill it with nervous laughter. I told them they didn't need to maintain eye contact the whole time and should really take some time blinking and looking away. No matter what, a decent number of people always would start cracking up because silence is terrifying for some of us. Try to sit in a room with someone you're talking to and just be silent in the middle of the conversation for one minute. You can look at each other, you can look away, you can't do something else like read a book or hop on your phone or email. Just maintain silence for a prolonged period of time and see how you both feel.

What happened? Did you get nervous and want to fill the silence with chatter about everything or nothing? Was it simple? Try it the next time you ask someone a question, and they don't immediately answer you. Take a few breaths and then rephrase or ask another question.

For the hundredth time in this book: you get the energy you put out. If you walk into a situation thinking the worst is going to happen, you might get that worst possible outcome. If you expect the best, with an understanding of the worst and negotiate to keep away from it, you'll end up with a better outcome. Essentially, you want to "Yes, and" versus "Yes, but." Keep the conversation as something that is continuously going versus something that is shot down because of someone not being able to work together.

"Yes" affirms the other person and how you are listening to them. Phrases like "Yes, I see what you mean," and "Yes, I understand," are excellent ways to show active listening skills in negotiation because you can then add your own thoughts and information with the "and." Statements like "Yes, I understand that you're looking to pay less for this, and I want to give you the best value for your money, how about $500?" are more effective than, "Yes, I know you want to pay less for this, but it's worth more." Again, saying "Yes" in "Yes, and" is never accepting blindly. It's acknowledging the other person. You're saying "Yes, I heard you," not "Yes, you're right!"

Another important tool to add to your negotiating toolbox is open-ended questions. Open-ended questions not only let the person you're talking to think about their answer, it also gives you time to listen to their response and pivot while they are talking. An open-ended question is a question that has many possible answers versus a closed-ended question, which again is something like a yes or no question—only one or two answers. While questions aren't always the best thing to use in improv, because they put the responsibility on the other person, and remove it from yourself, in negotiation an open-ended question gives the other person the illusion of control, because is it their control when you give it to them? Think about it like this: you know the other person likes to be the driver in conversations. You know what you want and what they want, and where the middle ground lies. So you ask an open-ended question to get more information from the other person and essentially give the decision to them to make. You've given them the control in the situation, but at the same time, you hold it, because it was yours to give. This is incredibly meta, so let's consider it in a real example.

A client was working on a new position at a start-up. The company had been in business long enough that no one was actively worried about an implosion, so she decided to ask for a raise and a new position. She had been there since the beginning and wanted to stay and grow with the company. She came to her boss with a specific number (important), and a specific position (also important), and she was told the number was a bit too high and the position wouldn't work for the structure of the company. A soft no, but a no still. So instead of taking it as a no, she thought about what to come back with. She dropped her number down a bit, added some responsibilities to her current position and came back to her boss, which is actually a great tactic because they didn't outwardly tell her no! Essentially the response had been, "This was not quite right." When she presented the new offer, her boss told her she was an incredible asset to the company, and they didn't want her to leave, but this was a little too high and a few too many responsibilities. The frustrating part was that her boss wasn't coming back with a counteroffer. He just simply negated her offer. A firm "no" would have been better than the "not quite." We talked about it and decided that the best thing to do in this situation was to come back with an open-ended question that put a lot of the focus and power in her boss's hands. We constructed a solid question that stated what she wanted and gave her boss the control to make the decision without deflecting.

She came to him with this email: "I'm looking for a raise of [her original offer] and [this position]. I understand that my two previous asks were too much, and I do very much want to continue working with [company]. Since my asks were too much, I'm curious to hear what you are willing to do when it comes to a raise and promotion, because I feel like I've earned both. Can we follow up next week and discuss your offer further?"

This might seem like a terrifying thing to send to someone, and it's because it's incredibly assertive, powerful, and direct. Things she did well: she stated what she wanted, summarized the situation up to this point, placed no blame or emotion on the other person, and gave them all of the decision-making power. She told them she would like to discuss their offer while they had never made one. She was essentially telling them to do it without ordering or threatening them to do it. She gave a very finite timeline for follow-up and asked the open-ended question (What do you think I deserve when it comes to a raise and promotion?) even though she didn't phrase it as such. She also used "Yes, and" in the situation. She affirmed the reality that the ask wasn't acceptable on their end.

All in all, an effective message. Who held the status in this? You might think it's the boss. He does have the ultimate say in this. But it could also be my client because she chose to give it to him, instead of coming back multiple more times with offers that might not go anywhere. The result: she got a decent raise, one that kept her in that job and additional responsibilities that echoed her first ask, the initial one she was told was "too much."

Again, this is a best-case scenario: she threw the ball; they caught it and threw it back. Some clients have done exactly this, and it didn't work out for them in whatever way. We learn from both though, and a lot of the "success" in this was simply chance. Her boss could have said, "I told you no twice before," and that would have been the end of it. Because she thought about the situation, and read the room and her chances, she decided to go for it.

When you're digging into the *who*, *where*, *what*, and *how*, be sure to eliminate as many emotional statements as possible. Often emotional statements are bullying tactics or a sign of insecurity. Stick to the facts, not the emotions behind them. The emotions only make the situation more difficult. Think of the previous example. She didn't show a moment of her frustration, and I *knew* she was frustrated. Who wouldn't be? She didn't let anyone at work see that. I've watched other clients let that frustration get in the way when they're negotiating for a raise or promotion. Letting those emotions into the conversation does nothing positive for anyone.

SPEAKING UP WHEN SOMETHING IS WRONG

When all else fails in good communication, you end up with a conflict. Workplace conflict is difficult, to say the least. It's idealistic to think you will never have conflict in the workplace. If you are communicating, it's a full-contact sport. You might try to avoid conflict, which is a terrible idea because you can't escape it once you're in it.

There are two major causes of conflict: communication and emotion. Think of the last conflict you had in the workplace. Was it because of poor communication? Low information? No information? Even if you got good information, and you had no idea how to handle it, you might end up with conflict. Emotion drives decision unless you consciously handle those emotions and remove them from the decision. When someone indulges in their emotions in the workplace, you usually end up with conflict. Out of all the points that guide the conversation, *how* you feel is often the most volatile one, mainly because emotions are so difficult for so many people and are often inappropriate for work situations.

But what happens when the communication fails or the emotions kick in, and you have to deal with the conflict? You need to develop conflict-resolution strategies, even if you are conflict avoidant. You can try to avoid it as much as you like, but you will have to deal with it at some point, so like all things in communication, preparation is key.

You'd be surprised (maybe not) how often improv conversations move to arguments and conflict. One of the biggest challenges for students is staying away from the argument in an improv moment. Whether it's because we try not to argue in public in real life, or because it's "easy" to have an argument (both things I really don't like to consider either as truth), it's a stretch to get people to not immediately go into a fight. Consider it though. You are finally firmly defining your *who, where, what*, and *how*, and if you don't discuss it beforehand with your partner, which you shouldn't, it's probably going to be two different things. Conflict is bound to happen when two or more people are fighting for two (or more) different things.

Real life has the same issues. Often we're looking for different experiences and things out of our professional life. On top of that, the competition that kicks in with career and work situations isn't helpful to a conflict-free environment. One way to handle conflict in the workplace has to come from a larger place than just you—acceptable behavior needs to be defined. If a group doesn't understand effective team communication or collaboration, there will constantly be conflict. Consider this strategy as more of a vitamin than a painkiller. You're preventing conflict as much as possible with an understanding of good communication and how to work together for a common goal. The other thing that happens when you define acceptable behavior: you actually give a structure for how to handle conflict when it happens.

When that conflict happens, you need to understand that other person, and "Yes, and" and negotiation come into full play. As learned earlier, that "Yes" in "Yes, and" isn't giving in and accepting what the other person wants—it's affirming their words, thoughts, and beliefs. Even if someone is getting incredibly emotional in conflict and upset you haven't done something or finished in time, and they haven't said they are upset, yet you see it, you can easily say, "I see that you're upset *and* I want to make this situation work." You're affirming how they feel—upset—and by that, you're letting them be heard. With the *and*, you can add your thoughts or questions to that affirmation and move the discussion forward.

What happens when something is seriously wrong at work? What about an ethical issue, like someone stealing money, or constantly leaving early but leaving their coat to pretend they are still in, or doing work for Company B while on Company A's time? Figuring out if it's worth it to speak up, how to do it, and to whom and protecting yourself from consequences is complicated. Generally speaking, most of us aren't in a life-or-death, jail-or-no jail situation if we speak up or not, but as we've both seen in the media and in high school, speaking up about even a small issue can have massive repercussions.

Mary Gentile, the author of *Giving Voice to Values*, believes that practice is the key to understanding how to both recognize and deal with these ethical issues that come up at work.[3] When dealing with ethics, according to Gentile, we tap into our emotions, tying it to moral identity. Think about everything up to this point: when you're dealing in the emotion space, we let those emotions drive—and considering we all share them in very different ways, we think that our emotions aren't as valuable as fact-based information. Even *if* the ethical violation is based in fact and not feeling, that decision about "right" or "wrong" is often several shades of gray.

Gentile offers excellent advice when it comes to practice. If we never deal with these situations—really deal with them, digest, and not just sit and wait for it to resolve itself—we make them terrifying. This is *just* like public speaking—you do it once or twice, it doesn't go perfectly the way you planned, and you deem yourself, "not a great public speaker." This is one of those places where improv-based thinking has to come into play, by tapping into "Yes, and" and imagining those best-case *and* worst-case scenarios as well as exploring the possibilities.

Another great tip from Gentile includes assessing the risk, and in the same moment, asking what you want from this. Her question of, "What is the value that's being violated here?" connects with what you want: what do you want out of this situation and why do you want it? Does it affect you if your coworker is doing another project for another company at work? If they are getting their work done, why does it matter? You're digging into *what* you want to accomplish, and why you want to accomplish it. If you're upset that they are doing two things at once, then maybe refocus that energy on to your work. If you're getting all of their work because they don't have time to finish it, that's a very different story.

Shifting your perspective is something that improv lends a hand to and is a strategy for this kind of speaking up at work. This can be accomplished by thinking about what the other person wants out of a situation, remember emotional intelligence? If you're looking at things from their risk and point of view, you might see why they are acting the way they are.

Most people aren't sociopaths or completely malicious in their actions, and often have a reason to do what they are doing, especially if there are emotions involved. Taking a moment to think about what the other person wants and why they want it will give you a better understanding of the situation. Look at their actions from a place of, "What's their motivation of getting what they want?" instead of "Why do they want to do this terribly wrong thing?"

After you've spent some time weighing out those wants—both for you and them—it's time to look at if it's worth it to you or not. If you spoke up, what would happen? If you didn't, would you care? Research by Thomas Gilovich and Victoria Husted Medvec shows that more people regret things they didn't do over things that they did—even when those things have poor outcomes.[4] The phrase, "Failure is never as bad as regret," comes to mind when thinking about that *if* jump. A newer study by Gilovich and Shai Davidai show that people regret actions that let them become their ideal self—a staggering 76 percent regret an action not taken that would have led to this "ideal self" as their biggest life regret.[5]

The phrase "ideal self" is an interesting one, given the context of the kind of professional development in this book. Have you sat back to look at what that ideal self is? If you don't have an idea, how can you get there? And placing this in perspective of this chapter, when you're looking to speak up, will you get closer or farther away from your ideal self if you do or don't decide to speak up? And on top of that, does achieving "ideal" matter to you?

TRY THIS

What *is* your ideal self? What are you working toward? Write down a few characteristics and guide points so you have something to work toward, and weigh when you're thinking about speaking up.

This helps you understand yourself. If you don't know what you're working toward, you can't improve what you want to improve. This activity gives you time to step back and examine what you're working on.

At the same time, much like ultimatums in negotiation, it's important to think about what you have to lose if things go badly. This is all a balancing act: if you don't want something selfish, if what the other person is doing is because of a self-serving act, if it's harming the company and your position as well and there is a small chance you'll face repercussions, then you'll want to say something. At the same time, if it's something that's affecting you, but there is a high probability you might lose your job or have another seriously negative consequence over speaking up, you'll have to compromise something. Role-play these as Sit-Prob-Sol—specifically looking into various "solutions" and what could happen in the situation, and balancing that against the need to speak up. Spend time with a friend, partner, improv class—run through some of the points you'd like to bring up. Often, you don't want to go immediately to HR or a boss; it's better to go right to the person and give them the chance to explain it themselves before it escalates into something larger.

While you're rehearsing your points, consider how you're saying what you're saying, taking care to keep it in a place of calm instead of a place of attack. Also, remember the power of questions. By asking those open-ended questions, you again are giving the control to them to justify their actions. They might not realize they are doing something wrong, and there might be things you don't necessarily see. Planning to use open-ended questions gives the person you're talking to the ability to explain and is a fairly safe way to see if they are open to having a conversation. If they respond to the questions in a negative way, they are probably not interested in having that conversation. If it's a positive, "Thanks for helping me," that's your ultimate best outcome.

If the response is negative, consider escalating it by to talking to your boss or their boss. Again, look at the consequences, the new information from the conversation, rehearse some open-ended questions, and see this more as looking for information than an accusation. If *that* doesn't work, consider your options. If it needs to be escalated further, think about that next step. If it's not worth it, take a moment and recalibrate.

I was coaching a guy in tech for almost a year, and he was working for a toxic boss. This person wasn't the person in charge of everyone. She had been there for about five years, and he was her direct report. She was in the process of getting her PhD and was writing her dissertation on company time. Like all on the company time. This client, since he was her direct report, got saddled with a lot of her responsibilities. She was using office time to write the dissertation and neglecting her other work, and when she did want things done, it was at times that were convenient for her with her schedule. When he couldn't make a meeting because it was held outside of his normal work hours, or couldn't make a strategy session she wanted to have on a *Saturday afternoon*, she would get upset with him and say he needed to care more about his job.

He started the conversation with her, asking her to think about his schedule and that he would be more than willing to meet during the day or to discuss things while he, and the rest of the staff, were in—Monday through Friday from 9 a.m. to 6 p.m. She got very upset about this, saying he wasn't in charge and it wasn't his job to determine when they met, it was hers. This particular conversation resulted in her saying he didn't value his job, and they clearly had different priorities.

The next step was going to her boss because after that initial meeting, retaliation was a very real thing. Every time he would speak up in a meeting she would snap back, and the passive-aggressive comments would fly. She also sent an email to her boss (who was also my client's boss) bringing in my client's wife, and saying she heard his wife making disparaging comments about the company. Retaliation happens, especially when people are upset or threatened.

The main boss was fairly ineffective in this: he basically told my client's boss to settle nonwork issues outside of work and everyone needed to act like adults. Funny story, adults often don't act like adults. All of this escalated up to the point where she would accuse my client of trying to take her job (he wasn't), and her passive-aggressive comments came to a head when she started to yell, then cry, then say, "Well, it's a good thing no one is here to see this," and then carry on with her work. And the cycle would continue. Since her boss was ineffective, we talked about going one higher, but for now, his job was to protect himself. He kept everything in writing, and after each interaction with his boss, he wrote an email to her boss, keeping as much emotion out of it as possible. Each email set up the situation, usually with an, "I am keeping documentation of this," and then the problem—what happened, and then leaving the solution to her boss.

Unfortunately, not much happened. He logged every interaction with her boss, who was also his boss. It all kept happening and escalating. After a while, her boss removed him from her direct report, which caused another situation. Document, discuss, exist. Wash, rinse, repeat. He was ac-cused of being smug and condescending when he used "Yes, and." When he removed emotion from conversations with her, she told him he didn't care about the job or company. And when he no longer answered to her, she would made passive-aggressive comments about how he "told on her."

Occasionally, you'll get in a situation where you do everything cor-rectly—you identify the issues, you connect with your wants and their wants, you keep things assertive, you do everything that looks great on paper and would work in most improv-based conversations—and it still goes very poorly. You work on the confidence and initiative to speak up to someone in your office, in HR, or higher. Still, no progress and the situa-tion is still awful and the conflict is still there. *This happens.*

So remember this: first, you aren't pizza and not everyone will like you. Second, you cannot control how people respond to you. You can do everything "right," and toxic environments are still toxic. Some people are simply toxic people. You can't change that and the sooner you recognize those situations for what they are and leave, the better.

How did my client's situation wrap up? The passive-aggressive PhD candidate got her PhD. Her boss ended up leaving. My client kept on track and started reporting the incidents to the interim. The interim sug-gested a reorg, and our PhD person quit. She "retired" officially because she could, but her exact comment was "I didn't want to deal with the reorg," and to my client, she said, "Now you can just take my job like you want to." He's still there, but working on his exit strategy.

Sometimes, speaking up doesn't work out the way we want it to. As we learned in the previous example, "success" might have been the retir-ing. Is that really successful though? My client endured months of her bad behavior, and nothing was assertively done to help the situation: just a lot of Band-Aids. Success could be the idea of improving your cur-rent situation by speaking up. Using that improv mind-set, you affirm your situation—"Yes"—then add and improve it—"and." Because in the end, you're looking to improve your communication style and be that best version of you. So go get appreciated for it and speak up if it improves your life.

YOUR CHEAT SHEET

Getting in your own way and realizing you are is frustrating to say the least. If it's someone else, at least you can write it off by not being pizza and walk away from the person or toxic job. Don't be the person who is their own worst enemy. This might come with a lack of prep or allowing that awful imposter syndrome voice to be louder than your own. Once you learn to get out of your own way, you can start to tackle the other—sometimes harder—issues that come up in your communication.

Remember:

- Know who, where, what, and how.

- Imposter syndrome isn't you and doesn't define you.

- Prep for raises and promotions—be your biggest ally.

- Negotiation is all about taking initiative.

And the biggest lesson from the whole book . . .

- *You can't change someone else's communication style.*

Presentation Skills

Whenever I start to explain what we do with EE, the first thing people usually say is "I hate public speaking." Chances are quite a few of you feel the same thing right now. Funny thing, I say it, too, and I teach it for a living. Speaking to a large group of people is *hard* and often really stressful. The cycle often goes like this:

- Get asked to lead a meeting for your team.

- Feel a little excited that you've been asked to step up.

- Feel a little panicked that you've been asked to step up.

- Write down some notes and run through it in your head.

- Make a PowerPoint with too much text.

- Go over the talk on the way to work.

- Give the talk, it's either OK or not the best—you tripped over words and had many of moments of "Why didn't I think of that when I was talking?" afterward.

- Feel disappointment and regret.

- Resignation: I'm just not great at this.

A few weeks or months later, you get asked to lead a meeting for your team . . . and it repeats all over again. Sound familiar?

We don't get better at it, because we tell ourselves we simply aren't good at it and the vicious cycle continues. Reality check: to be a better presenter, you have to work at it. It is *not* something people are automatically good at. When you're working on your own personal style, you need to immediately diagnose what you want to work on. After you've thought about the things you want to work on, you start working on those things, all while remembering you have to always practice and warm up before (and not just five minutes before!). You also need to continue to present—even when you don't want to—and the more you do it, the more you'll be able to improve.

WHO ARE YOU + WHO ARE YOU TALKING TO?

What is your presentation style? If someone had to describe it, what would they say? Are you funny, cracking jokes at the start? Do you like to tell stories and use metaphors to help the audience understand?

TRY THIS

Spend some time thinking what characteristics people might use to describe how you talk to a "large" (whatever that means to you) audience. After you make a list of a few characteristics, spend some time thinking about how you want people to see you, and if you don't have an idea, spend some time on the internet watching a few TED Talks. Pick one or two that seem interesting to you, and watch them, looking specifically for characteristics that you notice.

This helps you understand what kind of speaker you want to be. Words like *better* and *engaging* help only so much. What are you actually striving to be? This activity lets you step back to figure out what you're working on to improve.

One of my favorite talks is Amy Cuddy's "Your Body Language May Shape Who You Are." Aside from the awesome content, Cuddy immediately engages the audience and has them check in. She doesn't single out an individual and tell them they are doing it "wrong." She gives examples people might be able to relate to. You and she might use the word *engaging* when describing her style. She also smiles a lot while she speaks. Not a huge grin at the audience, more of an easy smile that brightens her voice and welcomes the audience. The word *friendly* might be used when describing her style.

Another great talk is Chimamanda Ngozi Adichie's "The Danger of a Single Story." Adichie stays behind her podium and speaks with great power and control: the words *powerful* and *grace* might be used to describe her style. In her other TEDx Talk, "We Should All Be Feminists," she has a slightly different style: still powerful, still standing behind that podium with presence, but this one is a bit more "playful" with smiles and a few moments of levity. If you watched one and not the other, what might you think? Would you use the word *playful* to describe someone who exudes power even over a computer screen? Probably not.

Find a few speakers you love, and start to pinpoint why you love them. Get really specific. Don't just write out "because they're good." What makes them good? What effect did they have on you? Did you laugh or cry listening to them speak? Really consider *why* they are powerful and *how* they have the audience hanging on every word. That's where you'll get some characteristics you might want to include. In most artistic professions, we joke that nothing is original and everything is stolen from someone else. I'm not advising you to simply steal a presentation skill or quality from another speaker. I do think the joke's validity is that something can be "stolen" and made unique by *you*.

Now that you have something to strive for, let's pull back and think on our public-speaking skills, which encompass more of the day-to-day communication. Again, this could be with your coworkers, in a networking situation, when you're interviewing for a job, in a staff meeting—any professional communication. Really dig into what you'd like to portray and what you currently portray. Maybe you really wish you could say that thing that you always think about after the fact. Many people take an improv class for that exact reason! Pro tip: that won't happen after one class. That flexibility takes time.

Some of this taps back into the audience: digging into what the audience might want from you and how you can provide it. A lot of it taps into the ideas behind what version of you needs to come out. All of this is constantly connected.

When you're prepping for a big presentation, you want to make sure to do a few things. First, you want to script out those points. Even if you're planning on flying by the seat of your pants, you need to know your talking points. If you get the panicky look when you're nervous, be sure you have these points written down. You're not writing things word for word. You're only noting the main ideas. The idea is to give yourself a cue line. If you have the whole paragraph written down, you'll have to review the information, figure out where you are, figure out what to say next, process that, and then get back on track. With talking points you have these cue lines to bring you back. Since improv is attending to the world around you and if the world throws you for a loop, you can take a breath, look at your points, and return to your thought.

This might sound funny from someone who advocates improv for everything, but you need to rehearse. The more you practice, the better you are. I performed off-Broadway for 10 years—every Friday and Saturday night, we had performances at 7:30 and 9:45. It was very much like "Whose Line Is It Anyway?"—all improv, and competitive at that. Nothing was scripted; everything was made up on the fly and on the spot, all while following improv rules.

We still rehearsed every Wednesday night. If you didn't rehearse, you couldn't perform. People hear this and constantly ask: "What in the world are you rehearsing if you're doing improv?" You're learning about one another. Aside from building trust in improv, you're learning how people respond to situations and playing with ideas, characters, and choices. If you're just going in cold to a performance, you're not going to do well, because it's a team sport.

Presentations are *also* team sports because it's you and the audience. If you don't rehearse and prep, you won't know what to do if something doesn't go quite right. On top of that, what if you say something you think is completely normal but your audience finds funny? Are you going to shut down their laughter by plowing through, or are you going to pause to take a moment to let them laugh and then pick up where you left off? Can you start and stop on a dime? This is why everyone needs to rehearse.

You're not only planning for the potential of things going "wrong," but you're also planning for things to go right! The more you understand the situation and the information you want to get across, the more confident you'll be in the moment.

Everyone is going to prepare for a presentation in whatever way they want, and that's OK. There are a few best practices of rehearsing and not going word for word, but whatever works for you will be what works for you. Whether you are giving a TED Talk or speaking at a high school (which actually might be scarier than a TED Talk), you have to figure out your best style of prep.

What happens when something goes wrong though? You know what I'm talking about: that moment when everything disappears from your head, and you have no idea what's next . . . and silence. More silence. Someone clears their throat. More silence.

What do you do when you have a brain lock? In prepping for a presentation you need to prep for those moments and know what you do when you're in the middle of a brain lock and you have to continue.

One of the first things to do when you get stuck is to take a breath—a nice, big, centering breath. Ask yourself, Where are you right now? Who are you talking to? Why are they listening to you? What do you want to tell them?

TRY THIS

Just stop and breathe for a little bit. Take a big breath in through your nose and then out through your mouth. Put one hand on your stomach and make sure your stomach and diaphragm expand when you breathe in and contract when you breathe out. Do this for a few moments. Next time you're panicky in a situation, remember, taking this breath will ground you.

This helps you realize if you're holding your breath. You might be and not even know it! This activity draws attention to your breathing in a way you probably haven't attended to before.

When you breathe in during a presentation, you're working on your mindfulness in this moment. When you're blanking in a presentation, your mind ends up going in a completely different direction from where it should be going. Something happened and it threw you off, so you kept going in the wrong direction. Checking in and asking yourself questions about the moment, some of the same questions from the last chapter can ground you in the here and now. You don't have to go through all of them or dive into specifics, because a group of people probably is watching you and waiting for your next word. Just a few questions to refresh your memory to where you are, as well as get you out of any irrational thought patterns like, "Oh, I'm failing."

After you've taken those deep breaths and connected back in the moment, be sure to take a look at those notes you made. There is absolutely *nothing* wrong with having a few notes to refer to and connect with when you're giving a presentation. Again, this is why you can't have pages on pages of notes—just a few key words that will cue you if you get lost. If you don't have notes, always remember one very important thing: the audience wants you to succeed.

No one wants to see you fail. This is a fact. Sure, there isn't a research study interviewing people going into or coming out of presentations, asking if they are interested in watching the speaker fall flat on their face, but consider that idea of getting the energy you put out. What does that look like when something awful happens? When a speaker feels awkward? When the whole audience watches that speaker feel awkward . . . they feel awkward.

Awkward isn't a good feeling, it's an awful feeling. No one *wants* to feel awkward. No one wants to watch someone struggle or stress in front of a large group of people. People want to feel good after listening to you. They don't walk into a presentation to see someone fail and make mistakes. The group wants you to succeed, no matter who they are. When you get stuck or things go awry, you can always remember the audience is rooting for you. They want you to do well.

A few years ago, a friend of mine asked me to coach her for her upcoming presentation—her email was pretty simple: "Hey Jen, I need some help on a presentation I have in about two weeks, can we meet?"

Sure! I usually don't help my friends, because it's a different kind of relationship, but why not? I wasn't doing anything.

Fast forward to us meeting up, and I asked what the gig was, fully assuming a conference.

"It's a TEDx Talk, I haven't started and it's in two weeks."

One of the reasons I actually don't work with friends is because I'm a hard coach, and sometimes friends aren't really thrilled with tough love. This friend mostly knew what she was getting into with me, so we decided to work together. We wrote, constructed, rehearsed, and launched a TEDx Talk in a little under two weeks. She was ready, in both of our opinions.

On the day of the talk, I snuck in to watch. I usually don't tell clients I'm going to be there, and usually I don't go, because I'm like a mom watching her kid play sports for the first time—cautiously optimistic and nervous because I know *anything* can go wrong.

She got up onstage and did such a lovely job, until about halfway through. There was a pause, and I knew it was the same spot that was tripping her up in rehearsal. I watched as she took a breath, centered herself with her feet under her knees, and picked things back up. The pause was unnoticeable to anyone but us, I'm sure. Her recovery was incredible. In rehearsal, she had to stop, look at her notes and come back to where she was. And on top of everything, her talk was extremely complicated: a high-tech concept that she was suggesting a very new application for. If she didn't think about where it was going and how to get there—and stay on track—she would lose the not-necessarily-tech-savvy folks who were in the audience. She knew this. We both did. So when we were prepping for this, we worked on what to do when she lost track, and she did exactly that.

Because my example is transparently here to make you feel good about prep and the things that go along with it, I have to include the whole story, as well as a counterpoint to see why having a plan is crucial.

My client and friend was also being considered for a position at the local university that was holding the TEDx program. A few months after the talk, she reached out to me to tell me she got hired and a few months after that the dean told her that during her talk, he texted another person at the university and said, "She's hired." She had a plan just in case things went awry, and while the university didn't mention her recovery, if someone was carefully watching, you could see she faltered and came back seamlessly. A pretty great skill for a young professor, if I do say so myself.

Take a moment and look up Michael Bay CES Meltdown. Please don't watch it before you have to do a presentation. This is what happens when you don't have a plan for going blank and everything goes to a worst-case scenario. Essentially, Michael Bay is doing a press conference and his teleprompter goes out. He was completely using it as a crutch and didn't prep in any other way. Sure, I don't know this for certain, but I do know that he couldn't recover in the moment and got so angry with himself and the situation that he walked offstage in the middle of the conference, leaving the host onstage by himself to deal with it.

When you don't have a plan for when things go wrong, you have to figure out what to do in the moment. In Bay's case, his teleprompter went out and that was his only option. So when he had nothing, he really had nothing. He also didn't know *how* to recover, because in a later interview about this conference (because his mistake went viral), he said he wasn't that good at impromptu speaking.

While Michael Bay can maybe get away with having nothing as a backup, you can't if you're like the rest of us. And if you have a plan for recovery like my friend, you won't end up crashing and burning in front of a large group of people.

That deep breath and moment to yourself will bring you back to center. Take it for yourself, and remember those points you practiced. And always remember: tech might go wrong.

Question Time: The Unexpected

Bad Q&A's post presentations make folks pretty apprehensive. The apprehension usually occurs because of the unknown—what if someone asks a question you don't know the answer to? What if someone tries to take over the presentation? What happens if they say you're wrong?

That unknown is incredibly anxiety-inducing for so many people, so how do you work past it to have a great Q&A as part of your presentation? It's often the part that the audience enjoys the most because they can ask the questions they are interested in, versus simply learning what the speaker thinks they should learn. Since the unknown is truly the issue with Q&A, knowing that the unknown is the only option, you're getting some control over the situation.

Think of the scary trope of running in the woods when someone is chasing you. If you don't look back, you have no idea what's there. They could have a knife! They could have a sword! It could be a bear! You get more and more caught in the unknown and blowing it out of proportion.

The moment you turn around and look at what it is, you can address it. So look at what a Q&A could be: what is the craziest question and what question will probably be asked?

When you're in the actual moment of the question, and it isn't something you're ready for, there are a few things you can do to ground what you're doing. The first, take that deep breath. If you need to hear the question again, ask and really listen. If it's something you don't know the answer to? Say, I don't know! Lying about something isn't good for anyone. Admitting you don't know is confidence. You're assertively communicating by using an "I" statement and owning it.

If you go blank, think about the question. Give yourself the grace to take some time with that answer, think about it, and respond. Go back to the core of improv: respond to the question you hear. If you're unsure if the answer is what they are looking for, button your answer with, "Does that answer your question?" You aren't saying this in a snarky or rude way, you are truly asking.

You might also get a person who tries to take over the conversation. This person might be extremely passionate about the subject, might be an expert in it, might have opinions—and really, none of this matters, because you can't change the way they respond to you. You can only change how you respond to them. Say, "Thank you so much for sharing—can we talk about this afterward?" You've acknowledged that you indeed hear they have something to share, and you will listen to it—just not now, because this is your show, not theirs.

TRY THIS

This activity works best with a friend. Have your presentation or talk at the ready, and start speaking. At any moment, your friend can call out "Fresh Choice," and you have to switch things up and substitute a word or phrase in your initial presentation for something else. For example, it might sound like:

> Person A: Improv is absolutely fantastic for all kinds of
> public speaking, because you're basically practicing
> how to show human behavior. When you're practicing
> improv, you're working skills that will help you with life.

Person B: Fresh choice!

Person A: When you're practicing improv, you're having fun.

Person B: Fresh Choice!

Person A: When you're practicing improv, it's nothing.

This is a really difficult activity. Even teaching it to a group gets rough sometimes because you're teaching someone to respond to an impromptu stimulus, pivot in the moment, and move along. It can be done by yourself as well; you can either set a timer for every minute and "Fresh Choice" yourself every time it goes off. The key to this activity is making a new choice when you hear or are triggered by "Fresh Choice." That choice can be anything; it just has to be different than what you just said. You're working the ability to pivot and respond to a stimulus.

This helps you work on pivoting in the moment. No one is going to actively ask you to do a 180 while you're speaking: sometimes we do need to quickly pivot. This activity lets you do it in a heightened state, making reality that much easier.

In the end, you can plan for the impromptu moments in presentations much like you can plan for the other situations that will come up when you're communicating. By having a solid plan in place—not 10 solid plans, just one—you'll handle many, if not all, situations that might come up with your presentation.

The key is in the prep.

WARM-UPS

If I told you to go outside and run three miles, would you start running before stretching and warming up? Well, you shouldn't. The same goes for speaking. You have to warm up your voice and body before you speak, in the same way you might warm up your body. Warm-ups are very personal. Try a few of these following activities, and then build your own warm-up routine to do prior to a big presentation (or even leading a meeting):

- **Start by taking those deep breaths.** If you aren't breathing, you won't be able to project, remain calm, or win your audience over. Unclench your butt and keep in mind you get the energy you put out.

- **Next, warm up your mouth.** When you get nervous, you trip over words. Work on being able to enunciate and mean what you say by warming up with some tongue twisters. You can choose from many. If you trip over one of them, that's what you should use. Say the words slowly and over-enunciate. Here are a few to start with:

  Irish wristwatch

  Red leather, Yellow leather

  The lips, the teeth, the tip of the tongue, the tip of the tongue, the teeth, the lips

  I slit the sheet, the sheet I slit, and on the slitted sheet I sit.

- **Now warm up your body.** Jump up, throw your arms out and your legs wide, and open your mouth as wide as you can. Now make everything as small as possible. Do this a few more times to get nimble and jazzed.

- **Finally, wake up your brain.** For this, I recommend Zip, Zap, Zop if you have friends who can help you; Last Word with yourself if you don't. Anything that will warm up your quick-thinking skills as well as your active listening and attention. Remember, even if you don't interact officially with the audience with a Q&A, you're still interacting with that audience. This also ups your presence.

After you try this prescribed warm-up, see what happens the next time you speak. Maybe this will be great, you'll get everything you need out of this warm-up, and you won't have to change anything! Chances are you'll pick and choose based on results. You'll assess your performance, think about what happened, and see where you still need to grow.

Make It Spicy

A few years ago I was presenting at a conference, and I snappily responded to a question that essentially questioned my authority. I said something along the lines of, "Well, I'm up here speaking and you aren't, so that should tell you something right there, no?" After my talk, a few people came up to me to congratulate me for putting the man who questioned my authority into place. One woman even called me "spicy." While I don't think you should call out people for the sake of calling out people (unless they question your authority in front of dozens of your colleagues, then go ahead), I do think there are other ways to spice up your presentation and presentation skills. When you've achieved a level of comfort, one that comes only with practice, you shouldn't just be comfortable with status quo in your presentation style. There are a few ways to spice up your presentation that are fairly easy and workable for everyone.

WALK AND TALK

Truth, did you read this heading and immediately think, "Oh, I do that!"

Repeat after me, pacing is not effective. I see so many people in our presentation classes, and they think that walking while they talk is a good idea. And they aren't wrong. The problem comes in when people are meandering or pacing while they are talking. If you're wandering or constantly moving when you're talking, it's going to be distracting. Swaying and rocking are self-soothing behaviors, things we do when we're nervous.

A quick fix? Stand with your feet planted. Make sure your feet are under your knees, under your hips, under your shoulders. Your feet should be pointed straight ahead, and your shoulders should be square to the audience. If you feel yourself starting to sway, you should take a step or two and then plant your feet again.

Jump in the air and land flat on your feet. Do it again, making sure you're not landing on the balls of your feet or your heels. One last time, really connecting with the floor. (If you have a bad knee like me, don't do this without good shoes on.) Feel that connection? That's how it should feel when you're standing squared off to the audience. Don't bounce or throw your weight, or do what I lovingly call the "youth hip," where you have one knee bent and your hip jutted out to the side. Solidly connected to the floor, weight evenly distributed.

This helps you connect with the floor and work on being grounded. Remember that best version of yourself: that version is confident and greeting the audience head on. This activity is a "quick fix" with an immediate result.

When you have the "no sway" youth-hip-free style down, you can try walking and talking. Again, you might be thinking, this is easy! I walk and talk every day.

Do you do it while you're presenting? When you walk and talk while you're presenting, you have to keep in mind a few key things. It's an incredibly confident and dynamic skill to add to your presentations, when done well.

- **Move and then stop.** Consistent motion is pacing. Walking and talking is not pacing. When you decide to try this skill, walk and then stop. Square off, plant your feet and talk a bit more. Then, move again. Wash, rinse, repeat: Walk and talk, stop and talk, walk and talk, stop and talk. By stopping and recentering, you're not only adding dynamism to your presentation, you're not pacing.

- **Move with purpose and intention.** When you walk, mean it. If you're making a choice to walk, *walk*. Don't take a few awkward steps or kind of walk. Do it or don't.

- **Move forward, not backward.** What causes us to move backward? Fear, shame, nerves—all things we don't want our audience to see. When we backpedal, we exhibit negative emotions. When you walk, walk forward, and if you have to move backward, make a conscious effort to turn around (with intention) and then turn back to face your audience. Don't awkwardly wander backward.

- **Move when you're transitioning.** Great presentations have transitions: same with stories. They don't just take you from point to point; you go on the journey together. If you're stuck and don't know when in your presentation to move or try walking, you can do it when you're transitioning (or moving) from point to point.

While walking and talking sounds easy, it's not once you start thinking about everything that goes into it. It's not as simple as walk while you talk, because you're doing it in front of a captive audience. The best way to start incorporating this into your talk? Just do it and see what happens!

PLAY!

Word of warning, this whole section is one big Try This. You can't write about play without playing. I am willing to bet quite a bit of my best houseplants that you take life way too seriously. I know I do. I have to remind myself of the fun saying that we aren't getting out alive.

This holds true for presentations, too. Whenever I'm working one-on-one, I usually try to shake things up by having the presenter do it while laughing or do it as if they are in a horror movie or a cartoon. And it never fails, I get a weird, "Why?" Then usually they resign to doing it just to be done. But magic happens when you play! Most people find a fun thing or two when they take themselves a little less seriously and have some fun.

Changing Genres is one of the best ways to "play" with a presentation, especially when you don't know how to take yourself less seriously. Of course, whatever you're speaking on is important, so playing with it might seem counterproductive, but studies show that playing can increase creativity, productivity, and feelings of well-being[1]—which are all things you should bring to a presentation to increase the dynamics!

Before you start playing Changing Genres, brainstorm as many genres of movies and TV shows that you can. Here is a list to get you started:

- Rom Com

- Horror

- Comedy

- Sci-fi

- Action

Now start rehearsing your presentation, either one you have coming up or something you've done before. At any moment, decide to adopt that genre. Say you're presenting the sales report from last year, and your first genre is horror. You can start presenting as if you are terrified that a ghost is chasing you. After a few moments of this, quickly switch over to Rom Com, where you talk as though you're recounting the tale of two star-crossed lovers.

While you are not going to do this in real life (ever, unless you want to make things really weird at the office), this is a great way to play with your talk or presentation. The likelihood of you finding a cadence, a pause, or a new dramatic technique through this activity is high. Even more so, you're going to have a lot of fun doing it. If you have fun practicing, you'll probably remember some of that joy when you're presenting for real. That will transfer to your audience; they'll feel great listening to you and want to continue listening to you. Win for all!

You're also going to come up with some junk. That's OK! Maybe you're not going to get anything *practical* out of practicing your sales meeting or elevator pitch in the horror genre. You will, however, laugh at yourself, and if you do it in front of another person like your friend, coworker, or partner, they will probably laugh too.

The more good experiences you have with public speaking, the less scary and intimidating it becomes.

DO SOMETHING THAT SCARES YOU IN MOMENTS WHERE RISK IS LOW

Do not try new things when the stakes are high, unless you enjoy the panic and fear of trying something new.

If you are giving a make-or-break presentation that a lot is riding on, don't try to pull out something you've never done before. This goes back to the whole wearing a new outfit for an important moment in life. Definitely not the right time to add stress to a situation that might already be stressful.

Be honest though: How many of those do you have a week? A month? Probably not a lot. Which means you have lots of precious time for experimenting. Those weekly meetings, weekly reports, monthly presentations that you have to give, and no one really likes? Those are the times for trying something new.

Think of it this way, no one probably likes the consistent meeting or presentation: it probably causes a lot of unneeded stress. Why not use it as your learning stage?

This comes back to the whole idea of this book—you actually can't learn all the things in a bubble. As much as I promote practicing in safe spaces, taking classes to learn these skills, and doing the homework before you're actually in the situation, you need to try these out in the real world. All of these spicy techniques and strategies? They might work great in the safety of your own home or office, and when put to practice in real life, something else might happen. This isn't a sign to quit; it is a sign to reflect. What worked, what didn't, and what can you do differently next time? How can you use this experience to learn, grow, and build, so you *can* use these higher-level techniques on a bigger stage for something that feels more important?

Everything has to be scaffolded to have a firm foundation and structure. Build yourself at your own rate, and keep reaching higher.

YOUR CHEAT SHEET

Presentations don't have to be this scary thing we dread. They may never be something you crave, but you owe it to yourself and your nerves to actively improve! Remember to:

- Think about what people want to see from you.

- Think about what you want to see from you.

- Big presentations require prep.

- Rehearse and warm up.

- When in doubt, remember: they want you to succeed.

- Add some spice where you can.

Conclusion

You did it, congrats!

Check-in. What were you working on in the beginning? How do you feel about it now? What were your glows and grows?

And again, congrats. Deciding to work on yourself is a major undertaking. When I was growing up and throughout all my career thus far (I know, I'm only 36), I realize some people are perfectly comfortable where they are. They don't want to be better. They like being exactly where they are and not moving any farther along the spectrum of improvement.

Then there are the people who want to be better. These people continue to grow and learn after school. These people want to constantly be the best version of themselves and they know that to do that, you have to do some hard things once in a while. We communicate constantly. Even now, you're reading the words I'm writing, and I write how I speak, so if we ever meet, you'll hear a lot of the same things. I'm communicating with you, and together we're working on making you the best version of yourself when it comes to impromptu communication. Even when it's prepping the planned communication so you are ready for the impromptu communication, you are working on the on-the-spot, seemingly on-the-fly moments some people are just so good at.

You can be good at it too!

A few things to remember:

1. You're incredible because you're choosing to work on who you are to be a better version of you.

2. This is a big step—go out and follow the fear and revisit that expectation from the beginning, and now go do the thing that you were too worried about doing. Or do the thing you've always been doing, and this time, do it better.

3. Continuing education continues. It's not done here, so this is very far from the end. More like a "to be continued" and instead of me telling you what's next, it's all on you.

So what next?

To be continued, by you.

What have you accomplished during this book?

What are you still working on?

What are you looking forward to?

What are you still dreading?

What's next?

Notes, References, Resources

Chapter 1: Attending to Your Audience: *Who, What, When,* and *How*

1. Deborah Friedman, *Influence for Nonprofit Leaders* (Greensboro: CCL Press, 2013).

2. Daniel Goleman, *Emotional Intelligence: Why It Can Matter More Than IQ* (New York: Bantam Books, 2005).

3. Paul E. Griffiths, *What Emotions Really Are* (Chicago: University of Chicago Press, 1997).

4. Ibid.

Chapter 2: Interpersonal Communication—the Everyday Professional Communication

1. E. T. Klemmer and F. W. Snyder, *Measurement of Time Spent Communicating* (*Journal of Communication*, Volume 22, Issue 2, June 1972, pages 142–158).

2. International Listening Association, www.listen.org.

3. Tina Fey, *Bossypants* (Boston: Back Bay Books, 2012).

4. Andrew Wolvin and Carolyn Gwynn Coakley, *Listening* (Madison: Brown and Benchmark, 1996).

5. Jon Kabat-Zinn, *Wherever You Go, There You Are: Mindfulness Meditation in Everyday Life* (New York: Hachette Books, 2005).

6. *OC Tanner Study: Appreciation Changes Everything*, 2012.

7. *Robert Provine Laughter: A Scientific Investigation*, 2001

8. Google Project Aristotle.

Chapter 3: Networking and Small Talk

1. *Linked In Job Report* 2019.

2. 2013 Harvard University Social Cognitive and Affective Neuroscience Lab, Adrian Ward.

3. Thanks, Tara!

4. Amy Cuddy, *Presence: Bringing Your Boldest Self to Your Biggest Challenges* (Boston: Little, Brown & Company, 2016).

Chapter 4: Leading a Meeting and Leading in a Meeting

1. John Antonakis, Marika Fenley, and Sue Liechti, *Learning Charisma* (Boston: Harvard Review, 2012).

2. Daniel Goleman, *Emotional Intelligence: Why It Can Matter More Than IQ* (New York: Bantam Books, 2005).

3. George T. Doran, There's a S.M.A.R.T. way to write management's goals and objectives *(Management Review*, 1981).

4. Martin Stack, *Inhibiting and Facilitating Conditions of the Human Smile* (1988).

5. Tara Kraft and Sarah Pressman, *Grin and Bear It: The Influence of*

Manipulated Facial Expression on the Stress Response (Association for Psychological Science, 2012).

6. Daniel Gatica-Perez, *Automatic Nonverbal Analysis of Social Interaction in Small Groups: A Review* (Idiap Research Institute, 2008).

7. Noah Zandan, *Eye Contact—a Declining Communications Tool?* Quantified Communications.

8. Arthur Aron, Stony Brook study, 1997.

9. Geoffrey Beattie, *Gesture Use in Social Interaction: How Speakers' Gestures Can Reflect Listeners' Thinking* (University of Manchester, 2007).

10. Vanessa Van Edwards, *20 Hand Gestures You Should Be Using,* Science of the People.

11. Kenn Adams, *Back to the Story Spine* (Aerogramme Studio, 2013).

Chapter 5: Interviewing

1. *LinkedIn Job Report*, 2017.

2. D. Byrne, W. Griffitt, and D. Stefaniak, Attraction and similarity of personality characteristics (*Journal of Personality and Social Psychology*, Volume 5, Issue 1, 1967, pages 82–90).

3. Career Builder, 2014.

4. Training Industry Report, 2017.

5. Ovul Sezer, Francesca Gino, and Michael I. Norton, Humblebragging: A distinct—and ineffective—self-presentation strategy (Harvard Business School Working Paper, No. 15-080, April 2015).

6. A. R. Feiler, and D. M. Powell, Behavioral expression of job interview anxiety (*Journal of Business and Psychology*, March 2015).

7. World Economic Forum, *Global Competitiveness Report*, 2018.

Chapter 6: Get Out of Your Own Way

1. Valerie Young, *The Secret Thoughts of Successful Women: Capable People Suffer from the Impostor Syndrome and How to Thrive in Spite of It* (New York: Crown Business, 2011).

2. J. Sakulku and J. Alexander, The imposter phenomenon (*International Journal of Behavioral Science*, 2011).

3. Mary Gentile, *Giving Voice to Values: How to Speak Your Mind When You Know What's Right* (New Haven: Yale University Press, 2012).

4. Thomas Gilovich and Victoria Husted Medvec, The experience of regret: What, when, and why (*Psychological Review*, 1995).

5. Shai Davidai and Thomas Gilovich, The ideal road not taken: The self-discrepancies involved in people's most enduring regrets (*Emotion*, 2018).

Chapter 7: Presentation Skills

1. Stuart Brown, National Institute of Play.

Resources and Further Reading

Charna Halpern, Del Close, and Kim "Howard" Johnson, *Truth in Comedy: The Manual of Improvisation* (Meriwether Publishing, Limited, 1994).

Tom Salinsky and Deborah Frances Wright, *The Improv Handbook: The Ultimate Guide to Improvising in Comedy, Theatre, and Beyond* (Bloomsbury Publishing, 2008).

Jill Bernard, *Jill Bernard's Small Cute Book of Improv* (yesand.com publishing, 2008).

Ann Libera, *The Second City Almanac of Improvisation* (Northwestern University Press, 2004).

Acknowledgments

Writing a book is neither glamorous nor easy.

I have to start by thanking my amazing husband Alex. From telling me to respond to the email from McGraw-Hill, to nudging me along to finish my manuscript. This book is the best it could be because you've made me the best I can be.

Thank you to Amy Li, my editor, for reaching out after taking classes in NYC with EE and for making me believe that I truly could write a book on improv.

My folks, Brian and Lisa, for letting me call and vent about running two businesses and writing a book at the same time, and for knowing that I would never, ever grow up—so of course my career involves full time play.

And finally, the countless women of Fearless Winston Salem, for asking me how it was going, bringing me tea and treats, silently walking into the space and asking if I was OK. We are all stronger, together.

Index

About the Author

Jen Oleniczak Brown, founder of The Engaging Educator (EE), has been teaching improv for over half her life. Through EE, her brand of improv-based training has reached over 50,000 people since 2012. She's done three TEDx Talks on the power of improv and truly believes it can change everyone's life for the better. Jen lives in Winston Salem, NC, and has a "Yes, and" tattoo—just ask.